D. H. Lawrence and Edward Carpenter

D. H. LAWRENCE AND EDWARD CARPENTER

A Study in Edwardian Transition

Emile Delavenay

HEINEMANN : LONDON

William Heinemann Ltd
LONDON MELBOURNE TORONTO
JOHANNESBURG AUCKLAND

First Published 1971

434 18620 1

Made in Great Britain at the Pitman Press, Bath

Acknowledgements

The author and publishers are grateful to Laurence Pollinger Limited and the Estate of the late Mrs Frieda Lawrence for permission to use copyright material by D. H. Lawrence, and to George Allen & Unwin Ltd for the quotations from the Works of Edward Carpenter.

The author expresses his gratitude to Miss Helen Corke, Mrs Olive Hopkin and Mrs Enid Hilton Hopkin, for permission to quote from letters and for information provided, and to Professor Edward W. Tedlock Jr of the University of New Mexico for allowing him to quote from one of his articles.

He wishes to render a special tribute to the memory of the late Norman Johnston, formerly of the Government Actuary Department, who first drew his attention in 1934 to certain striking similarities between *Women in Love* and Edward Carpenter's writings.

Contents

PAGE

Introduction 1

Chapter 1 INTERSECTING ORBITS 8

A Forgotten Pioneer (8), Approaches to a Comparative Study (10);

CARPENTER AND THE MIDLANDS INTELLIGENTSIA (12), Victorian Beginnings (12), Walt Whitman and Self-discovery (14), Socialism and the Fellowship of the New Life (15), The Midlands Sage (17);

LINKS BETWEEN LAWRENCE AND CARPENTER (21), Alice Dax and the Hopkin Circle (21), Home Thoughts from Abroad (25), *The Rainbow*, *The Intermediate Sex* and Officialdom (27), Carpenter and *The Rainbow* (30);

THE SLOW PARTING OF THE WAYS (33);

A TENTATIVE CHRONOLOGY (35);

WHY SILENCE? (39), Where Silence is Consent (41)

Chapter 2 THE ATTACK ON CIVILIZATION, ABSTRACT SCIENCE AND CONVENTIONAL MORALS 44

A Mirror of Late-nineteenth-century Advanced Ideas (44);

INTUITIVE REVELATION AND SOCIAL CRITICISM (47), *Towards Democracy* and the Cosmic Sense (48), A Turning-point (52), Indian Thought and Annie Besant (54);

CIVILIZATION, ITS CAUSE AND CURE (55), Civilization not Defined (56), Healthy Barbarian and Golden Age (57), Health and Civilization (58), The Fall and the Return to Paradise (59), Civilization and Sex (62), Civilization and Government (63), The Return to Nature (64), An "Advanced" Synthesis (66);

THE CRITICISM OF SCIENCE (67), Science and Feeling, Brain and Sympathetic Nerve (69), Yoga and the Science of the Future (72), Exfoliation and Perfect Man (74);

THE ATTACK ON CONVENTIONAL MORALS (76), Custom and the Free Individual (77), The 'Defence of Criminals' and the Apology of Greek Love (78), No Hierarchy of Actions or Passions (78), Human Service and the Expanding Circle of Consciousness (79), A Lawrence Parallel (80), Altruism and Passions (81), Perfect Man and the Superman (82).

Chapter 3 THE FREE INDIVIDUAL: MAN, WOMAN, LOVE AND MARRIAGE 85

Carpenter's Publishing Troubles (85);

LOVE'S COMING OF AGE (88), Teaching the Middle Classes the Meaning of Love (88), *Love's Coming of Age* and the 1913–16 Lawrence Novels (89), Sex and Hunger, Sin, the Mystic Balance (92), The Flower and the Seed (94), Acceptance of the Body (96);

THE FREE SOCIETY AND THE FLOWER OF ETERNITY (97), Love-making and Nature (97);

THE SOUL'S PROGRESS IN *THE SISTERS* (99), Gerald, the Ungrown Man (100), Birkin, the Prototype of Future Man (101), The Brangwens: from Golden Age to Paradise through Civilization (103), Ursula as Woman in Freedom (104);

MARRIAGE (105), *Egoïsme à deux* (105), Mystic Marriage (107), Reaching the Centre of Life (109);

A CHRONOLOGICAL RETROSPECT (110), German and Italian Translations (111), New Themes in 1912 and 1913 (112), The Rose and the Bee (114), Antinomianism (116).

Chapter 4 THE GODS IN THE BODY AND THE DISINTEGRATION OF THE PERSONALITY 118

A Precarious Balance (118);

THE ART OF CREATION (120), Three Ideas and a Syncretic Optimism (120), The Three Stages of Consciousness: from Separateness to Absolute Being (124), Finding a Physiological Basis for Cosmic Consciousness (129);

THE BODY AND THE UNIVERSAL SELF (131), Illusive, Separate Selves (131), Within Reach of Absolute Being (133), Perennial Bodily Cells and Race (135), Value and Limitations of the Brain (140), Thought as Disintegration of Being (143), The Temple of the Gods and the Road to Racialism (145), The Devils, Corruption and Disintegration (150);

THE NEW CONCEPTION OF PERSONALITY (154), The Individual and the 'World-self' (154), The Main Problem of the Age: a Programme for a Writer (157), The Ever-changing Ego (159), There is no Fixed Personality (160), The Non-human in Man (161).

Chapter 5 THE ART OF LIFE AND INDIVIDUAL EXPRESSION 164

Angels' Wings, or Justifying the Ways of God to Men (164);

THE ART OF DEMOCRACY (165), Beethoven, Wagner, Millet, Whitman (165), *Angels' Wings* and

Realism in Art (166), The Human Body in Movement (167), The Redemption of the Body (168), Tolstoy on Nudity (169);

LAWRENCE'S '*ART AND THE INDIVIDUAL*' (170), A Drawing-room Talk to Socialist Friends (170), Sources, Academic and Otherwise (172), The Undesirable in Art and Society (173), From the Drawing-room Table to the Language of the Masses (175);

CREATION OF THE INDIVIDUAL (177), Incompatibility of Expression and Conventions (177), Impressionism, Symbolism and Social Life (178), Art and Life: to Create Oneself (180), Aesthetic Theory in *Study of Thomas Hardy* (182), The Point of Divergence: Contempt of Men (184), The Aesthetic of Loneliness (186), Non-action, and how to Accept Evil in the Self (187).

Chapter 6 THE ANDROGYNOUS SUPERMAN 190

From Victorian Optimism to Georgian Pessimism (190), Faith in Organization (192);

CARPENTER AND ESOTERIC TRADITION (192), A Cautious Approach (193), Lawrence and Esoteric Lore (194), The Attraction of the Superman (194);

WHAT IS MEANT BY SUPERMAN? (196), Love's Aim is Religious (196), The Physiology of Love and Reincarnation (197), The Origin of the Individual Soul (201), Male and Female: the Mixture and the Balance (205), Melville and Michelangelo (205), Characteristics and Role of the Intermediate Sex (209), Vaticinatory Role of Intermediate Types (212), Some Additional Clues (214);

THE SUPERMAN AS ARTIST-HERO AND LEADER (215), Birkin's Secret: the Way to Permissiveness (215), From Permissiveness to Glorification (220), Walt Whitman as Preter-human

Hero (221), The Love of Comrades and the Mystic Circuit of Death (225), Whitman and Lawrence (230), Frustration and Withdrawal (234).

Chapter 7 CONCLUSIONS 236

NOTES 245

BIBLIOGRAPHICAL NOTE 268

INDEX 279

Illustrations

Between pages 146 and 147

1 D. H. Lawrence

2 Edward Carpenter outside his cottage at Millthorpe

3 The list of signatures to the 1914 Address

4 W. E. Hopkin and Florence Potter

5 Alice Dax with her daughter

6 Gal's cartoon of W. E. Hopkin in 1929

7 The Naples bas-relief of Paris and Helen

INTRODUCTION

This study is not meant to be a search for "sources" of the works of D. H. Lawrence, so much as an attempt to define a mental climate, to connect, historically and in detail the works of a great creative writer with ideas and conceptions detected in them yet never hitherto specifically related to his immediate surroundings. It aims rather at defining in the history of ideas not a main stream and filiation of philosophical thinking, but a pervading flow of mental representations at a given level of social life, at a given moment of English literature, and in a writer who at that moment gives these representations their most striking expression. It is a study of background and atmosphere, rather than of summits. It is concerned not with the values of ideas, so much as with their existence at the time of observation, and with their use in the hidden infra-structure of works of imagination.

If this study is viewed as a search for sources, then the word must be taken at its broadest sense, namely the recognition by a writer, in the works of another, of common preoccupations, common attitudes and assumptions; the discovery of a field to be ploughed and cultivated, in what Thomas Mann has called "the husbandry" of "an intellectual establishment".[1] A revelation often accompanied by contestation and debate, by a prolonged dialogue of the writer with his forerunner—so prolonged that it becomes impossible to distinguish the argument with itself of a split personality from that of the disciple with a kindred spirit. A discovery in which the genius, "by addition of *himself*, by stamping his own image on what he has picked up . . . can make the whole worth infinitely more than all the book knowledge in the world" and becomes "the king who mints the ducats".[2]

* * *

It is necessary at this early stage to dispose of the creative artist's diffidence and even prejudice about any study of "sources". This has been best voiced in recent times by Leonard Woolf in *Downhill all the Way*, with reference to the alleged influence upon Virginia Woolf of the "stream of consciousness" methods of James Joyce and Dorothy Richardson. "The idea that no one in the arts has ever invented anything," he writes,

> . . . or indeed has ever had an original thought, since everything is always 'derived' from something else in an unending artistic House that Jack Built, is extremely common and has always seemed to me untrue—and if not untrue, unimportant.[3]

We prefer to think, with Pierre Auger, that ideas remain latent like seeds until they find fertile ground in which to germinate again in human minds:[4] in this sense some writers are truly "seminal", and it is not unimportant to discover who sowed the seeds, even in cases when the writer thus fertilized remained unconscious of his borrowing, which ripened into a rich harvest. To discover which seeds were sown and how, in no way reduces the merit or the true human originality of the writer studied. There is no suggestion of plagiarism in a study of origins, a word which may be preferred to the invidious term "sources".

* * *

Another aspect of this vexed problem of "origins" and of the filiation of ideas deserves attention. With studied negligence, Lawrence, as he emerged from his emotional and intellectual nightmare of the war years, listed some of the "scholarly books" in which he admitted having found "hints" and "suggestions". While calling himself "an amateur of amateurs", he does not descend below the summits in his catalogue of sources, which runs "from the Yoga and Plato and St John the Evangel and the early Greek philosophers like Herakleitos down to Fraser and his *Golden Bough*, and even Freud and Frobenius".[5] He names the geologist Thomas Belt, without saying that he first found his name in the less respectable *Secret Doctrine* of Helen Blavatsky, to which the context none the less alludes. He does not claim James M. Pryse as the main source of his knowledge on Yoga and of his interpretation of St John's *Apocalypse*. He does not name Carpenter. And yet he might almost be quoting from *The Art of Creation*, when he asserts that "the intense potency of symbols is in part at least memory".[6]

The artist is not alone in such forgetfulness. When the critic wishes to relate a writer to his spiritual family, he also often tends to name and to see only the summits; for him, as for the tourist contemplating the mountain peaks brightly lit up by the declining rays of sunshine, the valleys and the lower ranges are hidden in shadow, and the paths leading towards the summits remain unseen. Unless he himself has followed the shadowy paths, the tourist will not really conjure up a clear picture of the chains and valleys. To say that Lawrence is close to Blake, to Carlyle, to Ruskin, to William Morris, and to Whitman, is surely to state truths of varying importance. But to discover the workings upon his creative imagination of a contemporary synthesis of ideas derived from those great authors, and from other less visible sources, should enable his reader all the better to follow his mental itineraries, and provide him with keener insights into those relationships.

* * *

For reasons inherent in the subject matter itself, the plan followed in this study has of necessity been somewhat circuitous. Apart from one essentially devoted to factual data and chronology, the chapters could not be cast into a rigid chronological sequence related to the life and works of either writer; nor could they conveniently be shaped according to some preconceived or even *a posteriori* logical framework of ideas. Neither Carpenter nor Lawrence ever followed such a pattern; so that to impose one's own analytical categories upon them would have tended to falsify and distort.

At the cost of some unavoidable repetition, an attempt has rather been made here to let the reader discover not only the deep resemblances which exist between their ideas, but also certain characteristic combinations and configurations of related themes and images. Except for the purposes of rhetoric and skilful exposition, Carpenter's thoughts tend to follow circular patterns, being rather exceptionally governed by emotional attitudes. To say the same of D. H. Lawrence would be an obvious understatement: he takes his passions for granted, and asserts with the vigour of the prophet. That force of conviction itself is not irrelevant to the idea that he had found many of his beliefs ready-formed in the works of Carpenter, and had absorbed them early as an integral part of his mental universe and an explanation of troublesome facts.

The compulsive or obsessive preoccupations which preside with both writers over the combination of themes and ideas may be a cause, rather than an effect, of their attributing such high priority in their psychology to the body and to emotion over the brain and intellect. Neither was equipped with the analytical tools of a psychology which could explain to them the feed-back effects of such a priority, leading to a weakening or destruction of intellectual structures by that modern form of quietism they both practised, and by their theory of abandonment to impulse.

By relating Lawrence's psychology to Carpenter's, we hope to show that it was essentially pre-Freudian, closer to the evolution of the declining years of the nineteenth century than to the discoveries or theories which spread widely in the second quarter of the twentieth. By pre-Freudian we do not mean non-Freudian; but we note that their conception, for instance of the character and personality, precedes, and owes nothing to, the genial synthesis of the founder of psychoanalysis. This is a question on which many misunderstandings and over-hasty generalizations subsist, which we may help to dissipate.

The two writers who are here compared are characterized by a common passionate desire to understand their own psychology. They hope to do so by relating their inner conflicts to an absolute essence, to some eternal and unitary being. Both were dissatisfied with the social environment in which they found themselves, and anxious to make one of their own liking not only in their immediate personal circle, but also on a larger scale. Both devoutly wished to return to the fundamentals of human existence, and tended to blame accidental circumstances or society for their inadaptation. It is not "unimportant" that one of them may have presented the other with a ready-made, instantly acceptable system, or mental attitude.

While this system does not "explain" the essential individual that is Lawrence, it enables his reader to penetrate closer to the inner mechanisms of his creative processes, to detect a pattern of interrelated ideas serving as a hidden carcass and framework under the flesh and skin of his novels. It throws light on the workings in his mind of esoteric doctrines which are concealed behind some of his more original creations. The underlying unity of thought behind his major novels, *The Rainbow* and *Women in Love*, is revealed in the light of a system of ideas which may have seemed to him highly modern in 1912, poised as it now appears between late-Victorian reaction against the closing nineteenth century, and the later evolution of Western thought and of modern art.

* * *

The method followed here has been as academic and traditional as the subject permitted: the search for facts on which to base comparisons has taken pride of place. But it has been necessary to supplement this factual approach with some sort of intuitive and interpretative reasoning, based on a familiarity acquired from his letters, novels and poetry, with the probable workings of the mind of Lawrence as man and artist. Whenever we have, so to speak, interpolated intuitive perception, we have rigorously refrained from drawing, and, we hope, from appearing to draw, any conclusions of a factual character. We have endeavoured to remain on the safe side of positive statement, using such terms as possibility, or hypothesis.

Carpenter strikes the casual reader as a lovable, balanced and well-integrated personality. Many have spoken of him as of a saint and an ascetic. He is in many ways the Victorian gentleman in revolt—but still the gentleman: the Anglican, the Cambridge wrangler, the curate in reaction against respectability and the stuffiness of Victorian interiors. To use one illustration of the limits of his practical revolt, his idea of "such a degree of nudity as we can reasonably attain to"[7] did not in practice go much further than the wearing of home-made Indian sandals and advocating for others the right to enter the Reading Room of the British Museum in sandals and without a tie. Victorian equilibrium still prevails, and moderation or reasonablenesss governs his contestation of moral codes and aesthetic rules. His deification of the sex instinct and his idea of the androgynous superman remain as remote from actual achievement as do his fantasies on nudity and groves sacred to Aphrodite.

In his vital formative and creative years, in the great ferment of his youth between 1906 and 1918, Lawrence appears as a transitional type between the gentlemanly Victorian revolt of Carpenter and the unconventional generations of Georgian and Elizabethan days in this century. He is struggling against the crippling social and religious conditioning of his Victorian adolescence, against middle-class patterns of behaviour which his generation and he himself had imitated in their aspiration towards social elevation. His reactions to nudity are almost as typical as Carpenter's. He frowns on Tolstoy's prudery, and will later advocate sun-bathing in the nude. But he cannot tolerate that Catherine Carswell should come from her bedroom into his sitting-room in long woollen underwear; and he turns Mabel Luhan's bedroom "into a brothel" by averting his eyes from her unmade bed.[8] Writing in times when people of Carpenter's natural mileu were relatively freer in their talk, and even in their behaviour, than the old Fabian himself, the much-hoped-for liberation from taboos is still for him a verbal and artistic act, designed to shock the bourgeois, rather than a new mode of conduct. And on the subject of comradeship or love between men he was undoubtedly more tortured and hesitant, and less courageous, than his Victorian model and mentor.

Thus in the slow process of disentanglement of the individual from artificial codes, in the search for new and spontaneous patterns of behaviour, which has so strikingly marked English life from Samuel Butler to our day, the part played by Carpenter the psychologist and mystic, at the side of the medical researcher

Havelock Ellis, and that played later by the prophet and creative artist Lawrence, may strike us today as morally hesitant, often intellectually indecisive, trammelled as they were by an obsolete psychology which could not separate observation from metaphysics, by hang-overs from nineteenth-century debates between Darwinists and theologians, by a naïvely materialistic approach to problems of individual psychic development.

It is hoped that this study may help the reader see them as they were; that is, as men struggling honestly with their problems, attempting to reconcile their instincts and passions with their codes and their metaphysics, and using for this purpose psychological tools which today have become museum pieces, as no doubt our own will before many years. These transition phenomena are a double lesson: one of doubt, since ideas which attracted one age seem idle to the next; and one of hope, because great art can be woven around such ideas, and can still be admired when one understands how it was woven, even if in the process one is led to discover the limitations of its practical import.

I

INTERSECTING ORBITS

A Forgotten Pioneer

"Edward Carpenter is rather forgotten to-day, partly because he was a pioneer whose work has passed into our heritage."[1] In these words, spoken by E. M. Forster in 1944 when celebrating the centenary of his friend's birth, there perhaps rang an echo of a metaphor used by the very man he was honouring. In his autobiography Carpenter modestly observed that his prose writings, "like the questions they deal with, have led a curious underground life in the literary world, spreading widely as a matter of fact, yet not on the surface".[2]

This worthy pioneering may well prove to have gone deeper and further than would appear at first glance today, when Carpenter is thought of, if at all, as an almost forgotten minor writer of the late Victorian age and a second-rate author of free verse in the manner of Walt Whitman. Because much of his prose writing was in close harmony with the general social evolution of the early years of this century, yet devoid of the imaginative power and driving force of prose fiction, his original and bold thinking has invisibly merged into the current of ethical ideas of the century, like the waters of a mountain torrent mixing imperceptibly with those of a lake, and wholly lost to sight in the vaster stream that issues from the lake.

Irene Clephane, in her remarkable study *Towards Sex Freedom*, while recognizing the significance of Westermarck and Havelock Ellis, rightly points out that their works did not reach the general public. Where William Morris in *News from Nowhere* had depicted, probably in the footsteps of Fourier and Engels, a society in which marriage would be free, it was left to Carpenter to have the possibly decisive influence on the change in the British attitude to sex:

> *Love's Coming of Age* (1896) . . . had an unexpected success, and, indeed, still continues to sell. Highly charged with emotion and often sentimental, yet it was, for the day in which it appeared, startlingly frank. It entered a world ashamed to discuss the intimacies of sex relationships, either verbally or in print. It went through one edition after another, and for twenty years after its appearance it revealed a new outlook on sex as something to be accepted and enjoyed instead of repressed and feared, to the impressionable young who read it.[3]

A so far totally unexplored instance of the deep undercurrent set up by Carpenter's prose writings is offered by the study of the part which they seem to have played in shaping the ideas of the forty-one years younger writer D. H. Lawrence, one of those "impressionable young", between 1905 and 1918, and indeed until the moment when all traces of an influence may be felt to have disappeared because they completely merge into the personality of Lawrence. From 1916 onwards, the streams of thought of the two men diverge in certain respects: Lawrence, finally wrenched away from his Eastwood background, had by then declared war on equality and political democracy, to which the veteran Sheffield Fabian and pacifist remained deeply faithful in spite of some deep differences. And yet we hope to demonstrate that many of the ideas which hurled Lawrence along his romantic and vitalist way into the search for a new creed were first found by him in the writings of Carpenter, with whom he was not only linked by extraordinary temperamental affinities, but whose social, philosophical and human orbit intersected his own in various ways and at different times.

Approaches to a Comparative Study

Several methods could be applied to the measurement of Lawrence's debt to Carpenter: the first test of all is the recalling of significant biographical data showing points of human contact, both direct and through intermediaries; another method is to analyse such aspects of Carpenter's thoughts, opinions and preoccupations, echoes of which, often reinforced by Lawrence's genius, vibrate in the works of the novelist; yet a third would be the close comparison of texts, which often provides striking evidence. While all three yield a rich harvest of comparative data, they can scarcely be applied in isolation one from the other; nor would it be convenient to work backwards from the works of Lawrence to the ideas of Carpenter, a method which could lead to the most arbitrary and artificial conclusions. In the interest of brevity, knowledge of the works of Lawrence will generally be assumed in what follows, and the plan of this study will be based, but only in so far as this is possible, on the chronological sequence of Carpenter's writings analysed from the point of view of their similarity with, and possible effect on, the formation of Lawrence's ideas, and of the suggestion or reinforcement of themes in his creative imagination.

The initial approach to this study came from the perception of marked similarities in the two men's views on sex and ethics. Textual analysis having given some surprisingly encouraging results, biographical inquiries led to the study, *inter alia*, of the Carpenter papers in the Sheffield Central Library, and to other specific inquiries in the course of the writer's study of D. H. Lawrence. Enough significant facts were brought to light to strengthen the case for a fuller literary study of the similarities between the works of Carpenter and Lawrence. It was then established beyond the shadow of a doubt that their paths had crossed, and that Lawrence had in fact read Carpenter at an early age; yet it cannot be proved that they ever met, except possibly in Lawrence's extreme youth, and without Carpenter registering the fact. It is important to note that Lawrence does not appear anywhere in his writings to have *named* Carpenter; this is not surprising, for a number of reasons which may in due course appear. But as we shall see, the intellectual and moral environment of Carpenter was for Lawrence synonymous with the circle of William E. and Sallie Hopkin and of Alice Dax; and whenever he turned in thought to these early friends, he very probably had in mind precisely the socialist and vaguely anarchist or libertarian climate which reigned in Carpenter's own circle.

Both writers lived and moved for a considerable period within the same geographical area; they had contacts with the same groups, they shared during years which were vital to Lawrence's development a social, ethical and intellectual climate which Carpenter largely contributed to create on the local as well as the national scale. Our concern here is not so much the detection of always debatable literary "sources", as the evocation of that climate, which happens to have fostered the unfolding of Lawrence's peculiar form of genius; and the examination of analogies up to the end of Lawrence's formative period.

We are dealing with the mental atmosphere of late- and post-Victorian socialist England in the working Midlands, of an intelligentsia (the word was first used in England about that time and in that circle) mentally evolving in the wake of Ruskin and William Morris and Annie Besant, of early Fabianism and the Fellowship of the New Life, when there began to spread widely among the élite of the working masses ideas of emancipation of the individual not only from political and economic dependence, but from the moral constraints of the Victorian middle class. In the movement for the liberation of the individual to which Bradlaugh, Annie Besant, Havelock Ellis and his wife Edith Lees, Olive Schreiner and others contributed in their various ways, nobody so much as Carpenter constitutes a link between the leaders and the working masses of the Midlands and the North, except perhaps, but some years later, A. R. Orage and his *The New Age*, to which Carpenter was an early contributor. No other figure of national repute offers locally a more complete synthesis of momentarily converging currents of thought in books and lectures which, up to and including his *Intermediate Types among Primitive Folk* (1914), define the range and content of the religious, social, ethical, aesthetic and sexual preoccupations of D. H. Lawrence up to the end of the Second World War. Personal relations in the neighbourhood would naturally and powerfully reinforce any more general influence of the writer on the young Lawrence. Carpenter was thus better placed than Havelock Ellis, or than any of their contemporaries, to exercise over Lawrence's genius a decisive influence by his development of themes which happened to fit in with the younger man's own preoccupations, if indeed they did not contribute to awakening them, and to offer explanations of some of his personal problems. The present study is thus conceived as a complementary survey of the evidence which shows how deeply Lawrence the Edwardian was rooted in his time and place, at least until such time as the uprooting of this child of the mining Midlands gave free play to the self-destructive forces which mark his middle years of wandering in search of strange gods.

* * *

Carpenter and the Midlands Intelligentsia

Only those biographical details which are indispensable to the current study will be recalled here; for additional material the reader is referred once and for all to Carpenter's autobiography, *My Days and Dreams.*

Victorian Beginnings

Edward Carpenter was born at Brighton in 1844 in a Victorian upper-middle-class home. His father, who belonged to a naval family, joined the navy only to leave it at twenty-five and read for the Bar. He soon gave up the practice of law to become a respectable *rentier* of Brighton, and a magistrate on the Bench of that city, looking after his stocks and shares and reading German philosophers. Carpenter notes that his mother, of partly Scottish parentage and Calvinistic education, was subjected to "a baneful parental influence—Scottish pride and puritanism" which severely restricted her ability to express any "tender feeling".[4] He appears to have been silently but profoundly devoted to his mother in his lonely and affection-starved childhood.

A conventional education at Brighton College was interrupted by one year's break at thirteen when his parents decided to take nine of their ten children to France. With his younger brother Alfred, he then spent a year at the Lycée Impérial (now Lycée Hoche) at Versailles, a distinction which he shares with another unconventional English writer, ten years his junior, Houston S. Chamberlain.

While his elder brother Charles made a rapid career in the Indian Civil Service until his accidental death in 1876, the second brother, George, joined the army, and Alfred resumed with success the family's naval traditions, Edward decided to pursue his studies at Trinity Hall, Cambridge, justifying his choice of a college by the conventional argument that the Hall was "gentlemanly"; he was also aware of the fact that the last Senior Wrangler was a Hall man, and that the college was Head of the River.

His own picture of himself in *My Days and Dreams* suggests he was an oversensitive and clinging child, who "early learned the profound lessons of suffering and of self-independence".[5] In the absence of his brothers, he was brought up, rather like Lawrence, in a household of sisters, and was deeply influenced by two of the elder girls, one of whom, Lady Hyett, encouraged his love of the open air, animals, nature and country walks, the other, Lizzie (Lady Daubeney), his taste for music.

At Cambridge he was tenth wrangler in the mathematics tripos, won prizes for English essays, and was elected to a clerical fellowship at Trinity Hall; this involved being ordained in 1870, and becoming curate of St Edward's, Cambridge, for a while under F. D. Maurice as vicar. He was interviewed by the Prince of Wales and Princess Alexandra as a possible tutor to their sons, the Duke of Clarence and the future George V—a position which was given to Hugh Dalton's father.[6]

Walt Whitman and Self-discovery

At the age of twenty-five Edward Carpenter had a revelatory experience when William Rossetti's edition of Whitman's poems came into his hands: he immediately fell under the spell of "the poems which celebrate comradeship", and, some time later, of *Democratic Vistas*. With a characteristic combination of reticence and frankness, he describes the "strange magnetism" exercised over him by a "succession of athletic and even beautiful faces" at Cambridge, and his sense of the "insurmountable barrier" which separated him from them:

> It was as if a magic flame dwelt within one, burning, burning, which one could not put out, and yet whose existence one might on no account reveal.[7]

He seems to have suffered from a nervous condition which, in *The Intermediate Sex*, but not in his autobiography, he imputes indirectly to the non-satisfaction of his spiritual and physical love needs.[8] Illness, and a sense of suffocation in his Cambridge surroundings, led him to abandon his church duties in 1871, and to take in 1873 a prolonged holiday in Italy, where Florence and Greek sculpture fully corroborated the effects of Whitman's poetry. Acting also under the liberating influence of an elderly and unconventional woman relative who seems to have persuaded him to face and acknowledge the true nature of his sexual desires, he decided to relinquish holy orders and his fellowship and started a new life in 1874 by going to teach astronomy at Leeds, Halifax and Skipton under the University Extension Lecture Scheme.

This decisive action opens up the long connection of Carpenter with the working Midlands and industrial North. He lectured for a while in Nottingham, York and Hull, then he was given in 1877 a regular tour including Sheffield and Chesterfield. After a pilgrimage to America and Walt Whitman in 1877, he settled in Sheffield, in an increasingly precise endeavour to lead a life which would accord with his convictions and inclinations.

That life, described in *My Days and Dreams* in terms which now seem exceedingly discreet (explainable by Carpenter's temperament, but also by the legislation of the time), was to be in keeping with his literary and philosophical models, Plato, Whitman, and, after 1883, Thoreau, as well as with the demands of his health and peace of mind. Tired of landladies and Northern city lodgings, he decided, with Albert Fearnehough, a bearded Sheffield scythe-maker and riveter, and his friend Charles Fox, a farmer, to go and live, together with Fearnehough's wife and children, in a cottage at Bradway, outside Sheffield; he became a vegetarian, worked on the farm, did other manual work, and wrote the long poem "Towards Democracy".

When in 1882 his father left him about £6,000, he bought some fields at Millthorpe near Holmesfield over the Derbyshire border, and began life all over again as a market-gardener with his working-class friends, overcoming what he calls his "nerve troubles" and immensely improving his health. He had come for some time past under the influence of Indian thought, through a Singhalese friend, and one of his occupations was to hand-make pairs of the Indian-type sandals which he wore instead of shoes, starting a substantial trade in this type of footwear. He remained at Millthorpe until 1922, when he moved to Guildford for the rest of his days.

Socialism and the Fellowship of the New Life

In 1883 he published *Towards Democracy*, his first book of poems in Whitman's manner; he then became acquainted with the socialist movement of Hyndman, William Morris, John Burns, etc., with the newly-founded Social Democratic Federation, and with the Fellowship of the New Life, founded in 1883 by Thomas Davidson (1840–1900) and Percival Chubb, for the purpose of "the cultivation of a perfect character in each and all" through "the subordination of material things to spiritual".[9]

Percival Chubb was then a clerk in the Local Government Board in Whitehall, and joint secretary with Havelock Ellis of the Progressive Association; he later migrated to the United States where he was active in ethical movements. Thomas Davidson, an Aberdonian philosopher and a much-travelled scholar, had in mind when founding the Fellowship, "the Pythagorean, the Socratic or Platonic, or the Epicurean brotherhoods",[10] and he expected manual labour from the members of the community which he strove to found "either in a village easily accessible from Euston or Charing Cross or . . . in some terrace or square in town where the members could live in adjacent houses".[11] There can be little doubt that Davidson had been under the influence of American communist societies such as Brook Farm during his stay at Harvard. Another possible link with nineteenth-century American socialism is a Miss Dale Owen, an original member of the Fellowship of the New Life, probably a granddaughter of Robert Owen.

The members of the Fellowship published a "perfectionist" manifesto entitled *Vita Nuova*, strongly reminiscent in certain details of the principles of organization of the Oneida Community, except for the rigorous nonconformist Christianity of Oneida's founder. While monogamy was a strict rule of the written constitution, this also prescribed that "the greatest freedom of intercourse between the sexes [was] to be aimed at", as conducive to the ethical ends of the New Life. Prayer was recommended, and defined as "the direction of the soul upon the infinitude and grandeur of Being". Socialism, based on the principle that "the only title to property is labour", was also a fundamental part of Davidson's creed as expressed in *Vita Nuova*, in the drafting of which Carpenter seems to have had a hand. Davidson soon left to found another Fellowship of the New Life in America, and ran summer schools at Concord, Farmington and Glenmore in the Adirondacks.

A majority of dissident members of the London Fellowship who were not content with its perfectionist ethical programme immediately seceded and founded the Fabian Society, leaving only four original members, including Chubb and Havelock Ellis. These four were soon to be joined by a young highlander, a protégé of Carpenter, named James Ramsay Macdonald, who succeeded Edith Lees as secretary of the Fellowship of the New Life, lived in a strange London phalanstery in Doughty Street, and plunged himself into the study of Swedenborg.[12] Such was the climate of this early English socialism, in which we find many trends of thought and aspiration familiar to the Lawrence scholar.

Carpenter spoke before the Fellowship, gave it his blessing, but did not join it: he met there Havelock Ellis and Ellis's future wife Edith Lees, and became their life-long friend; through Ellis he also became a close friend of Olive Schreiner. He was to co-operate with Ellis and John Addington Symonds in providing them with "case histories", including his own, for what became Volume 2 of the *Studies in the Psychology of Sex, Sexual Inversion*, first published in 1897.[13] George Bernard Shaw was to draw his portrait, as Morrell, the clergyman in *Candida*.[14]

The Midlands Sage

While Carpenter's career as an author begins in earnest at Bradway with the writing of *Towards Democracy*, at about the same time he becomes closely associated with Sheffield socialism and, through the Fabian Society, with the socialist movement on a nation-wide scale. At the same time, his friendship with Ellis, and his sincere and persistent determination to come to the assistance of sexual inverts, led him to assume an increasingly propagandist and scientific role in the revision of social ethics.

After several years devoted to market-gardening, in about 1888 he turned over the management of the land at Millthorpe to Albert Fearnehough in order to devote his time mainly to writing and lecturing. In his own words, he "spoke and lectured in the Socialist connection all round the country, at Bradfield, Halifax, Leeds . . . Liverpool, Nottingham and other places", his subjects being "the failures of the present Commercial system and the possible reorganization of the future".[15]

A visit to Ceylon and India in 1890, which gave birth to the volume *From Adam's Peak to Elephanta*, and his meetings with a Ceylonese *gñani*, greatly strengthened his interest in "pre-civilization man" and in the philosophic themes later popularized by theosophy and Annie Besant, but discovered by him a good deal earlier in the *Bhagavad-Gita*:

> After seeing Whitman, the amazing representative of the same spirit in all its voluminous modern environment—seven years before— this visit to the Eastern sage was like going back to the pure lucid intensely transparent source of some mighty and turbulent stream. It was a returning from West to East, and a completing of the circle of the Earth.[16]

D. H. Lawrence, after writing on Whitman in 1918–20, was in his turn to insist on completing the circle by beginning Eastwards.

The pattern of Carpenter's life as a North Country sage and lecturer in the causes of socialism and liberation of the individual is now set: his biography is largely the story of his books and friendships. From 1898 onwards, a kindred spirit named George Merrill becomes his companion and housekeeper at Millthorpe, which they make

> . . . a *rendez-vous* for all classes and conditions of society. I had by this time made acquaintances and friends among all the tribes and trades of manual workers, as well as among learned and war-like professions. Architects, railway clerks, engine-drivers, signal-men, naval and military officers, Cambridge and Oxford dons,

students, advanced women, suffragettes, professors and provision merchants, came into touch in my little house and garden; parsons and positivists, printers and authors, scythesmiths and surgeons, bank managers and quarrymen, met with each other. Young colliers from the neighbouring mines put on the boxing gloves with sprigs of aristocracy; learned professors sat down to table with farm lads.[17]

Millthorpe lies in Derbyshire, about half-way between Sheffield and Chesterfield, on the edge of the Peak District and close to the Derby and Nottingham coalfield, a mere thirty miles from Lawrence's birthplace at Eastwood. In every possible way the Carpenter of the years 1885–1922 is a prominent and characteristic local figure, well known to all, admired and discussed by the workers and Labour leaders of the district, and by the nonconformist preachers whom he occasionally joins for a Sunday lecture.[18]

His public addresses, his contributions to local journals, such as the *Sheffield Independent*, the *Sheffield Telegraph*, the *Sheffield Guardian*, his letters or articles in national papers or reviews, the *Manchester Guardian*, *The New Age* (before and during Orage's editorship), *The Labour Leader*, *The Clarion*, *The Progressive Review*, the *Daily News* (which Lawrence and the Chambers family read attentively), *The Albany Review*, etc., bring him regularly to the notice of the Midlands intelligentsia and Labour circles at a time of intense socialist development in Northern England.

His importance and influence in shaping the thinking of future Labour leaders is emphasized in the Yorkshireman Philip Snowden's *An Autobiography*; Snowden bought and studied Hyndman's *England for All* and *Historical Basis of Socialism*, based on Marx's *Capital*; but he did not "find these books so interesting and instructive as other volumes on the subject" which he read. "I derived much help and information," he goes on, "from the Fabian Essays and the Fabian Tracts, and from the books of Edward Carpenter, *England's Ideal* and *Civilization, Its Cause and Cure*."[19]

Carpenter belongs to the local colour, just as much as he himself, with his keen sense of the individuality of the common people of the North, appreciates the peculiar features and character of the local scene. What could be nearer to a description of the Lawrence environment, than this sketch of a miners' open-air audience addressed by a group of Sheffield socialists:

> We organized excursions into municipal politics; and country propaganda. . . . While, in the towns, as time went on, audiences grew in numbers and attentiveness, it still remained very difficult to capture the country districts. The miners would really not be uninterested, but in their sullen combative way they would take care not to show it. Many a time we have gone down to some mining village and taken up our stand on some heap of slag or broken wall, and the miners would come round and stand about or sit down deliberately *with their backs to the speaker*, and spit, and converse, as if quite heedless of the oration going on. But after a time, as speaker succeeded speaker, one by one they would turn round—their lower jaws dropping—fairly captivated by the argument.[20]

Carpenter would arrange to speak at the Nonconformist chapels on themes dear to his heart, on ethics, love, religion and philosophy. It is quite permissible to think that the atmosphere of culture and learning breathed by Ford Madox Ford in a Nottinghamshire chapel which he attended with Lawrence, was that prevailing at lectures given by Carpenter round Nottingham, Chesterfield and Sheffield and indeed much farther afield.[21] The meeting attended by Ford at a Wesleyan chapel included a sermon "almost entirely about Nietzsche, Wagner, Leopardi, Karl Marx, Darwin, the French Impressionists and the primitive Italians". It might well have been preached by Carpenter or by one of his Midlands disciples. On the back of Carpenter's notes for a talk, can be read the list of places where he had delivered it; this would range from ethical societies and theosophist temples, to branches of the Humanitarian League, university Fabians, Independent

Labour Party institutes, etc., all of which were traditionally and closely allied to Nonconformism.

* * *

Links between Lawrence and Carpenter

Even in the absence of any other evidence, one could estimate that the chances were exceptionally high of young D. H. Lawrence having come into contact with Carpenter's written and spoken word. But the evidence is there; Jessie Chambers, still by far the most thoroughly articulate and reliable witness of his early youth, assured us in 1935 that their mutual friend Alice Dax, the wife of an Eastwood pharmacist, owned most of Carpenter's works. Jessie was sure that Lawrence had read *all the books* on Mrs Dax's shelves, being a frequent visitor to her house at Eastwood and later at Shirebrook.

Besides, the personality of Alice Dax, whose interest in the women's movement is reflected in the portrait of Clara Dawes in *Sons and Lovers*, is one that fits perfectly into the picture of Carpenter's interests, influence and circle of cultural and political affiliations. So does, in so far as it is known from Lawrence's letters to her, that of her friend Blanche Jennings, the Liverpool postal worker of "advanced" views.

Alice Dax and the Hopkin Circle

In all likelihood Alice Dax was the "member of this little circle" of friends of Lawrence, "a socialist and a suffragette", who first showed him and Jessie Chambers, in 1908 or 1909, "A. R. Orage's *New Age*, which Lawrence took regularly for a time". Jessie Chambers emphasizes that "he liked it far more for its literature than its politics". She and Lawrence "used to enjoy particularly the 'Literary Causerie' of Jacob Tonson" (i.e., Arnold Bennett).[22]

Alice Dax lent Jessie Chambers Carpenter's book *Love's Coming of Age*, possibly in its 1906 enlarged edition. The evidence of the Jessie Chambers papers[23] suggests that this loan may have taken place around 1909–10; so does internal evidence in *Sons and Lovers*, found in the relationship between Miriam (Jessie) and Clara (Alice). Clara persuades Paul to try with Miriam "the great experiment of sex". It is safe to assume, from that triangular relationship, that Lawrence had also borrowed from Alice Dax and read *Love's Coming of Age*, the sub-title of which is "a series of papers on the relations between the sexes". We shall see, however, that his more systematic use and fuller understanding of its contents belong to a later period of his life.

Alice Dax was more than a voracious reader of books on the emancipation of women, a favourite cause of Carpenter's. She was an intimate friend of Sallie Hopkin, the first wife of Councillor William E. Hopkin, a former colliery clerk, cobbler and proprietor of a bootshop in Eastwood, later a magistrate and county councillor. Whether or not Hopkin sold Carpenter's Indian sandals we have not verified; but his name and address are to be found in Carpenter's address book in the Sheffield Central Library. That there are other and close links between the Hopkins and Carpenter will be seen below.

Alice Dax and Sallie Hopkin were active together in the cause of feminism. Enid Hopkin Hilton, daughter of the Eastwood couple, and co-editor with Aldous Huxley of Lawrence's first volume of *Letters* (1932), describes her mother's friend Alice Dax as being "*years* ahead of [her] time", "widely read", "advanced" in dress, thought and house decoration: in other words, a woman endeavouring at the beginning of the century to live according to Carpenter's doctrine of the "simplification of life".[24] She was, like him, reacting against late-Victorian formalities, stuffy furnishings and over-decorated interiors, against the excesses of middle-class gentility; and, in a more personal way, against "poverty . . . shut in behind clean faces and gloved hands, a father's silk-hat and frock-coat", against the desperate falsehood of keeping up appearances. From her own admission[25] she was also in vehement reaction against *men*, and she had sworn vengeance on her father's sex, rushing into marriage with "the first who offered" with the intention of wreaking her vengeance. She confessed to Frieda in 1935 that her love for Lawrence was one of the forms of that revenge against the male sex and a husband she did not love.

Enid Hilton's memories emphasize the link between the socialist affiliations of the Hopkin-Dax circle and their friendship with Carpenter:

> Philip Snowden, Ramsay MacDonald, Charlotte Despard, Annie Kenny, Beatrice and Sidney Webb, and others of the then "forward" group visited us frequently, *and these Lawrence met*. He was a silent listener or an almost violent leader in the conversation . . . Keir Hardie stayed with us, Ramsay MacDonald, Philip Snowden, *Edward Carpenter*, Margaret Bondfield—many others.[26] [*My italics.*]

Enid Hilton went to university in 1913;[27] she refers in the same document to "after the Boer War" and "before the great strikes" (of 1911); these would seem to date these visits during the period immediately preceding Lawrence's break with his Eastwood past, or at the most up to four years previously, when he left in 1908 for Croydon. The portrait of Lawrence which she paints in this passage, with his high collar, pale and thin face, certainly relates to the pre-Croydon period, i.e., around his twenty-first year or just later (1906–08).

The Carpenter link is further attested by Mrs Olive Hopkin, the second wife of William E. Hopkin, who has provided us with copies of letters from Edward Carpenter to her husband concerning *The Rainbow*, and volunteered the following information:

> The first Mrs Hopkin was Sallie Potter . . . The Potter family and Edward Carpenter were great friends, particularly Joe Potter [Sallie's brother] who spent some time in the East as a marine engineer. *I am sure that D. H. Lawrence would be present when Edward Carpenter and his books would be discussed.* I don't know whether Edward Carpenter ever came to Eastwood, but I do know that William visited Millthorpe. I am almost sure that Carpenter and Lawrence never met. I believe a meeting was arranged but it never happened.[28] [*My italics.*]

Such a meeting, however, may have been planned at a much later date, when Lawrence was already known as a writer, possibly after the suppression of *The Rainbow*. On this early period, the memories of Mrs Hilton are likely to be more first-hand than her stepmother's. In a letter to the author (18 January 1969) she recalls her parents' "frequent visits to Edward Carpenter's house", which she remembers as "rather austere, full of books, paintings, and quite unique":

> I can still see the long grass walkways between beds of delicious-smelling flowers, particularly roses and old-fashioned plants such as lavender. There was a stream at the bottom of the garden and Carpenter and his male companion (George?) had made a large swimming hole at a point where the stream was well concealed from neighbouring property. Here they swam in the nude . . . I remember Carpenter's gentleness and his patience with children.

One such visit at least, according to Mrs Hilton's memories, included Lawrence:

> My father and mother and I visited fairly often and one time I went alone with my father and was included in all the "talks" instead of being shunted out of earshot by my mother. It is my great regret that I was not five years older during those golden days. Other and more vital memories would remain now, and much of the conversation would have had meaning. Unless memory fails, I think that D.H.L. was with us on one of those visits. I have a mental picture of the two of them standing in the cottage doorway, under the arch of "climbers" over the door. The picture includes George in the background. Carpenter wore a beard but

in those days Lawrence had only a moustache. Lawrence wore immensely high collars, stiff and awkward. He reminded me of the Mad Hatter in *Alice*. He too was a very gentle person with children, standing no nonsense, but taking infinite pains to explain and answer questions.[28a]

If indeed Lawrence had then a moustache as well as a high collar, this would place the visit not very long after his departure from Eastwood for Croydon in 1908, where he grew a moustache but soon took to soft turn-down collars.

It is in any case likely that Lawrence heard Carpenter address Eastwood or Nottingham audiences, and there can be no doubt that he did discuss his books, his views and his person with his socialist friends of the Hopkin-Dax circle. Mrs Hilton does not positively remember their meeting at her parents' house but recalls that Carpenter would occasionally attend their Sunday "open-house", where Lawrence was "a frequent visitor", at the time when her mother and Alice Dax were "ardent supporters of the suffrage movement".

Faint traces of imitation of Carpenter's rhythms, themes and poetic diction can be detected in Lawrence's early poetry: especially in the 'Schoolmaster' poems, and '*Dreams, Old and Nascent*',[29] written in Croydon, which contain distinct echoes of *Towards Democracy*, a book which Lawrence brought to Helen Corke in his Croydon years.[30]

After 1912 the evidence of the intersection of the "aura" of both writers, to use a word which belongs to the vocabulary of both, is to be found mainly in their works. Yet there are significant signs of the continued interest of Lawrence in the actual circle of Carpenter's friends, as well as in his ideas and preoccupations.

Home Thoughts from Abroad

When Lawrence begins at the end of 1912 to plan the novel which he first calls *The Sisters*, and will rewrite finally as *Women in Love* and its introduction, *The Rainbow*, he writes to Sallie Hopkin; and as usual in those letters he is probably thinking of Alice Dax and of all that she had meant to him. "I shall do a novel about Love Triumphant one day. I shall do my work for women, better than the Suffrage."[31] He is already marking his preference for ethical rather than political theory. Two days later, thinking his letter has been mislaid, he phrases the same thought differently: "I'll do my life work, sticking up for the love between man and woman . . . I shall always be a priest of love, and now a glad one . . ."[32] Success in love, as opposed to the failure of "nearly everybody", will be his theme. This is the time when life with Frieda, in spite of their troubles, is at its happiest and provides a contrast with the old strains and failures of his early love-life, which will nevertheless rankle in his mind well into the years that follow: they are to be found all over again, with attempts at new explanations, in the '*Study of Thomas Hardy*' (1914) and the 'Prologue' written for *Women in Love* almost certainly in 1916. We shall find abundant traces of Carpenter's influence in all the essential works written between the date of these two letters and the end of the First World War.

Again, in January 1915, Lawrence wants to found "a little colony" of some "twenty souls", "away from this world of war and squalor", a colony "established upon the assumption of goodness in the members".

We have shown elsewhere the affinities of this project with American communities such as probably inspired the founders of the Fellowship of the New Life.[33] He wishes to discuss this scheme with William Hopkin. Is he putting out feelers to see how the idea will be received among the disciples of Carpenter? Is there any connexion in his mind between his dream of Rananim, the happy colony of free souls, and memories of the Fellowship of the New Life, the *Vita Nuova*, and the Free Society to which Carpenter refers in *Love's Coming of Age*?

He appeals to Hopkin again, this time much more explicitly, when in September 1915 he wants to "initiate . . . a new movement for real life and real freedom" and launches *The Signature*. He asks his Eastwood friend:

> Get me a few people *in Sheffield*, will you—people *who care vitally about the freedom of the soul*—a few people anywhere—but only those who really care. Ask Sallie to write to Mrs Dax—I would rather not open a correspondence with her again, after so long a silence . . . And perhaps she . . . will ask one or two people in Liverpool, Blanche Jennings for instance.[34] [*My italics.*]

In view of Carpenter's articles in the 1915 issues of *The English Review*, could there be a plainer appeal to see whether he is a potential ally in this revolutionary and pacifist movement Lawrence is starting with Middleton Murry? But again, the question must be asked, why not name him? Is he shy? What does he fear? Is he unsure of the elder writer's adhesion? A few days earlier he had stated his disgust with "Liberalism, Fabianism and democracy", as well as with "the Conservative", in a letter to Lady Cynthia Asquith, described by her as "full of bitterness and diatribe".[35]

The Rainbow, *The Intermediate Sex* and Officialdom

A few weeks later Messrs Methuen were prosecuted for having published "an obscene libel", *The Rainbow*; they pleaded guilty and surrendered all copies for destruction. At this point the destinies of Carpenter and Lawrence follow strangely parallel curves. W. E. Hopkin will now definitely act as a go-between. There is no record as to whether or not Lawrence actually knew of what follows, which we have brought to light thanks to the excellent memory of Sir Stanley Unwin and with the assistance of Mrs Olive Hopkin. The incident is potentially significant, because it evokes the possibility that Lawrence and Carpenter may have been associated in certain official minds as potentially dangerous and likely to hinder the successful prosecution of the war.

In *The Truth about Publishing* Sir Stanley Unwin relates, but without naming the author, how a police officer called on him shortly after the suppression of *The Rainbow*, with a marked copy of one of the books published by his firm.[36] The book was, he has now told the present writer, Carpenter's *The Intermediate Sex*. The policeman had underlined passages which he found obscene, and threatened prosecution if the publishers did not voluntarily withdraw the book from circulation. Sir Stanley noted the passages incriminated, and called upon the Commissioner of Police at Scotland Yard, in his turn threatening to prosecute the police for libel: he argued successfully that he had in 1912 purchased the book, originally published in 1908 by Swan Sonnenschein, with the goodwill of that firm, that several editions had been published without causing any offence, and that he failed to see why this scientific study should suddenly attract the attention of the police. The Metropolitan Police thereupon dropped the matter entirely.

Our investigations into the case of *The Rainbow*[37] have shown that the initiative for prosecuting Lawrence's publishers and thus labelling the novelist as an author of obscene and objectionable fiction, was taken by the Director of Public Prosecutions, Sir Charles Matthews. While it is true that, especially in wartime, the Home Office receives many complaints from busybodies wishing to "keep our boys pure", there is in the Home Office a department which specializes in sifting these protests and issues directives to the various commissioners of police as to the advisability of prosecutions. The official position tends to be that the normal duties of that department are restrictive rather than stimulative of police action, but there is no certainty that it was so in 1915.

Again, judging by the level at which parliamentary questions about the case of *The Rainbow* were handled in the Home Office, it can be assumed, although there is no absolute certainty in the matter, that the police had been given some sort of high-level policy directive concerning this type of prosecution; as early as February 1915 there had been rumours of threatened police action against Lawrence's volume of short stories *The Prussian Officer*.[38] What elements were then common to Lawrence and Carpenter, other than an interest in presenting in literature problems of homosexual attachments?

Suggestions of homosexuality in the German army could have been the only pretext for suppressing *The Prussian Officer*. The Lesbian scene in *The Rainbow* was the one selected by the prosecution to obtain from the magistrate the suppression of the book. But at the relevant times Lawrence was busy writing letters about revolution and pacifism to all and sundry, in particular to Bertrand Russell and Lady Ottoline Morrell, that rallying-point of leftist pacifists; and, as from September, he had embarked on the publication of *The Signature*, a short-lived periodical, the anti-war position of which shocked even the well-disposed Lady Cynthia Asquith as treasonable;[39] he was organizing anti-war meetings at No. 12 Fisher Street, London. The Home Office held a special report on his German wife; this was mentioned in red ink on a minute relating to Philip Morrell's question in Parliament about *The Rainbow*, and thus clearly drawn to the Secretary of State's attention when he drafted his own reply, as the Home Office minutes show. It thus seems that Lawrence was clearly noted as a potentially dangerous subversive writer, possibly as a conscious or unconscious agent of German propaganda.[40]

He was at the time also a contributor to the "advanced" *The English Review*, which had just published, in October, his short story 'England, my England', a tale which, even in its first published form, was unlikely to foster patriotism. *The English Review* had about the same time[41] published Carpenter's series of articles on the war and the "hidden sources" of the strife between nations, which were collected in a volume in 1915 by Allen and Unwin, and in New York by Scribner's, under the title *The Healing of Nations and the Hidden Sources of their Strife*; the book was thrice reprinted in 1915, and again in 1916, 1917 and 1918. A French translation which had been prepared apparently never found a publisher.

To the ordinary police mind, and possibly to minds at a higher level of responsibility in officialdom, it can be expected that, even with its "assumption" that Germany was the aggressor, such a book may have seemed dangerous for national morale. It appealed, with the socialist optimism of the early summer of 1914, to "the solidarity of workers" in all nations against class rule. It denounced German imperialism, pan-Germanism, and Houston Chamberlain's pro-German propaganda conducted from Bayreuth, but it also attacked the European "feudal social order", and it called on England to abdicate her claim to commercial supremacy; it asked for the recognition of "racial rights" (Ireland and India being sore points already), and opposed conscription in the name of anti-militarism.

If one considers the conduct of the Home Office in 1916 over the Diaries of Sir Roger Casement, and the fact that it was found expedient at a high level to try to discredit Casement before British and world opinion as a homosexual, is it absurd to conjecture that someone in the Home Office, prompted no doubt by some secret military authority, had hoped through such a timely attention to his apology of the homosexual in *The Intermediate Sex* to discredit Carpenter, the pacifist and the candid exponent and critic of national policies, influential as he was among the indispensable steel- and mine-workers of the North? The same action had just succeeded with Lawrence, whose publisher had neither the conviction, the courage nor the determination of the late Sir Stanley Unwin, and Lawrence had thus been effectively neutralized for the duration of the war. A police court case would have similarly dealt with Carpenter, had his publisher allowed himself to be manipulated by the police, as it now appears was the case with Methuen.[41a]

Carpenter and *The Rainbow*

Whether or not he was informed locally of this trial of strength of the authorities against his friend, W. E. Hopkin sent Carpenter a copy of *The Rainbow*, which was acknowledged on 28 March by the following letter. Its postscript suggests that Carpenter had requested the loan of the novel possibly on behalf of his friend George Merrill:

Dear Will Hopkin,

Many thanks for *The Rainbow*, duly received this morning—looks very interesting; and we will return it in a fortnight or so.

I don't see (at first glance) anything to baulk at, in the book, but then the morals of the Police are, we know, very superfine.

I'm glad you have stuck up on the Tribunal for Civil Rights. The latter seem to be rapidly disappearing. Good luck to your work.

Ever sincerely,
Edward Carpenter

P.S. I enclose stamps for the postage of the book and we are still in your debt for the trouble involved.

The book was returned on 4 April:

4 April 16

Millthorpe
Holmesfield
Near Sheffield

Dear Willie Hopkin,

I now return the "*Rainbow*" with thanks for loan thereof. I must say the suppression of the volume ridiculous. Some of the details are rather intimate certainly, but Lord have mercy on us! What is life if it is not intimate?

I don't find fault with the book on that ground at all; but I don't like the style. The style is jerky, and rather 'forced'—something artificial about it; also rather spun out. There is a cleverness certainly. Our 'cleverness' is apt to become a bore if indulged in too much. Still after all detractions and subtractions, there is authentic force and 'go' in the book, which raises it far above the commonplace, and as you say his drawing of women is good.

I am glad you have been whacking your Military Representative. How you got to be chairman of your Tribunal is a mystery to me!

George joins in congratulations.

Yours very sincerely
Ed Carpenter

P.S. I enclose a "Story of my Books". I hope you have plenty of friends with spare seven and sixes![42]

Nothing in Lawrence's rather scarce letters of those months suggests that this exchange had been prompted or solicited by him. He had of course visited his sister Ada Clarke at Christmas and almost certainly met the Hopkins. It is reasonable to assume that, if any one, Carpenter rather than Lawrence had associated the attempt to suppress his own book with the successful prosecution against *The Rainbow* and wished to see if there was any connexion between the two actions.

Carpenter did not meet Lawrence at that time. After Helen Corke wrote to him "in gratitude and admiration" for his autobiography *My Days and Dreams*, he said in his reply: "I have never met D. H. Lawrence, but should think he would be a rather 'difficult' person"—possibly an echo of conversations with Eastwood friends.[43]

At that time Lawrence was in rather strong reaction against the forms of advanced political thinking he had known in the mining country:

These men, whom I love so much—and the life has such a power over me—they *understand* mentally so horribly: only industrialism, only wages and money and machinery. They can't *think* anything else. All their collective thinking is in those terms only. They are utterly unable to appreciate any pure, ulterior truth: only this industrial—mechanical—wage idea. This they will act from—nothing else. That is why we are *bound* to get something like Guild-Socialism in the long run, which is a reduction to the lowest terms—nothing higher than that which now is, only lower . . . It is necessary to get the germ of a new development *towards the highest*, not a reduction to the lowest. That we must do, in Cornwall and Florida.[44]

Guild-socialism had for some years been expounded by Orage's *The New Age*: this is further evidence that Lawrence was dubious about the politics of that rather supercilious weekly: nor had *The New Age*, by 1912, a high opinion of Carpenter's later writing.[45]

* * *

The Slow Parting of the Ways

And yet Carpenter's influence on Lawrence is not at an end: the younger writer is more than ever evolving away from a mechanical concept of democratic action, which accepts compromise with the cash-nexus, but he pursues his search for "pure, ulterior truth", and Carpenter, through his original synthesis of leftist politics and religious mysticism, will continue to guide his quest at least for a while.

Lawrence will turn once or twice again towards the political left, but without deep conviction, and more in desperation than in hope. In July 1915 he had been advising Russell to get A. R. Orage, Bernard Shaw, "anybody", to help build "a new State" which in his conception was far from democratic and closer to the views of T. E. Hulme than to those of Orage. In November he had tried to enlist Shaw and Wells on his side for a fight against the *Rainbow* decision.[46]

In 1917 he wanted to initiate "a disruptive, pacifist and nihilist campaign in the industrial North, with a view to bringing a speedy end of the war";[47] nihilist describes his mood most aptly. In May he wrote to Sallie Hopkin:

> It is impossible to believe in any existing body, they are all part of the same evil game, labour, capital, aristocrat, they are the trunk, limbs, and head of one body of destructive evil. How can one say, the head is to blame, but the trunk is blameless? They're all one thing.[48]

Once more, in September 1918, he will wish to go into revolutionary action with the Labour leaders who are Carpenter's and Hopkin's friends, Robert Smillie, Snowden, Mary MacArthur, Margaret Bondfield; but nothing will come of this mood.[49] He has finally passed out of the orbit of socialism and Fabianism; but not quite out of that of the Fellowship of the New Life, or of what remains of it in the spirit of Carpenter's writings. It will take his new reading, the psychoanalysts, the ethnologists, the travellers, not to wean him from an early and lasting influence, but to help him follow it into new directions. Carpenter remains faithful to his original, in many ways surprisingly modern, and as we shall see essentially precarious, synthesis of progressive political thinking and erotic vitalistic mysticism; Lawrence accepts and pursues this latter path, but wants in politics "something new" and bids goodbye to "that old advanced crowd—Cambridge, Lowes Dickinson, Bertie Russell, young reformers, Socialists, Fabians—they are our disease, not our hope".[50] He is for "a new start . . ." and "damn humanity".

"Damn humanity" is what Carpenter would never have said, although he too was "for a new start"; this indeed is the real dividing-line between their two streams of thought on human destiny. But the link and the influence remain. Of far greater import than any political overtures is a reminder of Lawrence to the Hopkins of the special significance to them all of Whitman as man and poet. When finishing in 1918 the lost original version of his essay on Whitman, known today only by the second (1920) version published in *The Nation and Athenaeum* for 23 July 1921,[51] in which we find abundant traces of Carpenter's ideas, he writes to Sallie Hopkin: "The Whitman essay reminds me of Willie".[52] What can this refer to if not to his talks with Willie about Carpenter and Whitman? The similarities between that essay and a whole chapter of *The Intermediate Sex* suggest that the theme of male comradeship had been evoked and discussed between Hopkin and Lawrence. The revulsion from Whitman will come later, after the first visit to America, but will never be total.

In 1918 Lawrence tried to persuade a Charing Cross printer, C. W. Beaumont, a friend of Lady Cynthia Asquith's late brother Yvo Charteris, to print a private edition of *Women in Love*. Beaumont declined on the grounds that it might mean prison for the printer. He was the printer of the British Society for the Study of Sex Psychology, founded on 12 July 1914 with the advice and help of Edward Carpenter. Beaumont printed in 1917 the *Policy and Principles* of the Society, its first publication, and also publications No. 2 and No. 3. He also published (in 1919) Lawrence's booklet of poems *Bay*. He and Lawrence were in regular contact over nearly two years. Beaumont was thus a specialist in a risky type of printing and publishing, and it is difficult to believe that Lawrence could have been unaware of the existence of the Society and of Carpenter's vital role in its foundation at a time when he was deeply concerned with problems of sex psychology, evoked in *Women in Love* and other contemporary writings.

* * *

A Tentative Chronology

The factual basis, such as it is, of contacts between the two men or their respective circles being thus established, and before we delve into the similarities which exist between their works, it may clarify the following chapters if we now attempt to establish a first and approximate chronology of the manifestations of parallelism between Carpenter and Lawrence, partly based on external evidence, partly on summary anticipation of the results of the research which is fully developed in later chapters.

If Lawrence read Carpenter at an early age, from 1905 or 1906 onwards, from Alice Dax's bookshelves, we can expect to find traces of such reading in his first novel, *The White Peacock*, written between 1906 and 1910; this is very markedly reminiscent of the novelist's freshly acquired knowledge; we should find them there in diffused, and on the whole quite general, form. We have already pointed to some resemblances between *Towards Democracy* and Lawrence's Croydon poetry.

A second period opens with the letters of December 1912 from Italy to Sallie Hopkin, already quoted, at a time when Lawrence first conceives the new novel *The Sisters*, after writing the 'Foreword' to *Sons and Lovers*. Because of the extremely involved history of the manuscript of *The Sisters* through its various avatars from 1913 to 1916 and to the ultimate publication of *Women in Love* in 1920, and of its 'Prologue' in 1968, chronological study becomes at this point extremely difficult. Indeed it could well be that the traces in Lawrence's works of various aspects of Carpenter's thinking, from the exaltation of love between man and woman to that of the love between comrades, might hold some clues to the dating of the conception, if not the writing, of certain chapters of *Women in Love*. On the other hand *The Rainbow*, the first part of the double novel, was largely written *after* substantial parts of *Women in Love* in 1914, and was rewritten in 1915 immediately after the '*Study of Thomas Hardy*': in both these works, we find traces of Carpenter's prose writings and ideas. We would therefore tentatively suggest the following sequence:

Late 1912–1913: Foreword to *Sons and Lovers*, the first draft of *The Sisters:* traces of deep and consistent influences from *Love's Coming of Age*, *The Art of Creation*, *The Drama of Love and Death*.

1914: September to November, Lawrence writes '*Study of Thomas Hardy*', under several influences, in particular Carpenter's *Intermediate Sex, Intermediate Types among Primitive Folk* (reviewed by Havelock Ellis in *The Occult Review*, July 1914) and also Weininger's *Sex and Character* (quoted by Carpenter) and H. S. Chamberlain's *Foundations of the XIXth Century*, quoted by Weininger. Other mystical writers, and possibly theosophist works, also begin to act on his ideas.

1915: Lawrence rewrites *The Rainbow*, in which can be traced many ideas and themes of *Love's Coming of Age* and to a lesser extent of *The Intermediate Sex*. He may have read in *The Occult Review* for May 1915 an important 'Notes of the Month' article written on the occasion of the appearance of Edward Lewis's *Edward Carpenter: An Exposition and an Appreciation*.

1916: Conversations in Cornwall with Philip Heseltine, who, according to Robert Nichols, had read Havelock Ellis, Carpenter, Weininger, and Walt Whitman,[53] and was widely read in occult literature. Lawrence rewrites *Women in Love*, in which the influences of *Love's Coming of Age* and of *The Intermediate Sex*, become mixed together, and those of James M. Pryse, Helen Blavatsky, and possibly other occultists.

1917–1918: Lawrence pursues his occultist readings, and reverts to Carpenter in his Essay on Whitman (*The Intermediate Sex*), and in '*Education of the People*'.

1920: Contacts with Italian fascism may have influenced Lawrence's notions of male comradeship, as expressed in '*Education of the People*', *Aaron's Rod*, and in later works such as *Kangaroo* and *The Plumed Serpent*, but Carpenter's influence in this respect continues, mixed with Whitman's.

While the influence of Carpenter's studies and ideas is present from the very first in Lawrence's prose, its high-water mark would thus be between the end of 1912 and the end end of 1916, when it becomes merged with others such as that of theosophy, towards which Carpenter may easily have turned Lawrence's mind, through such books as *The Art of Creation* and *The Drama of Love and Death*. Whether Lawrence had any knowledge of theosophy between 1910 and his reading of Pryse and Blavatsky is directly relevant to the problem of Carpenter's general influence on his thinking. Miss Helen Corke assures us that he was not interested in theosophy or occultism at the time when she knew him, i.e. between 1909 and early 1912 at Croydon; although they almost certainly discussed the claims of spiritualism, which Lawrence appears to have opposed. On the other hand Mrs Hilton's memories would seem to be particularly reliable on this point. She definitely remembers Lawrence "speaking of Edward Carpenter's lectures on Theosophy, and vaguely of his theories of a second seat of consciousness", giving her reasons for this "imprint of memory":

> My father was quite a remarkable man and a great "feeler" into religious cults. I think that he wanted to "belong" but could not uncritically accept. So, in my early years we passed through some strange metamorphoses of belief. Passing from Church of England to Methodist, with overtones of Congregationalism, we proceeded to the Unitarian Church in Nottingham. This was followed by a thrust into the realm of Buddhism, and on to the teachings of Confucius . . . From this we gravitated to Theosophy, probably through the influence of E.C. . . . By that time I was old enough to absorb Theosophical theories and went through a violent addiction to the Church, one which lasted a number of years and was "studied". Interest in the Second Seat, etc., came much later, when I went to College . . . in Nottingham. But I *do* remember long talks on this more or less new subject, and I know that both D.H.L. and my father were deeply interested, especially so Lawrence.[53a]

The reasons why Lawrence is at first interested in the love between man and woman in 1913, to turn his attention later, in 1915–16, to what Carpenter called "homogenic love" and the "comradeship of males", are probably to be found in Lawrence's intimate experience during those years: whatever they may be, the above chronological analysis will have to be borne in mind in reading the study which follows of the traces of Carpenter's books in Lawrence's prose between *Sons and Lovers* and *Studies in Classic American Literature*. It may be that his borrowings from

Carpenter even partly hold the key to the idea which he formed during those years of his own nature and of his emotionally troubled youth.

* * *

Why Silence?

In so far as Carpenter belongs to Lawrence's old Eastwood self, and constitutes a link with that past, his direct influence will to a large extent wane after *Women in Love*, and even more after the 1921 version of the *Whitman* essay, with Lawrence's return to a saner and more peaceful view of life. But this is also the time at which some of the subjects to which Carpenter's books may have initiated Lawrence assert their hold on him in their own right: primitive man, Rosicrucian symbolism and theosophy, the alchemists and occultists, Helen Blavatsky's *Secret Doctrine* and *Isis Unveiled*, Pryse's *Apocalypse Unsealed* and its initiation into some of the more superficial aspects of Yoga. These may have then appeared to the novelist and author of the *Fantasia of the Unconscious*, together with St John, Plato, Herakleitos, Freud, Jung, Frobenius and Tylor, to be more creditable and original-sounding sources of his esoteric knowledge than the works of what may have seemed to him a local and secondary figure of the Midlands who still believed in equality and democracy, and may not have been felt to enjoy enough prestige as a passport to literary fame. Or perhaps Lawrence felt that his borrowings were so many that he had better be quiet and hope nobody would notice them?

There may be another reason for his complete silence on Carpenter. The latter was known to the world as the defender of the homosexuals. Lawrence and Frieda, in later years, hated any suggestion of homosexual inclinations or even interest in inversion, and Frieda after Lawrence's death took pains to pooh-pooh the evidence.

After the prosecution of *The Rainbow*, and when no publisher or printer would look at *Women in Love* for fear of being sentenced to prison,[54] Lawrence was not likely to admit openly any sort of connexion with the author of *The Intermediate Sex*.[55] It is not known at what time he decided to withdraw from publication the extremely compromising 'Prologue' to *Women in Love*, clearly written in Cornwall in 1916[56] and removed from the text before publication. In spite of this deletion, there remained enough in the Secker version of the novel to provoke hostile reviews accusing Lawrence of advocating homosexual practices and calling for police action against the book.[57]

Such considerations may in part explain the total absence of any direct references to or personal contacts with Carpenter, even when the Lawrences were living at Middleton-by-Wirksworth in Derbyshire, only a few miles away from Millthorpe, during most of 1918. And yet this is the period of his life in which, as we shall see, *The Intermediate Sex* exercised over him a special fascination, and is often echoed in his works.

Mrs Hilton does not understand Lawrence's failure to name Carpenter at any time in his books or letters. She is inclined to relate it to what she calls "the class-imposed codes of the time", and goes on:

> Lawrence himself stated . . . that to really enjoy life you had to be "common", or part of the freedom enjoyed by the "lower classes" who were not class-bound into dull respectability. Lawrence was never instinctively "common class". His mother was "a lady", which fact made it hard for her to tolerate her husband, at least at his worst. So—Lawrence went "up" from not very far down, in spite of himself. The Carpenter writings were not acceptable—homosexuality was not acknowledged. I wonder

if Lawrence preferred *not* to know Carpenter, publicly at least. He preferred his own twist to the theories of the other man. Naturally, I just *wonder*. There was a streak of Chapel-imposed morality about him, as with all of us of the period. He had that even whilst trying to free England from the constricting coils of hush-hush.[57a]

Where Silence is Consent

In his interesting study of Lawrence's annotations in a copy of Ouspensky's *Tertium Organum*, E. W. Tedlock[58] hints that Lawrence's silences could be misleading. Cecil Reddie,[59] in paying the tribute of the British Society for the Study of Sex Psychology to its founder Carpenter, after writing that "without him, we should probably never have come into being", mentions and lists the numerous references to, and quotations from, Carpenter's works in Ouspensky's *Tertium Organum*, among which are several allusions to his theory of "cosmic consciousness". It was in fact impossible to give serious attention to Ouspensky's ideas without taking an interest in the more extraordinary of Carpenter's theories, which happen on many points to have coincided with Lawrence's.

Ouspensky, who had in 1915 translated into Russian Carpenter's *Drama of Love and Death*, had formed in London in 1920, with A. R. Orage and an exponent of Jung, Dr Maurice Nicoll, a group to study Gurdjeff's ideas. Lawrence, it is true, became hostile to Gurdjeff's Fontainebleau group, at least in 1924 after the death of Katherine Mansfield. But sometime between 1922 and 1925 Mabel Luhan had given him the 1920 edition of *Tertium Organum*,[60] which he had annotated "rather extensively and vigorously".

His notes relate mainly to passages dealing with animal psychology. Tedlock points out that Lawrence's "belief that emotion is precedent and basic to reason seems to lie at the center of his objections—he resents the familiar dichotomy, and leans the other way".[61] This is a belief which he shares with Carpenter; he also follows Carpenter's teleological theory of the effect of desire on evolution, which is in contrast with Darwinism: "The most beautiful creatures", he writes marginally in Chapter VIII of Ouspensky, "brought about their rarity by their beauty, and the struggle towards that beauty was not expedient nor even strictly pleasurable—there is a deeper motive."[62] In this he follows the same idea of evolution as Carpenter, and carries it to the extreme which makes *Women in Love* a book deeply inspired by the same concept of beauty as *Birds, Beasts and Flowers*, a sort of prose poem looking forward to the near-extinction of the human race and to the creation or survival of a rare and beautiful new species arising from the best elements of the race.

Tedlock's highly appropriate comment runs as follows:

> Perhaps the most interesting aspect of Lawrence's treatment of Ouspensky's book *is his silence* about Ouspensky's heralding of a new consciousness and a higher race of men. . . . At first glance the terms of Ouspensky's prophecy seem compatible with Lawrence's. [*My italics.*]

Here Tedlock refers only to *The Plumed Serpent*, and fails to relate Lawrence's idea of consciousness to his earlier works, especially to *Women in Love*, of which *The Plumed Serpent* could be described as a long-delayed sequel.

Tedlock's comment runs on:

> After paying tribute to Bucke's *Cosmic Consciousness* [a favourite book of Carpenter's] and its identification of the men possessing such consciousness with the founders of world-religions, prophets, philosophers and poets, Ouspensky issues his *Manifesto*.[63]

What the Manifesto contains, in terms not of Ouspensky but of Carpenter and Lawrence, belong to the sixth chapter of this study. We need only report here that it announced a new race of men whose "spiritual eyes have opened" and who "have seen"; a race of which Edward Carpenter was a member, according both to Bucke and to Ouspensky.

Tedlock rightly thinks that

> It is impossible to believe that this did not interest Lawrence. Perhaps his deepest trauma was his haunting sense of the failure of his English and European past. It was precisely this that had sent him on his hegira around the world to New Mexico, and that . . . caused him to search through Mexico for a place to found a colony. He was seeking a new place, a new kind of man, a whole new way of life.[64]

So the American professor stressed that Lawrence "would like Ouspensky's notion of cosmic unity"; and he draws further parallels between *The Plumed Serpent* and Ouspensky's idea of "a new conscience" in the leaders of the new race of men. Indeed what strikes the reader of Ouspensky is the extent to which Carpenter's original views are explicitly and extensively developed in those chapters of the *Tertium Organum* which Lawrence read without a single mark of dissent or irritation.

It is permissible to think that by 1922 the thought of Carpenter on the new consciousness, on a new race of men, and on the special role of male comradeship, which we shall have occasion to analyse below, had become an integral part of Lawrence's own thinking, that he accepted the whole corpus of ideas as his own, and that he incorporated it as such in *The Plumed Serpent* as he had done in part in *Women in Love*, *Aaron's Rod*, and *Kangaroo*. In many ways, the concluding chapter of *Tertium Organum* was the more systematic exposition of ideas with which he had lived since his youth, and which had been central to the conception, and in part to the execution of *The Rainbow*, and of *Women in Love*: the expression of that Messianic belief in his own role as seer and as utterer, which alone explains his career as a writer. Perhaps some of the themes developed by Carpenter, in particular in his talks and writings on Whitman, contain, in their association between the theme of the seer and redeemer and that of male comradeship, the deep reason for Lawrence's silence on an early and durable influence on his thoughts and emotions.

2

THE ATTACK ON CIVILIZATION, ABSTRACT SCIENCE AND CONVENTIONAL MORALS

A Mirror of Late-nineteenth-century Advanced Ideas

Edward Carpenter's writings may be seen as a unique mirror of advanced social ideas in late-nineteenth-century England and at the turn of the century—but one which places unusual and prophetic emphasis on hitherto little-explored problems of the self and of consciousness, viewed from a simultaneously religious and would-be scientific attitude. A slow and prolonged period of maturation and self-understanding had brought Carpenter to full literary production during the 1880s; personal revolt against the more crushing aspects of Victorian life—and of longing for a new, freer, more human society—combined with a deeply religious and mystical temperament, produced this original synthesis of libertarian anarchism and Fabian socialism: a precarious compound, containing in itself the potentialities of its own destruction in any man less strongly assured than he was (by the very education against which he was reacting) of a perfect balance of character and control of his acts and ideas as well as of stable loyalties to his chosen comrades among Labour leaders, agri-ultural workers and industrial workers of the North Midlands.

In such a man, the ascetic temperament and stability of character to a large extent veil the fundamental inadaptation of the self to its social environment; and the ability to create a new environment of his own choice in a slowly changing world obscures the essentially temperamental nature of his inadaptation.

Carpenter has made it clear in his autobiography that his views and doctrines stem first and foremost from a revulsion against the upper-middle-class "Victorian" way of life, against his experience of its effects on family life and the lives of individuals. Not only his own intimate problems, which he was slow in understanding and solving, but those of the sex-starved existence of several of his sisters and of other women around him, condemned by social conventions to celibacy and idleness, turned him into a courageous, clear-headed rebel with a well-defined conception of what he felt needed to be changed, and an inexhaustible fund of optimism about the future of man and of society.

His attitude is admirably summarized by that other rebel and neurotic, Edith Ellis: "to be serene and brave enough to live out what we have discovered, through our introspection and destruction".[1] Carpenter was the kind of man who chooses the hard way, morally and intellectually; and he preferred to live as openly as possible according to his own nature and in complete dignity. It was difficult in the 1880s for a self-avowed homosexual to put his case against the social order of late-Victorian Britain rather than flee the country, as did others of less determined character. A man of deep integrity and ethical principles, he needed to express his ideas and his personality in coherent and rational terms, and to explore fully and deliberately those elements of emotion and mysticism which coloured his reactions to the accepted codes of thought and conduct. In his most irrational moments his thinking remained stamped, sometimes fallaciously, by his mathematical and classical education. His doctrine therefore expressed itself by degrees, slowly and surely, but almost always from the starting-point of a sudden revelation: the flash and illumination of intuitive discovery was followed by the patient working and reworking of his ideas in his essays over the years, each article or lecture being thought over and revised, meticulously adapted to the habits of thought of his readers, until its final publication in one of those little volumes which make up his prose works. The pressure of social and legal conditions was partly responsible for the patient and gradual exposition of original views, in a constant and measured effort to alter those conditions. Thus a general pattern slowly develops from his books, from the initial revelation to the gradual exfoliation of the full social and philosophical significance of his ideas. This slow development perhaps explains why the full import of his thinking appeared so gradually to a young reader such as Lawrence.

Towards Democracy, by far the least readable of his books today, contains the spontaneous but somewhat elusive assertion of his creed. "Whitman and water" was Havelock Ellis's first reaction to it; he changed his mind when he read it again, as indeed others might who study it in small doses, especially in Edward Lewis's subtle and sympathetic study of Carpenter's writings. His prose works, gradually assembled from short essays, constantly enlarged and clarified or supported by notes and quotations from other authors, regularly reprinted, some of them from 1887 up to the present, make up a remarkably homogeneous collection, with a progression from simple but thoughtful social and ethical studies towards philosophical meditations on *The Art of Creation* (which anticipates by several years some of Bergson's ideas in *L'Evolution Créatrice*) and *The Drama of Love and Death*, i.e., a cosmic view of the self and the universe and of the manifestations of the creative impulse through love and the final transfiguration of the self in death. Eros and Thanatos are, throughout, Carpenter's two great themes.

The main themes centre on a criticism of "civilization", the social incarnation of Thanatos, and on a desire to return to man's natural state of innocence; they are steeped in the romantic socialism of the nineteenth century, with a definite Marxist tendency, and they study the evil effects of society on the development of the individual. They analyse the effects of private property on sex life, and endeavour to define a new morality which would facilitate the complete liberation of man so that he might attain Carpenter's ideal of true democracy, profoundly influenced by Whitman's *Democratic Vistas*. They aim at, and they define, the "simplification of life", and search for ancient "cosmic" wisdom in the philosophies and religions of India. They even attempt to discover the physiological basis and centres of a "cosmic consciousness" which links man again, after the passage through his intellectualized self-consciousness, to the universe in which he lives. These themes develop with insidious mutual harmony, gradually, with admirable powers of exposition and persuasion well-exercised in the practice of public lectures. As the years pass, the emphasis is shifted to what Carpenter calls "the Eastern outlook", which he studied essentially in the *Bhagavad-Gita*, and to certain aspects of theosophy, but always without exaggeration, the critical sense almost always uppermost, at least in the exposition if not the intuition. No other English writer, except Annie Besant, combines in this way, in his generation, advanced political thought and Hindu mysticism.

Intuitive Revelation and Social Criticism

The starting-point is intuitive, and Carpenter never wavers or equivocates on this point:

> *Towards Democracy* came first, as a Vision, so to speak, and a revelation—as a great body of feeling and intuition which I *had* to put into words as best I could. It carried with it—as a flood carries trees and rocks and the mountains where it originates—all sorts of assumptions and conclusions. Afterwards—for my own satisfaction

as much as for the sake of others—I had to examine and define these assumptions and conclusions. That was the origin of my prose writings.[2]

At least before 1900, those prose writings are mainly devoted to a criticism of society and to forecasts of a democratic and socialist future, in the formulation of which free play is given to the author's personal preoccupation with a complete liberation from all external and artificial constraints of free and self-responsible individuals. The modern reader is irresistibly reminded of the author's early association with the Church, which he terminated not so much on account of unbelief, as of difference in belief. It may be said that his prose works are all dedicated to the definition and assertion of a creed; and that creed is a form of romantic vitalism, aiming at the reconciliation with religion, if not of science in its abstract and mechanistic form, at least of a science of life; of certain aspects of scientific materialism with a craving for the spiritual.

Towards Democracy and the Cosmic Sense

Written in the sentinel box which Carpenter had built for himself in the fields at Bradway under the combined influence of nature, of Whitman, and of the *Bhagavad-Gita*, *Towards Democracy* was also inspired by the severance through death in 1881 of "a strong invisible tie" with the poet's mother; the long poem which gives the full volume its title was composed in "a mood of exaltation and inspiration—a kind of super-consciousness—which passed all that I had experienced before".[3] Its message today may seem diffuse, and far less potent and immediately suggestive than Whitman's. Yet it is of direct relevance to the present study.

To begin with, *Towards Democracy* anticipates by many years much that is characterictic of Lawrence, in its insistence on the necessary integration of body and soul. Democracy is not for

Carpenter a matter of "States or Constitutions": that is "but the shadow" of that Platonic idea "which first expresses itself in the glance of the eye or the appearance of the skin".[4] For him, to quote his friend Edward Lewis, democracy is "self-utterance and self-realization . . . It is the 'Son of Man' which, ascending to its perfect blossom, exfoliates like a Tree of Life into human races (branches) and human individuals (leaves)";[5] or in Carpenter's own words, "a Celestial City of equals and lovers".[6] Equality and self-realization signify that the "freed soul" has "completed its relation to the body";[7] in order to do this it must acknowledge sex, and its priority over all other manifestations of the creative urge:

> Sex still goes first, and hands, eyes, mouth, brain, follow; from the midst of belly and thighs radiate the knowledge of self, religion and immortality.[8]

We have already indicated resemblances between the poetic treatment by Lawrence of "working men" themes in his early poetry and the Whitmanesque figures of workers and humble, ragged folk in *Towards Democracy*, with the same ambiguous haze of democratic feeling and sexual attraction. Ever present throughout *Towards Democracy* is this sense of the physical reality of bodies as materializations of the life impulse, so keenly felt by Lawrence. It expresses itself with particular force in 'The Ocean of Sex', which pictures "the great sea . . . within one":

> With flux and reflux pressing on the bounds of the body, the
> beloved genitals,
> Vibrating, swaying emotional to the star-glint of the eyes of all
> human beings,
> Reflecting Heaven and all Creatures,
> How wonderful!

The waves of this ocean vibrate, "a tremor travels across it", at the approach of "a figure, male or female":

> The glory of the human form, even faintly outlined under the trees or by the shore, convulses it with far reminiscences . . .
> Till may be to the touch, to the approach, to the incantation of the eyes of one
> It bursts forth, uncontrollable.

As the poet identifies himself with this ocean, he understands that he also is "of the dateless brood of Heaven and Eternity".[9]

Any reader in the least familiar with Lawrence's poetry of 1910–14 and with the '*Study of Thomas Hardy*' will feel how such passages may have encouraged the expression of his mystic attitude to love and sex, while also providing him with images which his poetic imagination could powerfully develop. Nor can one fail to make comparison between such a poem as 'Virgin Youth', in its original form[10] and this:

> The budding pens of love scorch all over me—my skin is too tight, I am ready to burst through it—a flaming girdle is round my middle. Eyes, hair, lips, hands, waist, thighs—O naked mad tremors; in the dark feeding pasturing flames.[11]

Swinburne himself had not dared so openly to express his auto-erotic raptures; and Lawrence, in the 1928 edition of *Collected Poems*, will carefully erase from 'Virgin Youth' the traces of auto-eroticism of its early version, which probably owe more to Carpenter than to Whitman.

Towards Democracy also contains much which might be echoed in the poems written after the death of Lawrence's mother, and in *The White Peacock*. More especially, in the diffused atmosphere of the soul's idyllic search for a lost secret and an earthly paradise. While the personal experience of the contrast between the ugliness of industrial surroundings and the beauty of nature is fundamental in Lawrence, and scarcely required external stimulation, his literary treatment of nature and agricultural life, and the ever-recurring pastoral tone of *The White Peacock*, including the chapter 'A poem of Friendship' in which the pastoral is allied to the theme of love for another boy, may easily have been if not inspired, at least made bolder by the evocation of Derbyshire landscapes and nature in *Towards Democracy*. In it are ever present nature and sun-worship, and its author tells how it was written

> . . . to the hum of the bees in the leafage, the robins and chaffinches hopping around, an occasional large bird flying by, the men away at work in the fields, the consuming pressure of work within me, . . . far, far away from anything polite or respectable, or any sign or symbol of my hated old life. Then the afternoons at work with my friends in the fields, hoeing and singling turnips or getting potatoes . . . everything turning and shaping itself into material for my poems.[12]

Many a page of *The White Peacock*, devoted to life in the fields, to agricultural labour and friendship with the young farmer, might be reminiscent of that atmosphere, or of such a stanza as this:

> Civilization sinks and swims, but the old facts remain—the sun smiles, knowing well its strength.
>
> The little red stars appear once more on the hazel boughs, shining among the catkins; over waste lands the peewit tumbles and cries as at the first day; men with horses go out on the land—they shout and chide and strive—and return again glad at evening; the old earth breathes deep and rhythmically, night and day, summer and winter, giving and concealing herself.[13]

It is true that such analogies remain very general, and that Lawrence could have inherited from the main romantic stream of thought and expression much of the sense of community with nature which inspired *The White Peacock*. But Carpenter's early works are dominated by the same sense of deep-seated conflict between natural man, cosmic man in instinctive touch with the pristine nakedness of nature, and the artificial state of "civilization" which is felt to be contrary to "the old facts". Rousseau, often named as a forerunner of Lawrence, may after all not have been so close to him in his youth as was the poet of *Towards Democracy*, the author of *England's Ideal*, and above all, of *Civilization, Its Cause and Cure*.

First published in 1887, *England's Ideal* is a collection of simple papers on social subjects, many times reprinted between the first publication in 1884 of the title-essay, and the ninth edition in 1919. Carpenter acknowledges in these essays the influence of Ruskin and that of Karl Marx.[14] The titles speak for themselves: 'Modern money-lending and the meaning of dividends'; 'Social progress and individual effort'; 'Desirable mansions'; 'The Simplification of life'; 'Does it pay?'; 'Trade'; 'Private property'; 'The enchanted thicket'. Fabian socialism is mixed with the assertion against landlords of the citizen's right of access to the woods and green fields (a theme which is evoked in *The White Peacock* by Cyril's and George's first encounter with the gamekeeper); and the simplification of life is offered as a reaction against Victorian middle-class manners and the rigid keeping up of appearances. These tracts, some of which deal with local problems, contain little which announces the future development of Carpenter's ideas; but they are strikingly suggestive of the problems of life in late-Victorian industrial and farming England.

A Turning-point

With *Civilization, Its Cause and Cure* (1889) comes the true turning-point of Carpenter's prose work, and the first attempt by him to make a synthesis of his poetical and ethical aspirations and of his abstract and social thinking. The first essay had been presented in 1886 as a Fabian lecture, and had attracted attention by its main thesis. The titles of the others are significant of the new attitude publicly taken by their author: 'Modern Science: a criticism'; 'The Science of the future: a forecast'; 'Defence of criminals: a criticism of morality'; 'Exfoliation: Lamarck versus Darwin'; 'Custom'. Later additions will be, in 1906: 'A Rational and humane science'; and, in 1920, 'The New Morality', with an 'Appendix' "containing notes and *data* on the life and customs of many 'uncivilized' peoples".

Around those subjects, and drawing from the very first many examples from the customs of primitive folk, Carpenter develops a coherent system of thought founded on the criticism of mechanistic science and of the social order founded on it. This system proceeds initially not from logical reasoning, but from a religious, intuitive and teleological conception of evolution, and of man's destiny and role in the universe. The intuitive nature of this revelation is stressed by the author in *My Days and Dreams*:

> The attacks on Civilization and Modern Science were both wrung from me, as it were, by some inner evolution or conviction and against my will; but in both cases the position once taken became to me fully justified.[15]

While admitting the great value of the scientific work of the nineteenth century, he continues:

> None the less the very decided criticism in *Civilization: Its Cause and Cure*, of the limits of scientific theorizing and authority had been quite necessary; as well as the forcible insistence on the fact that Science only deals with the surface of life and not with its substance. As to Civilization the advances of Humanity during the Civilization period have been largely bound up with the advance of Science and have chiefly consisted perhaps in increase of technical mastery over Nature and materials . . . During this period something of the intensity of the old tribal kinship and community of life has been lost, as well as something of the instinctive kinship of each individual to Nature.[16]

This criticism of society, of private property, and of mechanistic science, while it is in the tradition of Carlyle's attacks on utilitarian liberalism and commercialism, owes something to Marx, and much to Ruskin and William Morris—who was prevented by death from contributing an original essay to the collective volume *Forecasts of the Coming Century*, edited in 1897 by Carpenter for The Labour Press, Manchester, and the *Clarion*. But characteristically, the emphasis is on moral and religious values, rather than on the analysis of the mechanisms of alienation or on economic theory: the former curate of F. D. Maurice is closer to the chapel-going form of socialism than to any of its de-Christianized Continental forms. The numerous reprints of this book (eighteen editions between 1889 and 1938, six of which were issued, from 1889 to 1900, by Sonnenschein, the publisher of Karl Marx) testify to the success of the book among the "advanced" English public.

Indian Thought and Annie Besant

The first essay, originally prepared in 1886 as a Fabian lecture, is based on unstated but clear assumptions, a mixture of Marxism, Rousseauism or rather Whitmanism, and of ideas originating from Hindu religious sources. Carpenter's friendship with Annie Besant goes back probably to the time at which she joined the Fabian Society, in 1886 or 1887, and certainly to 1887, when she visited his socialist group at the Commonwealth Café in Sheffield.[17] Her interest in the more revolutionary forms of socialism began about 1895, at the time of her break with Bradlaugh. She joined the Theosophical Society in 1889, whereas Carpenter first read the *Bhagavad-Gita* in 1881; his visit to Ceylon and India took place in 1890. While he admired Annie Besant's "cool and intellectual temperament" and had nothing but scorn for "the rot and confusion" of Helen Blavatsky's *Secret Doctrine*, it is interesting to note his criticism of Mrs Besant's failure to penetrate "the ideas and inspirations of the ancient East". He does not claim to have preceded her in this endeavour, but he finds in her a lack of "the intuitive perception, the mystic quality of mind, which should enable her to reach the very heart of the old Vedantic teaching". His judicious criticism is specially valuable in that it so aptly defines his own qualities:

> She analyzes the composition of the human personality, or the order of general creation, or the various life-rounds of our mortal race; but in all she seems to be repeating or corroborating some

pre-established formula, never to be describing something which she has herself perceived; system and formula prevail, unseen 'authorities' are hinted at, the pages bristle with sanskrit jargon, but no living or creative *idea* moves among them, and the reader rises from their perusal void of inspiration or of any really vital impulse towards new fields of thought and life. Nevertheless, taking it all and all, and especially in her expositions of Socialism and Theosophy, Mrs Besant has done, as I have said, a great work.[18]

To what extent friendship with Carpenter may have contributed to accelerating the evolution of Annie Besant towards theosophy is thus a question worth asking: there is little doubt that his Fabian lecture of 1886 was already deeply influenced by Eastern ideas, and we find him at the very source of a current of English thought leading to the Lawrence of 1916–20. While the latter's reading of Helen Blavatsky can be dated approximately to 1916, there are earlier traces of theosophist and Rosicrucian ideas and terminology in his writings between 1912 and 1916; these may be responses to Carpenter, perhaps to Swedenborg, also named by Carpenter and available in cheap editions,[19] and possibly to other writers inspired by gnostic and Eastern traditions, although our evidence from Helen Corke suggests that by 1912 Lawrence had no special knowledge of such writers.

* * *

Civilization, Its Cause and Cure

In the essay on civilization, streams of thought which lead to Lawrence seem to converge significantly, as will be seen by this Whitman quotation on which it opens:

The friendly and flowing savage, who is he?
Is he waiting for civilization, or is he past it, and mastering it?[20]

Civilization not Defined

Here the poet states his English disciple's assumption: civilization is not defined otherwise than by this quotation, and as "a somewhat *peculiar* state of society . . . which . . . *does not seem* altogether *desirable*". [*My italics.*] It is seen as "*a kind of disease*" which the various races of man "*have to pass through*", and from which, so far, history suggests that nations do not recover.[21] [*My italics.*] In another essay, it is more clearly but not more positively defined as "a temporary alienation from true life".[22]

If civilization is a disease, it is also associated with a *sense of sin*. Faced with the necessity to define the term, Carpenter chooses not to use it in the sense of "a state of future culture towards which we are tending" but to "limit its use (as is done to-day by all writers on primitive society) to a definite historical stage through which the various nations pass, and in which we find ourselves at the present time".[23] Having thus postulated the restricted and pejorative use of the word, he associates it with the growth of wealth, the concept of private property, a society based on classes, and the destruction of "mother-right and inheritance through the female line" which "turned the woman into the property of man".

What would a psychoanalyst make of these associations, powerfully charged with emotions, and emanating from a man whose affective link with his mother was evidently as close as it was unable to find expression in life? In any event, this Fabian lecture groups together, as if at the compulsive dictation of its author's subconscious self, all the evils which he will spend the better part of his life impugning in urbane, almost always serene, but powerful language: the private ownership of land which has created "a class of landless aliens", slavery, serfdom, slave labour, the state, and the policeman. Such definition of civilization as is reached is therefore a denunciation of all these ills:

> We are justified therefore in calling civilization a historical stage, whose commencement dates roughly from the division of

society into classes founded on property and the adoption of class-government.[24]

Further evidence of the disease is sought in written history and written law (quoting Lewis Morgan's *Ancient Society*), in the existence of the merchant (Engels); and Carpenter mistranslates the French phase *les nations policées* as "policemanized nations", out of his wish to emphasize the "social degradation" which shows itself in the use of police.

Healthy Barbarian and Golden Age

Calling upon the evidence of the first ethnologists, prominent among whom is the American Lewis Morgan, he gives picturesque examples to show that barbarians are healthy in body and social structure, free from class division and from any contrast between rich and poor, as well as from all sense of sin. The myths and traditions of the Golden Age and of the Fall are pressed into service as further evidence of the superiority of the primitive state of man over that of civilization:

> That each human soul . . . bears within itself some kind of reminiscence of a more harmonious and perfect state of being, which it has at some time experienced, seems to me a conclusion difficult to avoid; and this by itself might give rise to manifold traditions and myths.[25]

Thus are the myths of the Good Savage and Golden Age powerfully revitalized by this association with advanced thought in Fabian England, backed up as they are by an early recourse to the infant science of ethnology in a context of Marxist criticism of private property. When, in 1906, Lawrence starts working on what became five years later *The White Peacock*, with its intense and haunting evocation of a "lost secret" and its denunciation of the ill effects on the natural instincts of social life, of convention and of private property; when he conceives the character of Annable the gamekeeper, "a man of one idea—that civilization was the painted fungus of rottenness"[26] when he stresses the incompatibility of civilization, academic culture, private property, with "the animal" in man, is he unconsciously drawing on memories of this essay, or perhaps on some lecture which he may have heard Carpenter deliver on similar themes? Does he have in his mind a personal picture of the bearded and sandal-wearing elder and market-gardener and nature-lover of Millthorpe, well known to the young Sunday ramblers of the district, and known to his friends as "the Noble Savage"?[27]

The character of Annable, while it owes much to George Moore's *Esther Waters*, is not without its analogies with the former curate of St Edwards, the Cambridge wrangler turned manual worker: he is a former Cambridge student and clergyman, and has become a gamekeeper after an unsuccessful marriage into society. He looks "like some malicious Pan".[28]

As for the tradition of the good savage, Lawrence has found it of course in Rousseau and Whitman, but the latter would seem to have been discussed by him with Willie Hopkin; and this tradition is here modernized and made locally accessible by Carpenter, who like Annable, puts his faith into practice in the vicinity: Cyril, the narrator in Lawrence's first novel, is passionately in love with farming and with a young farmer, and rather less in love with the latter's studious sister. The world-wide tradition of the good savage and the Golden Age is far less potent, far less well adapted to the universe of the young writer, than this native product, present either directly, or through close friends of Carpenter's in the immediate vicinity, and filled with the seeds of most other typically Lawrentian themes.

Health and Civilization

Civilization being a disease, what are health and illness according to Carpenter? Here again his assumptions are directly relevant to an underlying idea of Lawrence's, that of a permanently sick man who forges for himself a personal theory of health and disease.

From etymological reasoning, Carpenter concludes that health is *wholeness* and *holiness*: it is

> . . . a condition of the body in which it is an entirety, a unity—a central force maintaining that condition; and disease being the break-up—or break-down—of that entirety into multiplicity.[29]

The reader is thus presented with a positive conception of health; disease of body or mind is a loss of unity, the break-up into multiplicity; and death is "the loosening and termination of the action" of a unifying power in the organism. This power is like a sun "which illumines and gives unity to the man, whose warmth and light would permeate his system".[30] It has the power "to *expel* disease from its neighbourhood"; it means "unity, integration as opposed to disintegration".[31] Animals possess this unity, while civilized man has lost it but may reconquer it "when the more squalid elements of our present-day civilization have passed away".[32]

This almost Manichean dualism of integration and disintegration, so visibly inspired from Hindu religion, will be familiar to Lawrence's readers, and is almost entirely accepted by him as a fundamental belief. In a letter to Garnett on *Sons and Lovers* he states that "almost unconsciously, the mother realizes what is the matter, and begins to die"[33]; throughout '*The Crown*' and *Women in Love* forces of integration and disintegration are at work, and Birkin asserts that "one is ill because one doesn't live properly—can't",[34] in a conversation in which he expresses the wish to see not only civilization, but the whole of humanity destroyed, making way for a humanless world where the lark would rise happily every morning.

The Fall and the Return to Paradise

In spite of certain reservations, Carpenter accepts the theory of evolution, but it faces him with a problem: Why does man, placed as he is at the end of the evolutionary process, lose unity, lose wholeness, and *fall*? "What is the cause and purpose of this fall and centuries-long exile from the earlier Paradise?"[35]

The teleological assumption in the phrasing of the question is interesting, and so is the answer:

> There can be but one answer. It is self-knowledge—(which involves in a sense the abandonment of self). Man has to become conscious of his destiny—to lay hold of and realize his own freedom and blessedness—to transfer his consciousness from the outer and mortal part of him to the inner and undying.[36]

He will have much more to say on this process in *The Art of Creation*; the influence of that book on Lawrence may be more specific than that of *Civilization, Its Cause and Cure*. But this definition of the progress of the human soul through self-consciousness to assimilation into the 'Great Self' of the universe and to cosmic consciousness, this belief in the triumph of the self over its separateness *through* consciousness, is a theme familiar to readers of *The Rainbow* and *Women in Love* and of Lawrence's letters relating to the genesis of these two novels. The original idea of *The Sisters*, as exposed to Edward Garnett, and as executed in part in *The Rainbow*, is precisely that of the progress of the individual human soul through self-consciousness to a new and higher evolutive state in which there is a partial abandonment of self, and acceptance, in equilibrium, of the self of another. As we have shown elsewhere,[37] the development of this theme will be obscured by Lawrence's experience and conflicts between 1914 and the completion of *Women in Love* late in 1916, but it is likely that the general pattern of his idea of the soul's progress, of the Fall and the reconquest of Paradise, originates in the formulation by Carpenter, found here in its earliest form, of the theory of the Fall and the return to the Golden Age.

In *The Sisters*, Lawrence said that he wanted to describe the process of "woman becoming individual, self-responsible, taking her own initiative".[38] Carpenter shows the human soul gradually reaching "knowledge of its wonderful heritage" and becoming "finally individualized and free", until it can "know itself immortal, . . . resume and interpret all its past lives, and . . . enter in triumph into the kingdom which it has won".[39] This process of the fall through self-knowledge and of regaining paradise *through* self-consciousness, that is to say by overcoming it, of reaching at last the "disentanglement of the true self from the fleeting and perishable self",[40] is the very theme which constitutes the unity of *The Rainbow* and of *Women in Love*, through and in spite of all variations in the detailed execution over the successive stages of writing of the two novels. Success or failure in attaining this disentanglement in the three generations of Brangwens from Tom and Lydia to Ursula and Gudrun, is the key to the scale of moral values implicit in the two novels; and the character of Ursula, with its early insistence on knowledge and economic independence, leading to the discovery of an ultimate relationship outside human civilization, can be construed as an illustration of this conception of the Fall and the return of paradise.

The idea of consciousness, and of its central position in the process of fall and redemption, is indeed vividly presented in what is in all probability one of the chapters of *The Sisters* which constitute the original "nucleus" of the novel; it has become the third chapter of *Women in Love* entitled 'Class-room'. In it the didactic purpose of the novel shows itself clearly in the clash of ideas between Birkin, who embodies the theme of redemption by abandonment of civilization, and Hermione who stands for all that in Lawrence's youth which aimed at assimilation into civilization, and its attendant evils of split personality. Birkin reacts with unusual vehemence to Hermione's idea that it may be wrong to rouse young children to consciousness, and in particular to awareness of sex. The whole scene, which is central to the two novels taken as a single work, may be read again with its full significance in conjunction with this passage of *Civilization, Its Cause and Cure*:

> The animals and man, unfallen, are healthy and free from care, but unaware of what they are; to attain self-knowledge man must fall; he must become less than his true self; he must endure imperfection; division and strife must enter his nature. To realize the

> perfect Life, to know what, how wonderful it is—to understand that all blessedness and freedom consists in its possession—he must for the moment suffer divorce from it; the unity, the repose of his nature must be broken up, crime, disease and unrest must enter in, and by contrast he must attain to knowledge.[41]

The same mystery, the same ambivalent attitude to knowledge as being the first step towards redemption through the Fall, is common to both writers: neither offers a logical way out of the contradiction between self-consciousness as the sympton of the Fall, and a different level of consciousness seen as a stage on the way to Redemption, to "disentanglement": "I dream the dream of the Soul's slow disentanglement,"[42] writes Carpenter, accepting this mystery as part of the mystical process of experience.

Lawrence, at least in the opening chapters of *Women in Love*, is more impatient of mystery, and seeks an outwardly different, but just as mystical way out of the apparent contradiction. For him the equivalent of the Fall is knowledge "in the head"; redemption for him also comes from knowledge, but of a different kind.

"How can you have knowledge not in your head?" asks Hermione; Birkin retorts:

"In the blood, when the mind and the known world is drowned in darkness."[43]

But the problem is the same; when it come to an analysis of intuitive, instinctive, especially sexual behaviour, the difference between Lawrence and Carpenter will be found essentially in their modes of expression, in their varying degrees of audacity.

Civilization and Sex

For Carpenter, civilization is a "moment of divorce", a "parenthesis in human progress", co-extensive with history, of the "immense purpose" of which "civilization, and all crime and disease" are "only the materials". His Marxism, his Christian background and his Indian mysticism combine in the following synthesis: Civilization, founded on property, has disintegrated and corrupted man, has broken up "the unity of his nature":

> It begins with the abandonment of the primitive life and the growth of the sense of shame (as in the myth of Adam and Eve). From this follows *the disownment of the sacredness of sex*. Sexual acts cease to be a part of religious worship; *love and desire*—the inner and the outer love—hitherto undifferentiated, *now become two separate things* . . . It culminates and comes to an end . . . in a vast system of commercial love, bought and sold, as in the brothel and in the palace. . . . And so with this denial of Nature comes every form of disease.[44] [*My italics.*]

Those ideas will be expanded in *Love's Coming of Age*. The main theme of *The White Peacock*, in which Lettie sacrifices her deeper love to wealth and to the external trappings of upper-middle-class life, might be derived from this condensed formulation of Carpenter's ideas on sex; and the religious attitude to love is expressed by the character in that novel who exclaims: "I'll pray with kisses".[45]

Civilization and Government

Property separates man from Nature, draws him away from his fellow-men, breaks up "the unity of the old tribal society", leads to "the institution of government": and government is "the evidence in social life that man has lost his inner and central control, and therefore must resort to an outward one".[46] The true guide, the inward man, has thus made way for "an external law which must always be false". If all government is bad, monarchy is "the sincerest" form which it can take, because the monarch "represents the true Man and therefore the people".[47] The ideal leader is both king and priest, like the Greek *basileus*, or Moses.

Do we not find echoes of this in those pages of *Twilight in Italy* in which Lawrence discusses Hamlet and the significance of regicide in terms of the destruction of true man in each one of us?[48]

With significant references to Plato and Carlyle, the Fabian lecture goes on to contrast "the area of anarchy—the democracy of Carlyle; the rule of the rabble, and mob-law", with "the true Democracy" which "has yet to come". In civilization, "man has sounded the depths of alienation from his own divine spirit, he has drunk the dregs of the cup of suffering, he has literally descended into Hell", before he can "mount deliberately and consciously back again towards the unity which he has lost."[49]

Civilization not only means alienation from the proper function of sex, the creation of law and government: it produces an "abnormal development of the abstract intellect in comparison with the physical senses on the one hand, and the moral sense on the other".[50] Abstraction is "the great engine of that false individuality or apartness, which it is the object of Civilization to produce". Here again, is it necessary to stress how closely this resembles Lawrence's key ideas, and his chief message? And not so much the *individual* ideas, as their *combination* into a whole system.

The Return to Nature

Even more familiar to readers of Lawrence will be Carpenter's glimpses into the future. Quoting Thoreau on "the poem of creation", he outlines many themes to which Lawrence's novels and essays gave powerful impetus after 1920. He sees a future tendency towards "a return to nature and community of human life" as the way to "the new Eden". Man, he forecasts, will have to "emerge from houses", to unclothe his body so as to "deliver the divine image" within himself. Thus Paul Morel's love scenes with Clara Dawes take place in the open air; thus Birkin, the prototype of the man of the future, flees from over-conscious

Hermione's murderous and symbolic attempt on his life, and lies naked on the wet and prickly grass among the primroses, behaving in exact accordance with Carpenter's prescription for the recovery of the lost Eden.[51]

Simplification of housing, of garments; life and love-making in the open-air, in contact with nature; "familiarity with the wind and waves, clean and pure food, the companionship of the animals, the very wrestling with the great Mother for his food—all these things will tend to restore the relationship which man has so long disowned."[52] Vegetarianism and respect for animals, identification of man with the cosmos, the abandonment of private property, will lead to a new architecture, respectful of Nature, and to a new communal life. The cosmic self will take the place of self-consciousness, and the ancient nature religion will come back.

> On the high tops once more gathering [Man] will celebrate with naked dances the glory of the human form and the great processions of the stars, or greet the bright horn of the young moon which now after a hundred centuries comes back laden with such wondrous associations—all the yearnings and the dreams and the wonderment of the generations of mankind—the worship of Astarte and of Diana, of Isis or the Virgin Mary; once more in sacred groves will he reunite the passion and the delight of human love with his deepest feelings of the sanctity and beauty of Nature; or in the open, standing uncovered to the Sun, will adore the emblem of the everlasting splendour which shines within. The same sense of vital perfection and exaltation which can be traced in the early and pre-civilized peoples—only a thousand times intensified, defined, illustrated and purified—will return to irradiate the redeemed and delivered Man.[53]

There is of course an important difference between the *fin de siècle* romantic optimism of this Utopia, and the despair and pessimism of the later Lawrence: yet do not the echoes of this programme for a return to an Earthly Paradise ring from *The White Peacock* onwards, all the way to the short story 'Sun' and to *The Plumed Serpent*? With their heavier emphasis on certain aspects of man's sexual liberation, are these not the very themes of Lawrence's challenge to industrial civilization, and of his proffered remedies? Carpenter concludes with the suggestion that civilization might be "renovated by the influx of external savagery", and may find its cure "in these two movements—towards a complex human communism and towards individual freedom and Savagery".[54] So will Lawrence start his quest for Rananim, the Happy Isle, the communist society based on human goodness, which ends in his cruel Utopia of *The Plumed Serpent*. Here are of course current enough literary themes, which a voracious reader such as Lawrence could find in other books. But where, in his early formative years, could he have found them more closely, more systematically grouped together, in a synthetic pill more readily accessible to his youthful imagination?

An "Advanced" Synthesis

This original lecture on civilization contains the seeds of almost every one of Carpenter's ethical ideas. His admission that it was "wrung from him against his will" emphazises its character of an almost complete self-revelation expressing deep-lying convictions below the rational layers of the self. In prose aiming at rational presentation, it is the statement of a creed, and constitutes a powerful synthesis of "advanced" social views with much of Carlyle's, of Ruskin's and of William Morris's social and philosophical criticism, but combined with the deep influence of Hindu sacred literature. The poetical and irrational force of the argument is concealed behind a subtle appeal to the historians and the ethnologists made by a man well trained in mathematical and astronomical exposition. A façade of human sciences veils a subjective approach and religious motivations. The rejection of social values, the passionate assertion of anarchism, thus tend to be taken for granted, and to appear at first sight as being the result of a historical and scientific study of society, rather than of a temperamental inadaptation. Carpenter's socialism, his communism, are those of primitive life in a state of nature, not those of Fabian municipal reformism or of later English socialism. They have little in common fundamentally with the political work of the Labour Party and the trade unions, to which Carpenter was outwardly loyal and sympathetic. If Lawrence, as seems probable, read this paper in his early twenties, and promptly assimilated its substance and basic attitudes of mind, those would have become part and parcel of his own emotional background. His mental universe, as it reveals itself in *The White Peacock*, is fundamentally the same as Carpenter's. His later reading will develop and reinforce attitudes to society and civilization which are common to both men. Thus we are not so far dealing with a literary influence as such, so much as with a substantial and integral part of Lawrence's profound background of emotions and thought.

* * *

The Criticism of Science

Abstract knowledge being for him synonymous with civilization and the fall of man, Carpenter took care in *My Days and Dreams* to state that "no careful reader" would accuse him of "preferring ignorance to intelligence". In 'Modern Science: a Criticism', he had intended to mark "the limits of scientific theorizing and authority" and to insist "on the fact that Science only deals with the surface of life and not with its substance", in the hope that "a later age" might "combine some of the virtues of the more primitive man with the powers that have been gained during civilization".[55]

Nevertheless, for a reader passionate to the point of obsession, such as the young Lawrence, his criticism of science, especially coming from a former lecturer on astronomy, physics and other exact sciences, could be of decisive importance in marking the gap between "surface" and "substance". His essay on 'Modern Science', originally published as a pamphlet in 1885, opens on an admission of "failure" for science; the reason for this is found in

> the tendency . . . to separate the logical and intellectual part of man from the emotional and instinctive, and to give it a *locus standi* of its own . . . Science has failed because she has attempted to carry out the investigation of nature from the intellectual side alone—neglecting the other constituents necessarily involved in the problem.

It has attempted "an impossible task", because it is "simply impossible" to discover "a permanently valid and purely *intellectual* representation of the universe".[56]

Successive views of nature which men hold have no objective and definite basis: they belong "organically to the moral and emotional stage which has been reached", and they are "in some sort the expression of it". No explanation of phenomena is valid in itself "without reference to the mental condition of those who set it up". For instance, the notion of "species" is but "a fiction arising out of my own ignorance or arbitrary isolation of the objects observed".[57] Such a scientific law as Boyle's is "metaphysical. It has no real existence. It is a convenient view of a fiction . . ."[58] "In carrying out the process which is peculiar to it", science "necessarily leaves the dry ground of reality for the watery region of abstractions, which . . . ultimately fade out into mere ghosts".[59]

Having thus asserted the primacy of whole and direct psychic experience of nature over the mechanisms of abstraction which are the tools of scientific investigation, Carpenter shows how science tries "to enounce facts independent of Man, the observer,

. . . to produce something which would be exact and independent of human sensation", whereas "no statement obviously can be really independent of human sensation":[60]

> The whole process of Science and the Comtian classification of its branches—regarded thus as an attempt to explain Man by Mechanics—is a huge vicious circle. It professes to start with something simple, exact, and invariable, and from this point to mount step by step till it comes to Man itself, but indeed it starts with Man.[61]

Bringing Bishop Berkeley up to date, Carpenter sees in science not the path to ultimate truth but merely an expression of man's mind. His paper on science is intended to recall the need for a global, intuitive view of man and of the universe, in addition, rather than in opposition, to the fragmentary views afforded by scientific discovery; the problem of science cannot be solved by the intellect alone. His position is not anti-intellectualistic; he rather endeavours to complete intellectualism by what has to be called, for short, the religious outlook:

> There is no such thing as intellectual truth—that is, I mean, a truth which can be stated as existing apart from feeling.[62]

> The truest truth is that which is the expression of the deepest feeling, and if there is an absolute truth it can only be known and expressed by him who has the absolute feeling of Being within himself.[63]

Science and Feeling, Brain and Sympathetic Nerve

Characteristically, this belief finds its justification not in a purely abstract subjectivism like Berkeley's, but in an attempt to formulate a psychological and physiological theory: is this the source of one of Lawrence's most deeply rooted physiological ideas? The attitudes of the two men, both of them critical of science, and ready to advance a fanciful "scientific" explanation in support of their theories, are strikingly similar in their narrow and quasi self-contradictory logic. It is only fair to stress that the explanation may not have seemed as fanciful in 1889 or even 1910 as it does today in the light of recent neurological studies:

> That "the wish is father to the thought" is in its wide sense profoundly true. In the individual, feeling precedes thinking—as the body precedes the clothes. In history, the Rousseau precedes the Voltaire. There is, I believe, a physiological parallel; *for behind the brain and determining its action stands the great sympathetic nerve*—the organ of the emotions. In fact here the brain appears as distinctly transitional. It stands between the nerves of sense on the one hand and the great sympathetic on the other.[64] [*My italics.*]

Could this formulation of Carpenter's physiological theory of consciousness, which we shall find expanded in *The Art of Creation* after much research by him in books of neuro-psychology, be the very first germ of an idea to which Lawrence will revert in 1913 and more definitely in 1915, when, in a letter to Bertrand Russell, he recalls a belief of his youth? "I have been reading Fraser's *Golden Bough* and *Totemism and Exogamy*", he writes. "Now I am convinced of *what I believed when I was about twenty*—that *there is another seat of consciousness than the brain and the nerve system*."[65] [*My italics.*]

In 1918, when working on those parts of '*Education of the People*' which he will work into *Fantasia of the Unconscious*, he asks Barbara Low's sister, Mrs Eder, the wife of the psychoanalyst, for "a book which describes the human nervous system, and gives a sort of map of the nerves of the human body".[66] When he was "about twenty", that is in 1905–06, it is quite probable that either this passage of *Civilization, Its Cause and Cure*, or the corresponding developments in *The Art of Creation* were at the fountainhead of this unorthodox belief.

Far from being incidental with Carpenter, this idea is basic to his mode of thinking. He develops it further in the important essay 'Exfoliation: Lamarck versus Darwin':

> There is a kind of knowledge or consciousness in us—as of our bodily parts, or affections, or deep-seated mental beliefs—which

> forms the base of our more obvious and self-conscious thought. This systemic knowledge grows even while the brain sleeps. It is not by any means absolute or infallible, but it affords, at any moment in man's history, the axiomatic ground on which his thought-structures, scientific and other, are built.[67]

In his just quoted letter to Russell, Lawrence speaks of "blood-consciousness" and of "the sexual connection", while Carpenter, with his nineteenth-century reserve, at least when writing in prose, speaks of "consciousness of our bodily parts, or affections". These stylistic differences need not obscure the fact that they both have the same facts in mind, and that the one's "systemic knowledge" is the same thing as the other's "blood-precepts".

Indeed any distance separating the two ideas is entirely covered by Carpenter when he defines his vitalistic attitude, immediately after his reference to the great sympathetic nerve. Thought is for him "the expression, the outgrowth, the covering of underlying Feeling". Thought-systems change, they are replaced by new ones in a process of "new birth and inward growth":

> Like the new bud-sheaths and husks in a growing plant or tree they give form for a time to the life within; then they fall off and are replaced. The husk prepares the bud underneath, which is to throw it off. The thought prepares and protects the feeling underneath, which growing will inevitably reject it; and when a thought has been formed it is already *false*, i.e. ready to fall.[68]

Not only the botanical images, the husks, the buds, the new growth which makes the false old dead growth fall off, have a Lawrentian as well as a Bergsonian ring, but the idea that a thought is false as soon as formulated is the very essence of the aesthetic thinking of the '*Study of Thomas Hardy*' and '*The Crown*', in which many parallels to this passage could be found. The same thought assumes artistic form in the perception of vital change by Ursula at the end of *The Rainbow*, when in her fever she is aware of "the vivid reality of acorns in February lying on the floor of a wood with their shells burst and discarded and the kernel issued naked to put itself forth". All her past, her family, "and college and all her friends" are now "cast off like a year that has gone by, whilst the kernel was free and naked and striving to take new root, to create a new knowledge of Eternity in the flux of Time".[69]

Both writers think poetically, i.e. in images; both place growth and feeling at the centre of all perception: the vitalistic, botanical simile is fundamental to their mode of thought, because what they seek is "the centre of humanity" in spontaneous growth, while science searches for data "on the fringe of humanity".[70] Carpenter wants the science of the future to seek

> . . . not a shadowy intellectual generalization, but . . . an intense immutable *feeling* or state, an axiomatic condition of Being. Is it possible that here, blazing like a sun (if we could only see it—and the sun is its allegory in the physical world), there exists within us absolutely such a thing—the one *fact* of the universe, of which all else are shadows, *to* which everything has relation, and round which, itself unanalysable, all thought circles and all phenomena stand as indirect modes of expression?[71]

"I have found hints, suggestions . . . in all kinds of scholarly books, from the Yoga and Plato and St John the Evangel and the early Greek philosophers like Herakleitos down to Fraser and his *Golden Bough* and even Freud and Frobenius," Lawrence will write with affected modesty in *Fantasia of the Unconscious*:[72] did he not first assimilate Plato's imagery through such a passage as just quoted?

Yoga and the Science of the Future

Yoga and Plato are indeed closely associated in Carpenter's thinking. He sees the science of the future conducted away from "the gas-reeking, ill-ventilated laboratory" free from the "blasphemy" of vivisection; it will in fact be "the discovery of the nature of Man himself, and of the true order of his being".[73] Instead of breaking up the emerald in order to analyse it and its separate qualities, it will contemplate "how all these qualities are conjoined together, what their relation is which *constitutes* the emerald":

> Not till we know the law of ourselves, in fact, shall we know the law of the emerald and the orange, or of Nature generally; and the law of ourselves is not learnt, except subordinately, by intellectual investigation; it is mainly learnt by life.[74]

A religion of life, largely based on the idea that "man is the measure of all things", and that *I am* is the answer to all scientific inquiry, is thus what Carpenter wished to recall as the guide of all knowledge and supreme thought. Just as Lawrence in '*Study of Thomas Hardy*' makes "To be or not to be" the supreme question,[75] for his elder "The question is: 'What is the destination of Man?'": a religious-poetical appreciation of nature has claims superior to those of an analytical-scientific attitude; he reacts against the attempt by modern science

> to survey and to classify the phenomena of the world in the pure dry light of the intellect, uncoloured by feeling; . . . and . . . to separate the intellectual in man from the merely perceptive, the emotional, the moral, and so forth.

Mystical elements, such as the insistence on the nature and essence of the emerald, on the moral relation between, say, a bird and man,[76] are ever present and discreetly tipping the balance away from intellectual and mechanistic science towards the religious attitude.

India, and more specifically the yoga of the *Bhagavad-Gita*, provide the synthesis of rational thinking and mystic intuition. One of Carpenter's favourite themes being health, he is against vaccination, and opposes medicine based on analysis and dissection, offering in its place the example of the Eastern healers: their method of health

> . . . consists in rendering the body, by proper habits of life, pure and healthy, till it becomes, as it were, transparent to the

inner eye, and then projecting the consciousness *inward* so as to become almost as sensible of the structure and function of the various internal organs, as it usually is of the outer surface of the body. [*My italics.*]

This process "may need help and corroboration by external methods of study", but "there is no doubt that many of the Yogis of India attain of great skill in it".[77]

Thus Carpenter, starting from a criticism of the mechanistic exaggerations of nineteenth-century science, shows the way back to a religious creed different from the, for him, outdated Christian doctrine, with a strong injection of Indian mysticism. And there are at least suggestions that three of the essays in *Civilization, its Cause and Cure* may have started Lawrence on his search for a personal form of faith and equilibrium reconciling his deeply religious cravings and his modern education. Those essays, because they contain all the germs of Carpenter's later developments, may easily have had on Lawrence a fully seminal effect and prepared his mind almost unconsciously for its later unfolding. They may have shown him the way in his own search for his personal faith through the studies of ethnologists and the doctrines of theosophy and yoga, while presenting to him in pre-digested form as much of Plato as he would ever require in order to formulate his own doctrine. We are still in the area of general comparison, which would nevertheless be legitimate, even if limited, were not Carpenter's later works to offer more precise bases for comparison.

Exfoliation and Perfect Man

In his criticism of modern science, Carpenter emphasizes its "mechanical" outlook, which is contrasted with his own "human" approach. Science has looked at things "from the point of view of the non-ego, rather than the ego".[78] In 'Exfoliation: Lamarck versus Darwin' he attempts, while developing this idea, a reconciliation between a modified theory of evolution and a philosophy giving priority to the ego, that is to say, to desire, to teleological and vitalistic conceptions.[79]

Evolution he accepts as an established fact. But he prefers Lamarck to Darwin, summing up this view in the theory of exfoliation, "which was practically Lamarck's theory":

> There is a force at work throughout creation, ever urging each type onward into new and newer forms. This force appears first in consciousness in the form of desire.[80]
>
> . . .
>
> Every change begins in the mental region—is felt first as a desire gradually taking form into thought, passes down into the bodily region, expresses itself in action . . . and finally solidifies itself in organization and structure. The process is not accretive but exfoliatory—a continual movement from within outwards.[81]

Race growth or variation being thus "a process by which change begins in the mental region", evolution is the effect of *desire*: "desire precedes function", and therefore "organization is preceded by desire".[82]

"Vital" and "organic" are key words in Carpenter's vocabulary: they define his belief in a life-force which precedes all organization, and presides over all change. A single desire "runs through creation"; in man, it becomes "an absorbing power":

> Love becomes a conscious worship of the divine form; generation itself is the means whereby, in time, the supreme object of desire is realized. When at last the perfect Man appears, the key to all nature is found, every creature falls into its place and finds its interpreter, and the purpose of creation is at last made manifest.[83]

Lawrence will also show mankind accumulating upwards "through the zones of life expression and passionate consciousness, upwards to the supreme utterer, or utterers".[84] And for Carpenter, generation ultimately leads to the perfect man, the interpreter, the image of God. Who, what, is this perfect man? We shall find him in various contexts, and here already there is more than a hint that he is the ultimate goal of evolution, a man free from the burden of generation, capable of extracting mankind from the grip of civilization and history; the progression of the human mind "is a matter of growth from within, and involves a continual breaking away of the bases of all thought structures":

> It is then finally in Man—in our own deepest and lost vital experience—that we have to look for the key and explanation of the changes that we see going on around us in external Nature, as we call it; and our understanding of the latter and of History, must ever depend from point to point *on the exfoliation of new facts in the individual consciousness.* Round the ultimate disclosure of the essential Man all creation . . . ranges itself, as it were, like some vast flower, in concentric circles . . . and, as in the myth of the Eden Garden, [it is] *with the appearance of the perfected human form* that the work of creation definitely completes itself.[85] [*My italics.*]

The idea of the perfect man is not here further explained. It will be in 1924, in 'Some Friends of Walt Whitman', a paper to which it is unlikely that Lawrence ever had access.[86] But even here a key may be found in this vital passage on which the essay is concluded: Carpenter had begun 'Exfoliation' by quoting Whitman;[87] immediately before it he placed his 'Defence of Criminals'; to the careful reader these are significant clues to the importance he attaches to the idea of perfect man, not only in theory but in his personal manner of worship of the "divine form".

* * *

The Attack on Conventional Morals

In his discussion of civilization or of modern science Carpenter is relatively at ease, and working his way by slow stages towards the ideas dearest to his heart. Personal though the attack may be, and stamped with the seal of his own way of life, his subjects are such that he need not be particularly cautious. In his attack on custom and conventional morals his approach is necessarily more guarded, and those essays bear the marks of prudent circling round the real subject. They are none the less deliberate statements of a revolutionary attitude, more pointed than the general attack on civilization, and leading the way to his more outspoken books.

Custom and the Free Individual

'Custom', a short essay first published in 1888, opens with a quotation from Montaigne, followed by commonplace enough considerations on the varieties and mutual contradictions of human and animal customs: agriculture, cookery and food lead on to the attack on morals, which "also are customs", conditioned by "the class, the caste, the locality, the age in which we were born".[88] Like the caddis-fly larva, which leaves its tube behind and soars as a caddis-fly into the air, man must grow to manhood and leave his chrysalis; and then?

"Why he dies, and so becomes alive", is the Lawrentian reply. In other words, man having "run through every variety of custom, a time comes for him to be freed from it . . . At this point, 'morals' comes to an end and humanity takes its place—that is to say, there is no longer any code of action; but the one object of all action is the deliverance of the human being and the establishment of equality between oneself and another, the entry into a new life . . ."[89]

To free man from custom, to establish him in freedom and equality "with another", to enable him to associate as a full and free individual with whomever and however he may choose, here is Carpenter's moral ideal, which he will expound over the years in several books on sex and love.

The 'Defence of Criminals' and the Apology of Greek Love

His more important essay on morals in *Civilization, its Cause and Cure* bears the surprising title 'Defence of Criminals: a criticism of morality'. It was first published in *To-day* in 1889, the year of publication of the book in which it occupies a central position: all of which suggests that its author attached special value to it. It is in fact a tactful and remarkably outspoken effort, considering the times and the laws, to liberate homosexuals from crushing legislation and moral opprobrium.

To break the law, he points out, is in fact to prevent public opinion from ossifying, and society from dying. "The Outcast of an age is the Hero of another." Is this, a clear implication, the reply to the question, What is perfect man?

The proposed view of morality is essentially dynamic: "Society has an ideal in its mind. These ideals are tangents or vanishing points of the direction in which society is moving at the time."[90] Examples from primitive and modern societies having shown how varied are marriage customs, the writer comes to the point: the Greeks "did not hold marriage very high", partly because "the ideal passion of that period, and one which more than all else inspired it, was that of comradeship, or male friendship carried over into the regions of love".[91] After the classical examples of Harmodius and Aristogiton, the Theban legion, Greek statuary, etc., we come to this statement:

> In fact the most remarkable society known to history, *and its greatest men*, cannot be properly considered or understood apart from this passion; yet the modern world scarcely recognizes it, or, if it recognizes, does so chiefly to condemn it.[92] [*My italics.*]

No Hierarchy of Actions or Passions

After more general remarks, in particular to point out that the law is on the side of the rich, he concludes that there is no such thing as "a permanent moral code—at any rate as applying to *actions*". Then is introduced a distinction between "what is really good or evil *for the race* and what is reputed to be so": such action "must by nature vary almost indefinitely *with the changing conditions of the life of the race*": the "rightness or wrongness is *in the motive*".[93] [*My italics.*]

Is it then possible to find "a permanent moral code . . . among the passions?" Not at all; they do not lend themselves to the establishment of a hierarchy:

> . . . just as among the members of the body, the less honoured have their place as well as the more honoured, and could not well be discarded.[94]

This is no casual reference to members of the body: these are indeed the seat, or the allegory, of the passions. Passions are therefore neither right or wrong in themselves, but only in the use made of them: "it is really as impossible to draw a fixed line between moral and immoral actions". They have to be accepted and used, "redeemed" from their "narrowness and limitation", in the service of humanity. For "the evil consists not in the actions or passions themselves, but in the fact that they are inhumanly used".[95]

Human Service and the Expanding Circle of Consciousness

In what does this "human service" consist? In each age, while "moral codes" provide imperfect "approximations . . . to a statement of human service", there is a second, and better way to conceive it: that is, "by the expansion and growth of [man's] own consciousness", this being "by far the most important" way:

> Gradually, and in the lapse of ages, through the development of his sympathetic relation with his fellows, the individual man enters into a wider and wider circle of life; the joys and sorrows,

the experience of his fellows become his own joys and sorrows, his own experience, he passes into a life which is larger than his own individual life; forces flow in upon him which determine his actions, not for results which return to him directly, but for results which can only return to him indirectly and through others; at last the ground of humanity, as it were, reveals itself within him, the region of human equality—and his actions come to flow directly from the very same source which regulates and inspires the whole movement of society. At this point the problem is solved. The growth has taken place from within; it is not of the nature of an external compulsion, but of an inward compunction. By actual consciousness the man has taken an ever-enlarging life, and at last the life of humanity, which has no fixed form, no ever-valid code; but is itself the true life, surpassing definition, yet inspiring all actions and passions, all codes and forms, and determining at last their place.[96]

A Lawrence Parallel

This important passage, what it says, and what it begs, may be held to outline the initial and original theme of *The Sisters*, in so far as it relates to human consciousness: in *The Rainbow*, Lawrence insists, by twice using these words as a chapter title, on "the ever-widening circle"[97] of Ursula's consciousness; this ultimately, at the end of the book, leads to a crisis from which she emerges ready for the true life, and for her difficult accession with Birkin to a state of moral being in which "the region of human equality" reveals itself to them both. They can then regard "all actions and passions" and all forms of human love as equally legitimate, provided they are spontaneous and free from any externally conceived code. It is true that extraneous elements introduced by Lawrence in the course of drafting the two novels may disturb the reader and obscure this pattern, but if one concentrates on the main events in Ursula's life this general scheme will appear clearly.

In this light, Ursula's and Birkin's experiences with both sexes are by no means extraneous; indeed Lawrence's letters show that her story in *The Rainbow* was intended to give her experience which would make her meet for "her Mr Birkin".[98] Nor should one see extraneous elements in the homosexual attraction exercised by Gerald over Birkin, and in the insistence of the latter on the idea that "we should enjoy everything". Birkin and Ursula *are*, in Lawrence's scheme of things, approximations to perfect man of the future. Our further analysis will show how far the double novel appears to be indebted to Carpenter in its general conception; the passage just quoted, or the attitude of mind which it defines, being a possible early seed of the whole expanded conception of *The Sisters*.

Altruism and Passions

Carpenter pursues his exploration beyond good and evil by stating that we must "put *all* our qualities and defects to human use, and . . . redeem them by so doing", a programme worthy of Fourier. "Our very evil passions, so called, are not things to be ashamed of, but things to look straight in the face and to see what they are good for."[99] In the same way, "society also has to recognize its so-called criminals and discern their place and use".[100] Carpenter sees in the thief "that person who is protesting against the too exclusive domination of [the] passing ideal of private wealth"; in the prostitute,

> . . . that person who . . . has clung to a tradition which, in itself good, might otherwise have perished in the face of our devotion to the splendid ideal of exclusive marriage . . . In the future there will come a time when, as a free companion, really free from the curse of modern commercialism, and sacred and respected once more, she will again be accepted by society and take her place with the rest.[101]

"All through the Civilization-period, the so-called criminals are keeping open the possibility of a return" to the true democracy of pre-civilization days. They are preserving "the precious seed of a life which is to come in the future".[102] For moral codes, Carpenter substitutes humanity. Man has to "discover that there is no ultimate antagonism between himself and society" and, in the wake of Fourier, to find "that the gratification of every desire which he has or can have may be rendered social, or beneficial to his fellows, by being used at the right time and place".[103]

As one would expect from this religious moralist, he concludes with an appeal to "the subordination of the desires, their subjection to the true self", to "ascendancy over the passions",[104] and an altruistic morality: when "the true Democracy" succeeds "Civilization", these vexed questions of "morals" will cease to exist:

> The moral codes and questionings belong to Civilization, they are part of the forward effort, the struggle, the suffering, and the temporary alienation from true life, which that term implies.[105]

Perfect Man and the Superman

The idea of perfect man runs implicit throughout the book: it is often hinted at, never fully and openly defined. There are however enough suggestions that Carpenter believes in some sort of superman, freed from the notions of good and evil; he is in part defined by his concepts of democracy and equality. In the essay 'Morality under Socialism', first published in *The Albany Review* in 1907 (i.e., at the time when Nietzsche became known in England largely through *The New Age* and A. R. Orage) and added in 1920 to the *Civilization* volume under the title 'The New Morality', he takes care to criticize Nietzsche's "beyond-man" and "superman". His criticism, founded on Eastern thought, on the sense of the unity of man with nature, is also inspired by a genuine sense of democracy:

> The truth is that Nietzsche never really penetrated to the realization of that farther state of consciousness in which the deep underlying unity of man with nature and his fellows is perceived and felt. He saw apparently that there is a life and an inspiration of life beyond all technical good and evil. But for some reason—partly because of the natural difficulty of the subject, partly because the Eastern outlook was uncongenial to his mind—he never found the solution which he needed; and his outline of the Superman remains cloudy and uncertain, vague and variously interpreted by followers and critics.[106]

Faced with Nietzcheism, Carpenter restates his faith in socialism and the Indian inspiration of his humanism:

> Modern Socialism, in effect, taking up a position in its way somewhat similar to that of Eastern philosophy, says: Morality in its essence is not a code, but simply the realization of the Common Life.[107]

He sees hope for the future society in the joint embodiment of two principles:

> (1) the recognition of the Common Life as providing the foundation element of general morality, and (2) the recognition of individual Affection and Expression . . . as building up the higher groupings and finer forms of the structure.[108]

Thus by 1907, and even by 1920, the early motivations of Carpenter, his passionate desire to claim for the homosexual his place in society, had largely given way to a more serene, philosophical and dispassionate outlook and inserted itself in a broad moral scheme encompassing all human desires. He felt no sympathy for Nietzschean "blond beasts", and his idea of perfect man merged into his general socialism. Yet it should not be overlooked that the earlier essays of *Civilization, Its Cause and Cure*, were definitely written under the influence of Whitman and of his conception of a superman, and that Carpenter remained faithful to that inspiration and entirely consistent to the end.

Because of the soberness and broadness of his ethical position, we do not find in him a dogmatic public assertion that one or another type of man is perfect man. For Carpenter, the liberation of the individual from external, artificial constraints is enough. He admits, he proclaims, the need for and the reality of variety, as long as man may be free from the dominion of sin and of the law.[109] That does not mean, however, that in his early attempt to explain or justify homosexual love there was not a deep-lying idea of its superiority in the evolutionary scheme of things: this finds expression in the sub-title of one of his books, in the use of the words "transitional types" to designate members of the "intermediate sex".

3

THE FREE INDIVIDUAL: MAN, WOMAN, LOVE AND MARRIAGE

Carpenter's Publishing Troubles

The book of essays entitled *Love's Coming of Age* (1896) was Carpenter's first attempt to put together various papers on love, man, woman and marriage which had previously appeared in pamphlet form. It would be easy today to underestimate the moral courage this evinced in late-Victorian England. A short retrospect on the difficulties which he experienced in publishing at all will show to what extent he was genuinely a pioneer at a time when Oscar Wilde was in Reading gaol. He must indeed have seemed a daring innovator even in the early years of this century.

The second edition of *Towards Democracy* had been unfavourably reviewed by the London press, and especially *The Saturday Review* (27 March 1886). Apart from comments on its "blank monotony", attention had been drawn to "a few passages which it would be undesirable to quote, and which it is not wholesome to read" (*Saturday Review*). Such passages, very rare as they are, are occasionally of overt homosexual inspiration. Sales had nevertheless justified a third edition, which Fisher Unwin accepted to publish (1892). Meanwhile, Carpenter had begun through the Manchester Labour Press to publish pamphlets entitled *Sex-love*, *Woman* and *Marriage*. These sold well in socialist and advanced circles, and success encouraged him to collect them under the title *Love's Coming of Age*, which in 1895 Fisher Unwin also agreed to publish. In January of that same year, the Labour Press issued, "printed for private circulation only", a fourth pamphlet entitled *Homogenic Love*[1] which, Carpenter asserts, it was not his intention to include in *Love's Coming of Age*.

The condemnation of Oscar Wilde in April 1895 created, in Carpenter's own words, "a sheer panic . . . over *all* questions of sex, and especially of course questions of the Intermediate Sex".[2] On learning of the existence of the pamphlet on *Homogenic Love*, Fisher Unwin not only cancelled the agreement to publish *Love's Coming of Age*, in spite of the fact that the book was partly set up into type, but also "turned out of his shop" *Towards Democracy* and refused "to publish it any longer". Having failed to persuade "altogether five or six publishers" to accept *Love's Coming of Age*, the author went back to his little Labour Press at Manchester, with the effect that

> My book circulated almost immediately to some extent in the Socialistic world, where my name was fairly well known—but some time elapsed before it penetrated into more literary and more 'respectable' circles.[3]

Swan Sonnenschein, one of the houses which had turned it down, accepted it gladly in 1902, a member of the firm having noted with interest that at some Nonconformist chapel which he attended, the minister "quoted a page or two" from it and "spoke very highly of it", giving the publisher's address and the price. The book finally was taken over by George Allen & Unwin when they acquired the stock of Swan Sonnenschein sometime before the First World War: the book had thus hived back to the publisher who had originally accepted it in 1895.

Edward Carpenter was indeed at the spearhead of the movement for sexual freedom when he began, in 1894, to publish his essays on love. In that same year, Havelock Ellis, his friend since 1883, published *Man and Woman: A Study of Human Secondary*

Sexual Characters; Ellis describes his own book as "the prolegomena to the *Studies* [in *The Psychology of Sex*] . . . a book to be studied and read in order to clear the ground for the study of sex in the central sense in which I was chiefly concerned with it". In other words, he was still "slowly working [his] way towards . . . [his] chief life work".[4] He was of course, generally speaking, co-operating with Carpenter in preparing the public for that more outspoken attack on the whole problem of sex education and liberation of the individual, which his recent biography shows to have been one of his main concerns.[5]

Havelock Ellis's study on *Sexual Inversion*, which later became Volume 2 of the *Studies*, was to be rejected by several publishers in 1897, and in particular by Williams and Norgate, on the advice of the author's friend Dr Hack Tuke, who explained to him that "a book could never be confined to specialists, and so might exert a demoralizing influence. 'There are always', he said, 'the compositors'."[6]

The story of the publication of *Sexual Inversion* by the so-called Watford University Press, of the arrest and trial of George Bedborough, Secretary of the Legitimation League, in 1898, for selling a copy of the book to a plain-clothes policeman (he was prosecuted for "publishing an obscene libel"), too long to be related here, places strong emphasis on the various dangers that beset the daring authors of studies on sex and its anomalies. A writer and his work could easily be compromised for life by an unscrupulous and dishonest adventurer-publisher, for instance the notorious de Villiers, alias Springmühl, or by a weak or pliable ally, such as Bedborough, too happy to plead guilty when the police prosecuted in an effort to strike a blow at his anarchist associates. Carpenter's skill in managing to publish unscathed through the small Labour Press at Manchester is as remarkable as the close association thus established between his campaign for sexual liberation and the socialist movement in Northern England.

* * *

Love's Coming of Age

The papers which compose the original edition of *Love's Coming of Age* are: 'The Sex passion'; 'Man, the ungrown'; 'Woman, the serf'; 'Woman in freedom'; 'Marriage: a retrospect'; 'Marriage: a forecast—the free society'; 'Some remarks on the early star and sex worships'.

Other papers now included in the current edition were added in 1906 (a chapter on 'The intermediate sex') and 1923 ('The beginnings of love', and 'Love's ultimate meaning', both from *The Drama of Love and Death*). A note on 'Preventive checks to population', advocating *inter alia* Mrs Alice B. Stockham's method of "prolonged bodily conjunction" based on J. H. Noyes's Oneida method of male continence, would seem to have been added in 1909 in the sixth edition, and was reprinted by Methuen in 1914 and 1915 in a pocket edition, but omitted in 1916 from their third edition, possibly as an afterthought following the magistrate's decision on *The Rainbow*, or possibly out of regard for wartime demographic considerations. It is difficult to date other notes: 'The primitive group marriage', 'On jealousy', and 'On the family'.

Teaching the Middle Classes the Meaning of Love

The real and deep meaning of *Love's Coming of Age* appears more clearly in the light of later works, *The Intermediate Sex*, *The Art of Creation* and *The Drama of Love and Death*. In its background of 1895, as a small book intended to educate the public into a more liberal attitude towards sex and marriage, it has considerable value, especially if one bears in mind the audience at which the author was aiming: "the middle and well-to-do classes" among which "the conditions of high civilization" increase sexual difficulties, and where "the special evils exist of sex-starvation and sex-ignorance on the one hand, and mere licentiousness on the other".[7]

This then is the book which Alice Dax, an emancipated and advanced married woman, gave Jessie Chambers to read about 1909, having in all probability prompted D. H. Lawrence to read it first. It is not our intent here to analyse it from the angle of the development of Carpenter's thought, it being admittedly a pedagogical rather than a self-revealing book, but from the point of view of what Lawrence, apart from his own and not very successful early sex-education, may have remembered from it, in the light of his later writings. It seems as if the lessons of Carpenter's essay on love had not been fully assimilated by him until a later period, ranging from 1912 to 1916; and yet as if echoes of this and other books had then resounded in the works of Lawrence, after a long period of gestation during which his unsolved personal and sexual problems prevented him from fully mastering the import of Carpenter's small treatise. It took him some years before he attempted to define his own attitude, often in contrast with the mystique of love and sex prevalent in Carpenter's writings. As is often the case with Lawrence, the assertion of the favourite themes of a writer whom he remembers is almost concomitant with his effort to state a position of his own, which may differ in significant aspects from that writer's.

Love's Coming of Age and the 1913–16 Lawrence Novels

The papers composing *Love's Coming of Age* are presented by their author as "an attempt to indicate the inner laws which, rather than the outer, may guide Love when, some day, he shall have come to his full estate".[8] Similarly, *The Rainbow* and *Women in Love*, at least in their original intention, were conceived as the progress of several generations of Brangwens, up to the moment when Ursula Brangwen and her lover Rupert Birkin reach a state of fully-grown, adult equality in love. Quotations can best illustrate the parallel:

Birkin, who takes the lead in teaching Ursula what he is seeking, meditates on love in the seclusion of his sickroom:

> On the whole, he hated sex, it was such a limitation . . . he wanted sex to revert to the level of the other appetites, to be regarded as a functional process, not as a fulfilment. He believed in sex marriage. But beyond this, he wanted a further conjunction, where man had being and woman had being, two pure beings, each constituting the freedom of the other, balancing each other like two poles of one force, like two angels or two demons.[9]

Carpenter undertakes to treat of love without "fetishism", as an important but natural appetite:

> Next to hunger it is doubtless the most primitive and imperative of our needs. But in modern civilized life sex enters probably even more into consciousness than hunger. For the hunger-needs of the human race are in the later societies fairly well-satisfied, but the sex desires are strongly restrained, both by law and custom, from satisfaction—and so assert themselves all the more in thought.[10]

It should be remembered that "civilized", "law", "custom", are with Carpenter derogatory words, representing what he is aiming to control or evade, just as Birkin wants to renounce civilization once and for all in the quest for an earthly paradise. Birkin wants to find Ursula "where you don't know your own existence", beyond her "common self":

> What I want is a strange conjunction with you—not meeting and mingling;—you are quite right:—but an equilibrium, a pure balance of two single beings—as the stars balance each other.[11]
>
> . . .
>
> I meant two single equal stars balanced in conjunction.[12]
>
> . . .
>
> One must commit oneself to a conjunction with the other—for ever. But it is not selfless—it is a maintaining of the self in mystic balance and integrity—like a star balanced with another star.[13]

And a constant theme of *Women in Love* is Birkin's need for the love of a man, which is complementary to his love of Ursula. He finds himself

> . . . confronted with another problem—the problem of love and eternal conjunction between two men. Of course this was necessary—it had been a necessity inside himself all his life—to love a man purely and fully. Of course he had been loving Gerald all along, and all along denying it.[14]

In defining the marriage of the future, Carpenter advocates the possibility of men and women forming "strong attachments to persons of their own sex";[15] he wants to see established in marriage itself "a freer and broader and more healthy relationship than generally exists at the present time",[16] avoiding "*égoïsme à deux*", each partner being free "to reach a hand to others, or even to give a boon of affection to those who need it more than themselves":

> A marriage so free, so spontaneous, that it would allow of wide excursions of the pair from each other, in common or even in separate objects of work and interest, and yet would hold them all the time in the bond of absolute sympathy, would by its very freedom be all the more poignantly attractive and by its very scope and breadth all the richer and more vital—would be in a sense indestructible, like the relation of two suns which, revolving in fluent and rebounding curves, only recede from each other in order to return again with renewed swiftness into close proximity—and which together blend their rays into the glory of one double star.[17]

And stressing "the failure of the Monogamic Union" and "the immense *variety*" of love in human nature, he forecasts the possibility for "intimacies" for married people "with outsiders" and "in rare instances for triune and other such relations to be permanently maintained".[18]

These quotations fully outline the parallel intentions of the novelist and the essayist, which we shall further compare after an analysis of Carpenter's main themes in *Love's Coming of Age*. Not only are images and phraseology strikingly similar, but there is also in the novels a basic pattern of events which can be shown to run very close to his main ideas.

Sex and Hunger, Sin, the Mystic Balance

First of all, Carpenter singles out the main difference between sex-needs and hunger-needs: "food . . . has no moral rights of its own",[19] while "the object of sex is a person".

"The moment Man rises into any sort of consciousness of the equal rights of others with himself his love-needs open up this terrible problem" of equality.[20] He discovers that there is something even greater than his needs. Sexual and socio-moral instincts become differentiated, and "both the satisfaction of the passion and the non-satisfaction of it are desirable and beautiful". Carpenter is at pains to show that physical passions are "admirable [and] desirable in their place",[21] asceticism and libertinism being two sides of the same shield.

This leads him to a definition of sin as "the separation or sundering of one's being", which consists in "*seeking* those external things and pleasures";[22] this is what Lawrence will call "sex in the head".

Pleasures should come "as the natural . . . accompaniment of life", and should not "be sought as the object of life". Sex is felt to be unclean because it is "slimed over with the thought of pleasure".

Foreseeing that with an increase in "the capacity for true companionship . . . the importance of the mere sex act will dwindle till it comes to be regarded as only one specialized factor in the full total of human love" (a sentiment which chimes with Birkin's wish to reduce sex to the level of the other appetites), Carpenter emphasizes that "this means . . . a free people, proud in the mastery and the divinity of their own lives, and in the beauty and openness of their own bodies", a thought which again should be kept in mind in order to understand the strange conversations and actions of Birkin and Ursula's courtship. He goes on:

> Sex is the allegory of Love in the physical world. It is from this fact that it derives its immense power. The aim of Love is non-differentiation—absolute union of being; but absolute union can only be found at the centre of existence. Therefore whoever has

truly found another has found not only that other, and with that other himself, but has found also a third—who dwells at the centre and holds the plastic material of the universe in the palm of his hand, and is a creator of sensible forms.[23]

Is this not what Birkin seeks, "beyond the common self" of Ursula, "where [she] doesn't know [her] own existence"? This "mystic balance and integrity"? Birkin rejects "merging" and "mingling" at the vulgar, daily-life level, the commonplace assertions of love, but he seeks "a pure balance of single beings". If we disregard the means by which he tries to find it in the chapter 'Excurse', is there not a close relationship between "absolute union at the centre of existence" and his definition of "mystic integrity"?

The mystic nature of the love and sex union is made clear by Carpenter in words which again arouse deep Lawrentian echoes. The reproduction of the race is not the primary object of love or of sex:

> . . . taking all together I think it may fairly be said that the prime object of Sex is *union*, the physical union as the allegory and expression of the real union, and that generation is a secondary object or result of this union.[24]

In other words, the satisfaction and regeneration of the individual takes precedence over the generation of new individuals. The sex act becomes not gratuitous, but primarily directed to the well-being of the lovers. It consists in an exchange of cells between the male and female, and "even without the actual sex-act, there is an interchange of vital and ethereal elements"—an idea on which, as later found by him in Weininger, Lawrence will expatiate in the '*Study of Thomas Hardy*'. Implicitly, Carpenter proclaims that the race may end when certain individuals reach an appropriate level of evolution. The reader will compare this with Birkin's frequently expressed ideas about the wiping out of the human race and of civilization, which he mentions at least once almost in the same breath as "perfect union with a woman—sort of ultimate marriage": "Let mankind pass away—time it did."[25]

The Flower and the Seed

The belief behind Carpenter's and Birkin's statements is essentially the same, with the difference that the former's general philosophy is one of very long-term optimism, while that of *Women in Love* is more tinged with immediate hatred and contempt of mankind than with the hope of a genuinely evolutionary process.

On the other hand, the theme of generation being the secondary object of love and sexual union is not new in *Women in Love:* Lawrence has already expressed it, probably in 1913, in the poem 'Rose of all the World':

> The seed is purpose, blossom accident.
> The seed is all in all, the blossom lent
> To crown the triumph of this new descent.
>
> Is that it, woman? Does it strike you so?
> The Great Breath blowing a tiny seed of fire
> Fans out your petals for excess of flame,
> Till all your being smokes with fine desire?
>
> Or are we kindled, you and I, to be
> One rose of wonderment upon the tree
> Of perfect life, and is our possible seed
> But the residuum of the ecstasy?[26]

This theme of the flower and the seed, of the perfection of life in the excess of the flower, is also amply developed in the '*Study of Thomas Hardy*', composed at the time of the final rewriting of *The Rainbow*, and in which can be detected gnostic and theosophic influences which ran in the same direction as Carpenter's thought. The words the 'Great Breath' have been quoted[27] as evidence of Lawrence's theosophic reading, which however would from other data appear to have been somewhat later. They are synonymous with the 'Universal Self' and the 'All-Self', constantly used by Carpenter in *The Drama of Love and Death*. Lawrence may have found them in *The Occult Review*, sometime before he had access to the works of Madame Blavatsky. This seems to be one of the cases where the converging influences of Carpenter, theosophy and occultism can scarcely be separated.

The point of divergence is found when the influence of Helen Blavatsky introduces different esoteric concepts or images less well assimilated into a modern system of thought than those accepted by Carpenter. We have studied elsewhere the traces in *Women in Love* of the reading of *The Secret Doctrine* and of James M. Pryse's *Apocalypse Unsealed*.[28] Making full allowance for the fact that Lawrence is a novelist, and must translate ideas into actions and concrete situations, there is a moment when he falls a victim to the "rot and confusion" of Madame Blavatsky, to use Carpenter's own phrase, and loses the poise and serenity of the elder writer before Eastern concepts and the gnostic tradition. Some of the semi-comprehensible jargon of *Women in Love*, and of the mock-mystic behaviour of Ursula and Birkin in 'Excurse', denotes the passing over the borderline from an intellectualized mysticism into a world of daemonic black magic, in part inspired by occultism, in part by some obsession with anal contacts, which finds justification and reinforcement in Pryse's chart of the *chakras*.[29]

But the exaggerations and obsessions introduced into the book in 1916 need not obscure the pattern of ideas which seem to correspond to an earlier conception, that of 1913–14, when *The Sisters* was intended to delineate the progress of the human soul towards true love. And this progress was undoubtedly through individual development towards a mystical conception of the relation of the self to others (especially if the poem 'Rose of all the World' was written at the time of the conception of the double novel).

Carpenter's doctrine may here be assumed to have provided the pattern of events and ideas in the two novels. Love, he states,

> is doubtless the last and most difficult lesson that humanity has to learn: in a sense it underlies all others. Perhaps the time has come for the modern nations when, ceasing to be children, they may even try to learn it.[30]

Lawrence's letters of late 1912 are full of a sense of his being "a priest of love", of his "doing [his] work for women, better than the Suffrage", and "sticking up for the love between man and woman";[31] he wants to save "thousands of young men in England" from the "tragedy . . . [of] Ruskin, and men like him":[32] in other words, he wants to teach humanity the lesson of love, and in particular of successful physical love. The theme of psychological impotence haunts his short stories of that period.

Acceptance of the Body

If, as seems at least probable, *Women in Love*, under the title *The Sisters*, was written in 1913–14, and the 1916 rewriting consisted of the addition of a certain number of chapters and short scenes and of extraneous material, e.g. from H. Blavatsky and J. M. Pryse, it may be possible to trace to the early draft a number of themes which, in that hypothesis, might spring straight from Carpenter, reinforced of course, as is the rule in any work of imagination, by personal experience and memories of actual scenes in the writer's own life.

One such theme is that of "acceptance" of the "physical body", closely allied to that of nakedness in natural surroundings. Carpenter advocates sexual intercourse "in the open air, in touch with the great and abounding life of Nature" rather than "in closed and stuffy rooms, the symbols of mental darkness and morbidity, and the breeding ground of the pettier elements of human nature".[33] He sees a possible change in our estimate of the place and fitness of "the various sex-relations", if

> . . . the sense of cleanness in sex ever does come in, if the physical body ever becomes clean (which it certainly is not now-a-days), clean and beautiful and accepted, within and without—and this of course it can only be through a totally changed method of life, through pure and clean food, nakedness to a large extent, and a kind of saturation with the free air and light of heaven. . . .[34]

We have shown elsewhere how the idea of acceptance of the body and all its functions is a basic theme of Lawrence's works and in particular of *Women in Love*[35] as indeed in his later years, of *Lady Chatterley's Lover* and *A Propos of Lady Chatterley's Lover*. Birkin and Ursula, like Paul Morel and Clara, make love in the open air, and the theme of "acceptance" of the bodily functions is present in several such scenes of *Women in Love*.[36] In many ways the novel appears to be an illustration in action of the ideas expressed in *Love's Coming of Age*.

* * *

The Free Society and the Flower of Eternity

Love-making and Nature

The link between love-making and nature is not fortuitous either: Carpenter wishes that "sexual embraces" might "receive the benison of Dame Nature, in whose presence, under the burning sun or the high canopy of the stars and surrounded by the fragrant atmosphere, their meaning can be fully understood".[37] He sees in the Bacchanalian festivals of earlier nations "an element of Nature-sex-mysticism, which has become lost in modern times".[38] And in his description of "the Free Society" of the future, the link between this nature-sex-mysticism and gnostic mediaeval ideas is clearly expressed, as is also a connexion between this mysticism and socialism.

The free society will, he thinks, "lovingly embrace this great soul [of humanity] within it" and "recognize the variety of needs of the human heart and of human beings". This moral freedom will go with economic freedom and the solution of the industrial problem: "and in such economically free society human unions may at last take place according to their own inner and true laws".[39]

Then the science of love will cease to be neglected, and man will discover in himself "most distinct and inviolable inner forces, binding him by different ties to different people . . ." He will find "that there is in fact in that world of the heart a kind of cosmical harmony and variety, and an order almost astronomical".[40] He will discover "planetary laws of distances in the relations of people to one another" and "a cosmic world of souls . . . whose relations are eternal and clearly defined".[41]

From there Carpenter plunges into Dantesque imagery which, while being structurally supported by Platonic concepts, is very close to that of Lawrence's images and thoughts in 'Rose of all the World' and to his concern with the flowers he uses as symbols of eternity and the "Mystic Now" in '*Study of Thomas Hardy*' and '*The Crown*':

> Is it possible, we may ask . . . that there really *is* a Free Society—in another and deeper sense than that hitherto suggested—a society to which we all in our inmost selves consciously or unconsciously belong—the Rose of Souls that Dante beheld in Paradise, whose every petal is an individual, and an individual only through its union with all the rest—the early Church's dream, of an eternal Fellowship in heaven and on earth—*the Prototype of all the brotherhoods and communities that exist on this or any planet;* and that the innumerable selves of men, *united in the one Self*, members of it and of one another (like the members of the body) stand in eternal and glorious relationship bound indissolubly together?[42] [*My italics.*]

Carpenter accepts this mystical interpretation, if not necessarily of society, at least of the union of two lovers:

> In the inner world . . . we divine that we and our mate are only *two little petals that grow near each other on the Great Flower of*

> *Eternity;* and that it is because we are near each other *in that unchanging world*, that in the world of change our mortal selves are drawn together, and will be drawn always, wherever and whenever they may meet.[43]

This image of the rose is one to which Carpenter lovingly returns on many occasions: "In whatever race or nation or language a great work may appeal, lo! it is but another petal of the same red rose, a leaf of the old World-tree," he writes in *Angels' Wings*,[44] and there he states explicitly a thought which will be echoed by Lawrence, that the emotion conveyed by such art "is and remains beyond the reach of Time".

From 'Rose of all the World' to '*The Crown*', throughout 1913, 1914 and 1915, these images of the flower of eternity and the rose haunted the prose and poetry of Lawrence. They were certainly reinforced by other reading, but it is probable that they had visibly struck the imagination of the young poet when he first read *Love's Coming of Age* and learnt to associate love with a religious attitude which, for being free from, and even hostile to, Christian tradition, was none the less mystical and tending to deify love, life, and the sex instinct.

* * *

The Soul's Progress in The Sisters

We have so far attempted to show how the whole background of religious-emotional attitude to love is moulded on a similar pattern in the works of Carpenter, and in those of Lawrence at the vital creative period between 1912 and 1916. Further examples could be advanced, especially from the '*Study of Thomas Hardy*'. In this, however, other influences are at work, not all of which converged with Carpenter's on all points. It remains to be shown how the initial plot of *The Rainbow–Women in Love*, which we shall here call *The Sisters* for short, tallies with the analysis of love and marriage made in *Love's Coming of Age*

Gerald, the Ungrown Man

"Man, the ungrown" is the title of the second paper of the original edition of *Love's Coming of Age*. By man, Carpenter means "the ordinary human male", with all that the first adjective implies. His opening paragraph could be a faithful description of Gerald Crich in *Women in Love*, and it may indeed have suggested the prototype or basic idea of this character:

> While mastering the world with his pluck, skill, enterprise, he is in matters of Love for the most part a child. The passion plays havoc with him; nor does he ride the Leopard, as Ariadne is fabled to have done.[45]

Gerald, the industrial magnate, has been an explorer and a soldier; his passion for Gudrun will play havoc with him, even though he can by will-power and force master the Arab mare he is riding, and dominate the miners. In matters of love, he remains a child, "in the last issue . . . wavering and lost", a "clumsier, cruder intelligence" than Birkin's, a "limited soul".[46]

In *Love's Coming of Age* the adolescent youth is shown "burning to master a real quadruped"; and to the grown ordinary man "passion is the little fire with which he toys, and which every now and then flares out and burns him up". The parallel with Gerald Crich could be pursued almost throughout:

> The men who have the sway of the world to-day are in the most important matters quite ungrown—they really have never come

> of age in any adequate sense . . . Remove the distinctive insignia of their clique and office, and you find underneath—no more than a public school boy.[47]

In contrast with this "ungrown" man, in the woman "the coming of age of Love (which harmonizes all the faculties in the human being) may take place early". But because Man has "dominated the other sex, and made himself the ruler of society", society itself is "advanced in mechanical and intellectual invention" but is "ungrown" and "on its more human and affectional side seems at times an utter failure".[48] This is the human failure of Gerald's life as the leader of industry, which Lawrence depicts as a complete vacuum in human relations.

Birkin, the Prototype of Future Man

Carpenter sees a hope for the future in an alliance of "the women and the workmen". This is perhaps merely a thought for his socialist audience. On this point the anti-feminist Lawrence of the '*Study of Thomas Hardy*' and of *The Rainbow* does not follow him. But if we try to revert to the original intention of *The Sisters*, which was to show the diverging and indeed opposed conceptions of love of two couples, Ursula–Birkin, and Gudrun–Gerald, we may have a clue to the original pattern of the opposition in his mind. Birkin, the school inspector, is of unspecified social origin (he has £400 a year private income, not unlike Carpenter). His nature is "grown" as opposed to the "ungrown" character of Gerald. In the newly-published 'Prologue' to *Women in Love*, which may partially hold the key to the unelucidated differences between the original draft of 1913 and the 1916, or rather 1920, text as finally edited and cut, Birkin is presented as of a deeply homosexual nature, tied to Gerald by a "subterranean kindling", "a strange, embarrassing fire".[49] At the same time, he, the poet who seemed "almost weak, passive, insignificant", is "in the last issue . . . callous, and without feeling, just as Gerald Crich in the last issue was wavering and lost".

> He knew how to pitch himself into tune with another person. He could adjust his mind, his consciousness, almost perfectly to that of Gerald Crich, lighting up the edge of the other man's limitation with a glimmering light that was the essence of exquisite adventure and liberation to the confined intelligence.[50]

Here we have the contrast between Carpenter's "ungrown" man of action, and the more feminine, more perceptive nature of Birkin, whom Lawrence has definitely presented as a prototype of the man of the future.[51] We shall see later how closely the portrait of Birkin resembles Carpenter's description of the mental qualities of the Urning, or man of homogenic nature.

If our thesis is correct, it is not by accident that Lawrence has endowed Birkin with sexual ambivalence, with the gift to love both male and female and to awaken love in them both. He is deliberately creating a character moulded on the ever present, but not always fully expressed, thought of Carpenter, that the "intermediate" type is closer to the paradisial future of mankind than the ordinary male. What else can be the meaning of Carpenter's essay "Man, the ungrown" if woman "is the more primitive, the more intuitive, the more emotional",[52] "comes of age", "harmonizes all the faculties in the human being",[53] sooner than man? if the more feminine types of men are considered to have attained a further degree of evolution than the men of action, the athletes, the Empire-builders?[54] An ideology of sex and social categories transcending class underlies *Women in Love*; much of that ideology appears to be directly inherited from *Love's Coming of Age*. And because Lawrence is what he is, the emphasis is placed by him on sexual relations and sympathies, the class element being on the whole secondary, though always present, in his analysis of the character of Gerald. The uprooted miner's son tries to state eternal values expressing his sense of superiority over the mine-owner.

The Brangwens: from Golden Age to Paradise through Civilization

Our analysis resting on the characters of Gerald and Birkin is fundamental because it shows that Lawrence shares with Carpenter, at least in the deeper imaginative processes at play in *The Sisters*, certain assumptions relating to the psychological pre-eminence and capacity for sympathy of the homosexual, indeed to his divine nature. But there are many more aspects in which *Women in Love*, and, in that order, the early chapters of *The Rainbow*, owe a tremendous debt to Carpenter. We may now proceed more allusively, letting the reader make for himself detailed comparisons on the basis of our indications.

Developing in *Love's Coming of Age* ideas already outlined in *Civilization, Its Cause and Cure*, Carpenter sees in "a half-grown man" a tyrant: Man in his ascendancy relegates woman to "the seclusion of the boudoir or the harem, or . . . to the drudgery of the hearth": whereas she should be "the interpreter of Love to Man, and in some degree his guide on sexual matters",[55] woman "the serf" is reduced to the status of either prostitute, lady, or drudge.

The Rainbow was conceived and written as the introduction to *The Sisters*, and the three generations of Brangwens depicted in it were meant to lead to the perfect couple, Ursula and Birkin. The evidence for this is ample in Lawrence's letters. Seen from this angle, *Women in Love* being in large part the original *Sisters*, presents not only the women of the future (women in freedom, to use Carpenter's terminology), but the "drudge" who has spent her life breeding children and doing household work: Anna Brangwen, dominated by the ungrown domestic tyrant, Will Brangwen. The novelist also shows in action the prostitute, Minette, in the London chapters; and the lady, Hermione Roddice, with her ambiguous, wilful and dishonest attitude to love and sex, her love of abstraction and false spirituality. Gudrun is a more complex image of a type of woman having attained false freedom, an aesthete, morally and aesthetically "bound" rather than "loose", to quote Birkin. There are of course differences in detail, but it can be argued that the basic pattern of contrasts is between these various feminine types, with two predominant favourable portraits: those of Lydia Lensky in the first generation, and of Ursula in the third. Both make a success of their sex and love life, after trials and errors; both reach some sort of paradisial blessedness and freedom.

In many ways, the progress of the human soul from the early Brangwens, earth-oriented and living in a pre-civilization age, to the "post-civilization" couple Birkin and Ursula, who choose to live on Birkin's £400 a year in freedom from all the trammels and encumbrances of civilized life, is that of mankind as seen by Carpenter from the noble savage through the industrial and commercial age to the goal of freedom and simplification of life. It is scarcely necessary here to discuss the paradisial state which Tom Brangwen and Lydia finally attain, except to recall that Lawrence refers, with respect to it, to a quotation from Swedenborg which he may have read in *The Drama of Love and Death*: "Those who are truly married on earth are in heaven one Angel."[56]

Ursula as Woman in Freedom

'Woman in Freedom', the next chapter of *Love's Coming of Age*, opens with the statement "what woman needs most to-day . . . is a basis for independence for her life" which will enable her "to face man on an equality . . . and to dispose of herself and of her sex perfectly freely".[57] This can be achieved by doing away with "our whole commercial system", by the destruction of "the poor little pinched ideal of the 'lady' which has ruled society so long", and by a new code of manners between the sexes. Improved house construction, reduced and simplified housework, shared by the male, will reduce drudgery. Here again we have in two or three pages the pattern of life chosen by Lawrence, and much noticed and commented on by his acquaintances.

"Free woman" and "free love", Carpenter pursues, have to be restored to their "*true* and rightful significance . . . . only when the free woman is honoured will the prostitute cease to exist".[58]

Ursula Brangwen remembers that she has in her femaleness an ultimate weapon in her life struggle: "In her femaleness she felt a secret riches, a reserve, she had always the price of freedom".[59] Yet she fights for her economic and social independence, and truly becomes a free woman, in Carpenter's sense: the part of *The Rainbow* in which she achieves against great odds this precious independence is among the best and most convincing, and corresponds to deep and mature conviction on the part of Lawrence. If it does not by itself testify to a study of Carpenter, its place in the general scheme of the development of the characters towards true equality in love corresponds entirely to the general conception of *Love's Coming of Age*. Lawrence however—and the subject and mood of final writing of *Women in Love* did not lend themselves to it—does not follow Carpenter in his forecast of a new "neuter" sex of female workers, nor into his analysis, on the whole favourable, of the women's movement which the author of *The Rainbow* came to scorn as much as did his heroine Ursula.

* * *

Marriage

Egoïsme à deux

We now turn to Carpenter's criticism of marriage and his forecast for the future of that institution. Contrasting what it could be and what it is, he points out that it cannot be expected to be successful "as long as man is only half-grown, and woman is a serf or a parasite".[60] He goes on to plead for easier divorce and better sexual education, particularly of men, recalling the importance of initiation ceremonies in primitive societies. But apart from "difficulties arising from personal ignorance and inexperience",[61] there are other, social and economic, reasons which tend to turn marriage into "a death-struggle". In *The White Peacock* Lawrence had defined it as "more of a duel than a duet".[62] Public opinion draws round the married pair "a ring-fence", isolates them in "fatal boredom", without the enrichment of "outside personal interests". Marriage becomes a narrowing experience "a mere *égoïsme à deux*". Bourgeois marriage "carries with it an odious sense of stuffiness and narrowness, moral and intellectual". The conclusion is that "marriage must be either alive or dead".[63]

We find in *Women in Love* a very closely similar criticism of marriage, culminating in Chapter XXV, 'Marriage or not'. In it the attitudes of Birkin and of Gerald to marriage are sharply contrasted, and, with the difference that this is a novel, expressing ideas mainly (though not only) through characterization, the whole chapter could be directly derived from *Love's Coming of Age*. Gerald, for instance, sees in marriage a "*pis-aller*", whereupon Birkin, the champion of the new, living marriage, uses language very similar to Carpenter's:

> Then don't do it . . . I tell you . . . the same as I have said before, marriage in the old sense seems to me repulsive. *Egoïsme à deux* is nothing to it. It's a sort of tacit hunting in couples: the world all in couples: each couple in its own little house, watching its own little interests, and stewing in its own little privacy—it's the most repulsive thing on earth. . . . One should avoid this *home* instinct . . . One should never have a home . . . In fact, because the relation between man and woman is made the supreme and exclusive relationship, that's where all the tightness and meanness and insufficiency comes in.[64]

But Gerald, the man of action, the ungrown public-school boy, is doomed:

> Marriage was like a doom to him. He was willing to condemn himself in marriage, to become like a convict condemned to the mines of the underworld, living no life in the sun, but having a dreadful subterranean activity . . . But he would not make any pure relationship with any other soul . . . Marriage was not the committing of himself into the relationship with Gudrun. It was a committing of himself in acceptance of the established world, he would accept the established order—in which he did not livingly believe, and then he would retreat to the underworld for his life.[65]

The addition to this theme of the problem of the love between the two men is very far from lessening the probability of a use by Lawrence of a whole chain of ideas set in motion by Carpenter. But it belongs to the next stage, i.e. the positive conception of marriage. On the negative and critical side, examples could be multiplied from *Women in Love* and *The Rainbow*, replicas of the analysis made by Carpenter of what is wrong with bourgeois marriage. The atmosphere of the home of Will and Anna Brangwen, especially in *Women in Love*, the stuffiness and closeness of their house and of their minds, the hatred of "houses and furniture and clothes" which are "terms of a base world, a detestable society of man", associated with the criticism of "mechanism, the very soul of materialism",[66] all these are severally, and in their combination, reminiscent of Carpenter's general line of thought as expressed in *Love's Coming of Age*.

Mystic Marriage

With 'Marriage, a Forecast', Carpenter comes to his positive view of the perfect union. Like Birkin, he accepts "the compulsion of the marriage tie", while he wishes to see it made more free; he believes in "permanent and life-long union—perhaps a many-life-long union—founded on some deep elements of attachment and congruity of character".[67] Man is by nature polygamous but with a trend towards unitary alliances; woman is not by her physical nature polyandrous; both tend towards "the formation of this double unit of wedded life";[68] he advocates freedom: freedom of choice and experience in youth, leading to a freed form of marriage allowing "for its reasonable development and growth".[69]

His forecast for successful marriage is based on four conditions:

(1) the furtherance of the freedom and self-dependence of women;
(2) the provision of some rational teaching, of heart and head, for both sexes during the period of youth;
(3) the recognition in marriage itself of a freer, more companionable, and less pettily exclusive relationship;
(4) the abrogation or modification of the present odious law which binds people together for life, without scruple and in the most artificial and ill-sorted unions.[70]

We have already quoted [71] his development on the third point and his plea for "wide excursions of the pair from each other", for the recognition of "the remarkable and immense variety of love in human nature"[72] and for "triune relations". We have stressed the resemblance between this passage and its intent (marked in later editions by the juxtaposition of the paper entitled *The Intermediate Sex*) with the general plan and intention of *Women in Love*. We need only quote here the most relevant passages from that novel.

In the chapter 'Marriage or not' Gerald, faced with his doom, sees another way, but does not accept it:

> The other way was to accept Rupert's offer of alliance, to enter into the bond of pure trust and love with the other man, and then subsequently with the woman. If he pledged himself with the man, he could later be able to pledge himself with the woman: not merely in legal marriage, but in absolute, mystic marriage.[73]

After Gerald's death, Ursula asks Birkin whether he needed Gerald:

> "Yes", he said.
>
> "Aren't I enough for you?" she asked.

"No", he said. "You are enough for me as far as a woman is concerned. You are all women to me. But I wanted a man friend, as eternal as you and I are eternal" . . . .

"To make it complete, I wanted eternal union with a man too: another kind of love", he said.[74]

Reaching the Centre of Life

It might be unfair to Lawrence, as indeed to Carpenter, to place the emphasis only on the "triune" marriage. For both authors, true marriage is a state of union reached beyond the personalities of the lovers; it represents the attainment of a supreme and higher state of being, the accession to "another world",[75] the "paradisal entry into pure, single being".[76] Making allowance for the destructive influence of the novelist's own experience of love and marriage, and for the dubious magic of bodily approaches by which Ursula and Birkin reach their spiritual consummation; also allowing for the fact that Lawrence is never at his best when describing a *positive* love experience, and provided we give our attention to the general pattern of *Women in Love* rather than to the details of its execution—it must be recognized that in the chapter 'Excurse' we have an attempt to express in words a state of being such as Carpenter tries to describe in 'The Sex Passion', when he asserts that "absolute union can only be found at the centre of existence",[77] and therefore identifies love, as does Lawrence, with the life force and ultimately with the Divine. The passage already quoted above, in which he asserts that "whoever has truly found another . . . has found also a third—who dwells at the centre and holds the plastic material of the universe in the palm of his hand",[78] is the text for many a Birkinian sermon. When Birkin had reached with Ursula the "gladness of having surpassed oneself, of having transcended the old existence", when they could no longer say "I" because "This I, this old formula of the age, was a dead letter", they experienced

> . . . a peace superseding knowledge, there was no I and you, there was only the third, unrealized wonder, the wonder of existing not as oneself, but in a consummation of my being and of her being in a new one, a new, paradisal union regained from the duality.[79]

A Chronological Retrospect

Our analysis, which has reaped a rich harvest of similarities of thought, image and expression between *Love's Coming of Age* and Lawrence's double novel, has been conducted without regard for considerations of chronology. And yet *Women in Love*, from which most of our quotations have been culled, was finally rewritten after other books by Carpenter had made an impression on Lawrence: some of them published later than *Love's Coming of Age*, such as *The Art of Creation* and *The Intermediate Sex*, which the author of *Women in Love* could have read in early youth even if their full impact, like that of *Love's Coming of Age*, was not manifested until after 1912; others such as *The Drama of Love and Death*, published that year, or *Intermediate Types among Primitive Folk*, which only appeared in 1914.

Thus the question now arises of the reasons which may have provoked in 1912, or early 1913, a resurgence and deepening of Lawrence's interest in Carpenter. They are not known, in the absence of any direct references to the Sheffield writer in the letters of Lawrence. His influence is nevertheless present, very palpably as we hope to have shown, in the very conception of the main characters of the double novel. We now propose to show that it is present in the last days of 1912 and the beginning of 1913, and permeates the whole new Messianic orientation of Lawrence's vocation as a writer.

German and Italian Translations

A few biographical details may help here. From May 1912 to September when he settles in Italy, Lawrence is on the move with Frieda, and hardly sees an English book, by his own admission in a letter.[80] What he read from among the books of Alfred Weber when living in his chalet at Icking, nobody has recorded; it may however be relevant to note that as a sexologist Carpenter was almost better known in Germany than in England and that his books, translated from 1895 onwards, may have been on the shelves of the German sociologist. Moreover, they were also translated into Italian, and the translator Guido Ferrando relates that when the English writer visited him in Florence in 1911 he had the pleasure of showing him in a bookshop a prominent display of his own books, *L'Amore divinta maggiorenne* (1909) and *L'Arte della Creazione* (1909). In 1909 the *Revista della Società internazionale degl' Intellettuali* had published a translation of an extract from *Towards Democracy*, and in 1912 Teresina G. Campagni Bagnoli also published a translation of *Verso la Democrazia.*[81]

It is possible that Italian acquaintances may have discussed these books with an English writer living in Italy in 1912, and so contributed to renewing his interest in what must have seemed from afar a familiar figure. The publication in March 1912 of *The Drama of Love and Death* at a time when Lawrence was himself living the drama of his own love, and, while rewriting *Sons and Lovers*, painfully reliving the days of his mother's death, may have led him to procure a copy of this new book, which many signs in his writings of that period suggest he had read. Some friend such as Sallie Hopkin may have thought of sending it to him, in response to some of his letters in which he spoke of the joys and stresses of his new passion.

None of these suppositions is completely to be excluded from consideration until some definite clue either confirms or denies any one of them. However that may be, it is clear that the complete list of all books and reviews named in Lawrence's and Frieda's letters between May 1912 and July 1914, and indeed later, does not give anything like a full account of his reading, nor indeed of his exceptional faculty of seizing upon an idea which coincided in the slightest degree with his preoccupation of the moment and of exfoliating it into appropriate imagery.

New Themes in 1912 and 1913

In an analysis of the evolution of the themes of Lawrence's short stories of this 1912–13 period, undertaken quite independently of the present study and indeed before this was conceived, we have shown, in the final pages of *Sons and Lovers* and the stories of the same period, the sudden appearance in Lawrence's mind of certain themes on consciousness, love, death and the self which are highly relevant to the present discussion.[82] These can be very briefly summarized here.

The new themes first appear in the final chapters of *Sons and Lovers* and in the 'Foreword' written at the end of 1912 and sent to Edward Garnett in January 1913; they are also found in letters to Ernest Collings, of approximately the same period, to which attention is given in the next chapter. Very briefly, they centre on an opposition between the Lawrentian concepts of being and not-being, the first associated with the flesh and the blood, the other with certain forms of consciousness in connexion with mental, social, and mechanical activities. Darkness, death of the conscious self, in this system, relate to being, while the word, the law, light, and their corresponding symbols, whiteness, cold, and ice, stand for not-being. A fragment from *Sons and Lovers* which was probably written in November 1912, when the true meaning of the novel seems to have struck Lawrence, who then gave it its new title, sums up these themes:

> To him now, life seemed a shadow, day a white shadow; night, and death, stillness and inaction, this seemed like *being*. To be alive, to be urgent and insistent, that was *not-to-be*. The highest of all was to melt out into the darkness and sway there, identified with all the great Being. . . . To be rid of our individuality, which is our will, which is our effort—to live effortless, a kind of conscious sleep—that is very beautiful, I think; that is our after-life,—our immortality.[83] [*My italics.*]

Without unduly anticipating the next chapter, it may be recalled here that the love scenes between Paul Morel and Clara are the first occasion for Lawrence of describing the lovers' accession to a sort of cosmic consciousness, to the sense of "their own nothingness": through passion they came to "know the tremendous living flood which carried them away, gave them rest within themselves"; they became identified with "so great a magnificent power" and they "knew they were only grains in the tremendous heave that lifted every grass blade its little height, and every tree, and living things".[84]

Autobiographical elements, of course, predominate in the formation of these themes, as we have shown elsewhere in our analysis of the 1913 flowering of new ideas in Lawrence's writings and of some of its sources; these, as could be expected, are many and varied: from Schopenhauer and Nietzsche through Whitman and Carpenter, to Bergson and secondhand echoes of Freud via Otto Gross and Frieda. While Whitman images predominate, glad leaves and trees, gates of the body and of the soul, it is almost impossible to distinguish between Whitman and Carpenter in this imagery inspired from botany and the love of nature; but what matters supremely is the *combination* and the symbolic *meaning* of images, rather than the words and visual import.

Those ideas and images are thrown together in a ferment in the

'Foreword' to *Sons and Lovers*, which was not intended for publication, but is essentially, like the '*Study of Thomas Hardy*' nearly two years later, Lawrence's 'Confessions of the Heart', an intimate and self-revealing document: "I should die of shame if [it] were printed", its author wrote in February 1913.[85] While some of its language and content is closely allied to *The Art of Creation* and as such belongs to the next chapter, several passages appear to contain reminiscences of *Love's Coming of Age*.

The Rose and the Bee

The image of the apple-blossom, and that of the rose, prevalent in Lawrence's poems of 1913, at least in their mystic implications and symbolism, are possibly reminiscent of that "rose of Souls that Dante beheld in Paradise" mentioned in 'The Free Society'.[86]

In *The Art of Creation* Carpenter uses the image of the bee and the hive, in a chapter from which we draw several important parallels with the 'Foreword', to express this sense of cosmic communion with the 'All-Self' or 'Great-Self', which is common to that book and to Lawrence's new thinking of 1913:

> The ego of the Bee . . . is in its essence one with the 'Spirit of the Hive' (whence comes the utter readiness of the Bee to give its little body for the safety of the Hive). The particular hive or colony of bees again is affiliated to the whole race of domestic bees, and this to the further back race of wild bees: and when our little friend comes humming along the southern wall among the early blooms in the February morning, she brings (as we feel) a message not of the moment, but of things aeonian slumbering deep in our hearts as well as hers.[87]

At the end of his note 'Early Star and Sex Worships' in *Love's Coming of Age*, having recalled that asceticism is "a curious part of all the old religions", that it is "a basic thing in human nature" which "gives man supremacy, not only over the beasts of the fields, but over his own bodily and mental powers", he describes the opposite mood of hedonism, in which man "gives the rein to his desires to chariot him to the extremest bounds of his Kingdom". He then expresses this necessary opposition in a complex image:

> Are not these two moods both necessary—the great rhythmical heart-beat, the *systole* and *diastole*, of the human soul? The one, a going forth and *gathering of materials* from all sources, the other an organizing of them under the most perfect light, or rather (it may be said) a consumption of them to feed the most perfect flame, the one centrifugal, the other centripetal; the one individual, the other universal; and so forth—each required for the purposes of the other, and making the other possible?[88] [*My italics.*]

In the "Foreword" Lawrence compares man to a bee out of a hive, coming backward and forwards to his woman, the queen, who is also the father; he comes to her "for suggestions, and renewal, and identification", before he goes to "his Uttering, wherein he is masterful and proud". He has, just before, misquoted Whitman, which suggests he did not have *Leaves of Grass* at hand but remembered his reading very generally. He goes on:

> But not only does he come and go: it is *demanded of him* that he come and go. It is the *systole* and *diastole* of the Heart, that shall be. The bee comes home to the hive, and the hive expels him to attend to the flowers. The hive draws home the bee, the bee leaps off the threshold of the hive, with strength, and is gone. He carries home to the hive his essence of flowers, his joy in the word he has uttered, he flies forth again from the hive, carrying to the flowers the strength and vigour of his scrambling body, which is God Almighty in him. So he *fetches and carries*, carries and fetches.[89] [*My italics.*]

Admittedly the thoughts are dissimilar, in spite of a probable reminiscence of *The Art of Creation* in the Lawrentian context. But could it be that the Lawrence of 1913 had absorbed the imagery of *Love's Coming of Age* in his early days to the extent of echoing it unconsciously? Or was the substance and form of Carpenter's writings very near to his conscious preoccupations of the time? There are other, and more significant resemblances which suggest the latter.

Antinomianism

The idea of the free society, symbolized for Carpenter as for Dante by the 'Rose of Souls', is associated both by him and by Lawrence with a form of antinomianism: the spirit of the early Church, its "dream of an eternal Fellowship in heaven and on earth"[90] is evoked in Carpenter's chapter *The Free Society*. Lawrence's 'Foreword' is placed under the aegis of "John, the beloved disciple", and its incessant references to the Father, the Son, the Word and the Holy Ghost, testify to its author's immersion in Christian symbolism. It is the first of his "philosophic" papers which attempt to rejuvenate and interpret anew Christian and Jewish religious concepts: these themes will be reworked by him in '*Study of Thomas Hardy*', and, just before his death, in *Apocalypse*. The 'Foreword' to *Sons and Lovers* is in this respect a key text for the understanding of Lawrence, of his effort to free himself from his puritanical education by hammering out the concepts of the religion which has so profoundly marked him, and to reconcile them with his emotional and physical needs.

With the greater serenity of a former Anglican churchman, Carpenter distinguishes between the artificial laws of society, and some "inner laws" in matters of love and sex; he concludes that

> . . . the inner laws of the sex-passion of love and of all human relationships—must gradually appear and take the lead, since they alone are the powers which can create and uphold a rational society; and the outer laws—since they are dead and lifeless things—must inevitably disappear. Real love is only possible when love is a

> reality. The subjection of sex-relations to legal conventions is an intolerable bondage, but of course it is a bondage inescapable as long as people are slaves to a merely physical desire.

He looks forward with confidence to a time "when love becomes sufficient a reality" for "the absurdity of the Law to be at an end" since "sincere Love is . . . a real fact and its own justification . . . a law unto itself, probably the deepest and most intimate law of human life".[91]

In his tremendous effort to shake free from the fetters of a Congregationalist moral education Lawrence goes much further than Carpenter; he tears at the law, and deifies the Flesh at the expense of the Word:

> The Father is the Flesh, the eternal and unquestionable [we shall show in this idea a possible echo of *The Art of Creation* and *The Drama of Love and Death*], the law-giver but not the law, whereas the Son is the mouth. And each law is a fabric that must crumble away, and the Word is a graven image that is worn down.[92]

In the name of the Flesh (which is his own word for Love) he condemns the law of marriage,[93] making the agreement of flesh with flesh the deep and only true law of human life.

Carpenter's sober, moderate, spiritual late-Victorian doctrine is carried to the extreme of finding in physical passion alone the justification of marriage. What is significant, however, is the use by Lawrence, of the religious Christian phrases to reach his goal, and his sustained use of the image of the rose[94] to convey his identification of the divine and of beauty with the flesh. This remarkable convergence of imagery and concepts, in spite of permanent differences in the temperaments of the two writers, would in itself have suggested a deep and sustained renewal of interest in Carpenter at that critical period of Lawrence's career.

4

THE GODS IN THE BODY AND THE DISINTEGRATION OF THE PERSONALITY

A Precarious Balance

The sudden irruption in Lawrence's mind, during the last months of 1912, of ideas about race and the blood, and of a new conception of human character, might seem incompatible with our working hypothesis, namely that when Lawrence conceived his double novel at about that time he was going through a period of renewed interest in the works of Carpenter. An illustration of this incompatibility could, superficially, be sought in the difference between Lawrence's new beliefs and Carpenter's humanitarian and democratic creed. It is a fact that there were at that time new and perhaps decisive influences at play in Lawrence's life and in his reading. Nevertheless, two of Carpenter's books, *The Art of Creation* (1904) and *The Drama of Love and Death* (1912), may have contributed to preparing the way for Lawrence's anti-democratic evolution. It is indeed possible that they also sowed the seeds of other ideas, more sinister in retrospect after the events of the last fifty years, which the present analysis may help place in better perspective by showing how they relate to the development of Carpenter's system of thought.

Carpenter was, of course, always highly sensitive to the new ideas of his time; his interest in the psychology of sex and in inversion kept him in close touch with the literature of psychopathology and neurology. At the same time, his syncretic mind and philosophical bent always led him to seek the reconciliation of ideas, rather than their clash and opposition, and his deliberate modernism and Hegelianism tended to make him try to marry opposites in a unified system. His religious nature also encouraged this effort to effect a synthesis, satisfactory to his metaphysical aspirations, between a science built on the observation of material phenomena, and his philosophical leanings.

In this way, his own development largely prefigures and anticipates that of the literature of the early twentieth century and of Lawrence. But he manages to maintain more severe critical control over his interest in psychical research, in spiritualism and in some aspects of theosophy, for instance, by going to the fountainhead of these doctrines, rather than by following more or less blindly in the footsteps of less-critical adepts such as Helen Blavatsky or even Annie Besant. The ideas which we now propose to analyse in two of his later books may nevertheless to some extent have prepared the ground for Lawrence's further and less critical evolution. They may, so to speak, have acclimatized in his mind modes of thought which Carpenter's name and personality would then endow with a minimum of scientific respectability: in late 1915 his letters show that he still cared about "what science says about these things", and even in 1917–18, when he wrote some of the early versions of the American Studies, the word "scientific" still had some prestige in his eyes.[1]

Foremost in this train of thought are the conception of the self and of the three stages of consciousness, the related idea of the Gods as dwelling in the physiological centres, and the notion of an inherited race mentality, itself closely associated with Carpenter's identification of mind and matter. We are here in the domain of pre-Freudian psychology, in which the materialism of mechanistic science is characteristically allied to an idealism and spiritualism derived from Plato, Berkeley, and the *Upanishads*. What later psychology will explain genetically and structurally in the individual, Carpenter tries to explain by a sort of analogical or metaphysical-cum-physiological reasoning, through cells and a micro-organic form of heredity. Even the 1920 revolt of Lawrence against Freud is in part built up on some of these materialistic-spiritualist explanations of the human self. At the very least, it derives from the same attempt to carry the reasonings of mechanistic science into the field of interpretation of the spiritual. In any event, his conception of character, as expressed in 1913, bears very close resemblance to Carpenter's basic views on the self and its affiliations, as we now propose to show.

* * *

The Art of Creation

The Art of Creation consists of thirteen 'Essays on the Self and its Powers', first published in 1904, enlarged in 1907, reprinted in 1912 and subsequently. It is conceivable, in view of the fact that its ideas do not seem to have penetrated deeply into Lawrence's thinking before that date, that he may have read it in 1912 in that second reprint, which was discussed, in relation to Bergson's *L'Evolution Créatrice*, in the *Christian Commonwealth* between 29 May and 10 July 1912.[2] Lawrence's interest in Bergson at that time might have prompted one of his friends in England to draw his attention to Carpenter's book, which on many points had anticipated the ideas of the French philosopher.

Three Ideas and a Syncretic Optimism

Three ideas are developed in *The Art of Creation*: we shall see how each one of them has its replica in Lawrence's outlook and writings. To use Carpenter's own summary, the first idea, which ran all through *Civilization, its Cause and Cure*, was "that of there being three great stages of consciousness":

> the simple consciousness (of the animal or of primitive man), the self-consciousness (of the civilized or intellectual man), and the mass-consciousness or cosmic consciousness of the coming man.

Having emphasized that this idea is more fully developed in *The Art of Creation*, Carpenter goes on in his autobiography:

> Relating itself closely and logically with the idea (1) of the three Stages of Consciousness is that (2) *of the Berkeleyan view of matter*—the idea that matter in itself is an illusion, being only a film between soul and soul: called matter when the film is opaque to the perceiving soul, but called mind when the latter sees through to the intelligence behind it. And these stages again relate logically to the idea (3) of the *Universal or Omnipresent Self. The Art of Creation* was written to give expression to these three ideas and the natural deductions from them.[3] [*My italics.*]

The third idea, derived from Hinduism, was in Carpenter's opinion bound "to revolutionize . . . all our views of science" when "the coming man" had arrived. The passage quoted below gives the tone, conceived as it is in the spirit of boundless optimism of Victorian times: written probably in 1916, it also contributes to the understanding of some of Lawrence's wildest ideas of 1917–18, when he was writing 'The Two Principles':

> Such matters as the Transmutation of Chemical Elements, the variation of biological Species, the unity of Health, the unity of Disease, our views of Political Economy and Psychology; Production for use instead of for Profit, Communism, Telepathy; the relation between Psychology and Physiology, and so forth, must take on quite a new complexion when the idea which lies at the root of them is seized. This idea must enable us to understand the continuity of Man with the Protozoa, the relation of the physiological centres, on the one hand to the individual Man and on the other to the Race from which he springs, the meaning of

> Reincarnation, and the physical conditions of its occurrence. It must have eminently practical applications; as in the bringing of the Races of the world together, the gradual evolution of a Non-Governmental form of Society, the Communalization of Land and Capital, the freeing of Woman to equality with Man, the extension of monogamic Marriage into some kind of group-alliance, the restoration and full recognition of the heroic friendships of Greek and primitive times; and again in the sturdy Simplification and debarrassment of daily life by the removal of those things which stand between us and Nature, between ourselves and our fellows—by plain living, friendship with the Animals, open-air habits, fruitarian food, and such degree of Nudity as we can reasonably attain to.[4]

Indeed Carpenter hopes in this book to produce, or pave the way for, "a great synthesis of all human thought on the ancient and ever-engrossing problem of Creation", ranging from the *Upanishads*, Buddha and Lao-Tze, through Plato, Jesus and St Paul, the fourteenth-century mystics, Spinoza, Berkeley, Kant, Hegel, Schopenhauer, James Ferrier, Whitman, to modern science and psychology. He wants this synthesis to lead to the practice of the art of creation "in ourselves". Take away the late-nineteenth-century optimism, and you are not far from the spirit of *Women in Love* and Birkin's attempt at renovating life.

Related motion, which is almost synonymous with desire, is for Carpenter "the ground and foundation of Life". Is consciousness *prior* to the material world, or does it come *after*? "Mind and matter are simultaneous and co-extensive".[5] They are distinct, but not separate; but the fact that they are distinct "forces us to conceive . . . of a 'stuff' prior to both", primitive being, or will, known to a cosmic consciousness "transcending our ordinary consciousness".[6] These concepts seem quite near to Lawrence's "flesh", "word" and "Holy Ghost".[7]

Feeling comes before intellect, just as desire arises in the mind before thought; and since the problem of the universe is insoluble "without the introduction of some transcendent factor—will, being, the ego . . ." the hierarchy between feeling and intellect is clearly marked by this priority of the one over the other. "The Ego, a transcendental being, descends, and manifests itself in our ordinary world of Time and Space."[8]

Is it necessary to look very far for the train of thought which manifests itself, at the end of 1912, in Lawrence's 'Foreword' to *Sons and Lovers*, and is resumed and amplified in the '*Study of Thomas Hardy*' at the end of 1914, in '*The Crown*' of 1915? For a detailed analysis, showing its many similarities with the guiding ideas and themes of *The Art of Creation*, the reader is referred to our study *D. H. Lawrence: l'homme et la genèse de son œuvre*. We may limit ourselves here to a few essential comparisons.

Whether we call it will, being, ego, there is thus a transcendental being which is eternal and outside space and which manifests itself in the ordinary world of time and space: a "creative source", present in man and in all beings, for instance in a tree: "a dominant Idea informs the life of the Tree; persisting, it forms the tree".[9]

Creation is thus "a process by which forms are continually being generated from feeling and desire", in the world of man, in art, and in the natural world. Between "the intelligences which constitute the Universe", there must exist "a common purpose and object of existence".[10] Creation is "a stupendous and perpetually renewed work of art, an everlasting evolution and expression of inner meanings into outer form, not only in the great whole, but in every tiniest part".[11] Messages of innumerable intelligences flash through the universe.

Critics have tended to credit Bergson, for whom Lawrence did not care much,[12] as the main external influence on the aesthetics of D. H. Lawrence, and especially on his vitalistic beliefs, and on his tendency, already asserted in *The White Peacock*, to extract the maximum of symbolic meaning from descriptions of objects and beings. It should not be overlooked that his perpetual endeavour to see in nature and in persons deep underlying motives and messages of subconscious recognition, may have been encouraged by this very concept of "the Art of Creation" which implicitly, and also explicitly, contains a conception of artistic creation. This is more specifically stated in *Angels' Wings*, discussed in the following chapter. This process, "which we can see at any time going on within our own minds and bodies, by which forms are continually being generated from feeling and desire . . . is the foundation of all human art."[13] Carpenter, the poet whose message was, so to speak, unconsciously forced out of him in his hut in the fields, anticipates on such conceptions as will find modern expression in Bachelard's *Poétique de la Rêverie*. Lawrence's reflection on art and form in '*Study of Thomas Hardy*' and '*The Crown*', with its rejection of external form or "law", and its insistence on each work of art creating its own form, runs very close to this Lamarckian doctrine of aesthetic creation. It is true that by 1912 Lawrence had read Bergson's 1911 Huxley lecture; but it is permissible to think that its effect was mainly to reinforce in his mind ideas he had already derived from earlier reading and reflexion on artistic creation.

The Three Stages of Consciousness: from Separateness to Absolute Being

Carpenter's Berkeleyan Platonism leads him to take a pre-Freudian interest in dreams, which are "evoked by dim underlying feelings", and also in the growth of thought out of unconscious desire.[14] He does not appear to have known Freud in 1904, when his interest in the unconscious was focused on the problem of the three stages of consciousness; this, fundamentally, was for him the romantic problem of attaining union with the desire which impels the cosmos. His psychology is that of materialistic science combined with Platonism—that is to say, an idealism or spiritualism dominated by bio-physical conceptions of the nervous system, of cell biology, of the identity of matter and mind, and of heredity as the transmission of combined physiological and psychological characters. The revolution in psychological thought which developed from the Freudian analysis of the development of the individual psyche, was alien to him, as indeed it will be to Lawrence for the most part, because both essentially belong to the same pre-Freudian universe of thought, seeking a metaphysical synthesis of spirit and matter rather than the understanding of psychological processes in themselves: Freud is closer to behaviourist observation and cybernetics than either of them. Carpenter's attempt to reconcile mind and matter, to see them as manifestations of the same transcendental being, answers a need created by the deficiencies of the mechanistic, abstract science against which he is reacting, a need which can be met in part by a more flexible genetic and cybernetic approach to the formation of the psyche.

Like Lawrence he seeks this reconciliation by postulating a third, mediating, transcendental essence, which encompasses both. Their imagery is sometimes strikingly similar.

From a consideration of things known, knower, and knowledge, Carpenter concludes that matter does not exist independently of a knowing mind: "dead matter" is nonsense, and so is "unconscious thought". Because he sees thought as an absolute essence, he postulates that, if there is thought, there is consciousness of some kind: with the emphasis on the last three words—since his vocabulary, like Lawrence's, is not always up to the subtleties of his meaning. "We are therefore compelled to adopt the supposition . . . that 'unconscious thought' is really conscious thought of some kind, but inherent in or related to another self than our own".[15] "Knowledge, Perception, Consciousness (in its ordinary form) are messages or modes of communication between various selves",[16] nature being a "countless interchange of communication between countless selves", one ego underlying "all thought and knowledge" and the whole of creation being "self revealment". He is now ready to develop fully his idea of the three stages of consciousness.

In the first stage, simple consciousness, "the knower, the knowledge and the thing known are still undifferentiated".[17] It is found in animals and young children. It has a "cosmic universal quality", carries with it "a kind of *aura* or diffused consciousness extending far around it", and is "daemonic or quasi divine" (a definition which the reader of Lawrence will be well-advised to remember). It is lost in the second stage, but restored in the third.[18] This will be the "aura" of Lawrence's animals, e.g. the stallion St Mawr, and of his primitive males; this daemonic knowledge is that which Lawrence attributes to the bees and to primitive man in his essay on Hawthorne[19] and to plants in 'The Spirit of Place'.[20]

The second stage is, in both Carpenter's and Lawrence's words, that of fallen, i.e. civilized, man: "in which the differentiation of knower, knowledge and thing known has fairly set in".[21] "The mind itself", says Lawrence, "is one of life's later-developed habits".[22] In this stage, "the consciousness of self becomes more and more distant, and with it the consciousness of an object antagonizing the Self". It is followed by "a kind of fatal split between (the Self) and the objective side of things"—which is described in *The Rainbow* by Ursula's education at university and her early experience of the world of men:

> The self is left face to face with a dead and senseless world. Its own importance seems to increase out of all reason; and with the growth of this illusion . . . the knowledge itself becomes dislocated from its proper bearings, becomes cracked and impotent and loses its former unity with Nature. Objects are soon looked upon as important only in so far as they minister to the (illusive) self; and there sets in a stage of civilization, *when self-consciousness becomes almost a disease.*[23] [*My italics.*]

So with Ursula and Skrebensky in the last stages of their love affair: she is pursuing a mere phantasm of her self-consciousness instead of love of a real being. And when Lawrence tried in 1917 to restate, after much esoteric reading, what he had intended to do in *The Rainbow*, he wrote:

> I knew, as I revised the book, that it was a kind of working up to the dark sensual or Dionysic or Aphrodisic ecstasy, which does actually burst the world, burst the world-consciousness in every individual.[24]

In its Nietzschean clothing the thought is the same, and Lawrence's vocabulary in the period of writing *The Rainbow* and *Women in Love* shows acute awareness of the problem in the very terms of Carpenter—for whom "the second mode [of consciousness] is sheer illusion . . . is all built upon the separation of the self from the knowledge and from the object [i.e. from other selves] . . . Its form is not true knowledge, but *Thought*. Thought is an aspect; it is the last disintegration of knowledge".[25]

Conscious thought is "the fact seen from just one . . . separate point of view"—and in "reintegration", in the third stage of consciousness, thoughts "fusing in the intense heat of union lose their separateness and merge in perfect light": separate, separateness, these are words which Lawrence uses in mainly pejorative contexts, already in '*Study of Thomas Hardy*', and increasingly so as he progresses in the description of his characters in *The Rainbow* and *Women in Love*.

This second period, that of self-consciousness, is marked—and here again we might be hearing Lawrence preach—"by the growth of the Brain", which "rises into immense importance" in man, whereas in animals "the great sympathetic system of nerves and the cerebro-spinal system are relatively large".[26] Owing to this growth "the emotions and the intellect of man for a long period are at variance", this leading to distress of mind, and to disease.

The coming of the third stage is a flash, an illumination, which takes place "when the illusion of separation is complete and the man has sounded the depths of grief and pain which accompany" thought and the illusion of knowledge.[27]

"The object suddenly is seen, is felt, to be one with the self. . . . This form of Consciousness is the only true knowledge—it is the only true existence."[28] It brings with it "a strange illumination". If the reader of *The Rainbow*, in the light of this passage and of the next quotation, turns to the scene of the "transfiguration" of Tom and Lydia Brangwen,[29] he will see how the first generation of Brangwens, in their own way, achieved an approximation to this third stage:

The true knowledge . . . is that in which the subject and object are known as one, and is of course a much higher and more perfect form of knowledge than the first—as in the animals—when subject and object *are* one, but never having been distinguished are not known as one. . . . A circle is, as it were, completed, and the external act of knowledge is no longer merely external, but is transformed into a symbol of a vast underlying life. The *aura* of the animals returns with greatly increased intensity. . . . It is not merely that the object is seen by the eye or touched by the hand, but it is felt at the same instant from within as a part of the ego; and this seeing and touching wake an infinite response—a reverberation through all the chambers of being—such as was impossible before. The knowledge, in fact, loses its tentative illusive form of *thought*, and acquires a cosmic universal character. It becomes luminous with far-reaching interpretations.[30]

Naturally, Carpenter assimilates love to such knowledge: a fact which strengthens the analogy with the experience of the elder Brangwens:

When two folk know each other in the sense of *love* (love being a consciousness of the third kind), instantly a word or a glance of the eyes, in the external world, reveal abysmal depths in the two selves, and a sense of age-long union.[31]

And to complete the likeness, just as Tom and Lydia form over the child Anna an arch, pillar of cloud and pillar of fire, that meets "to the span of the heavens",[32] so in Carpenter's metaphoric language "the luminous arc springs into being when the circuit is complete and is the evidence and manifestation of that completeness".[33] Images of rainbows, arcs, circles and auras abound in his prose, symbolizing as in Christian iconography, integration, unity, as opposed to the disintegration and dissociation of thought, the sunderer.

For Carpenter, all things, "the whole universe of space and time", have their real existence "in the third stage":

This is the state of absolute Being in which all things *are*, and *from* which the things which we ordinarily see and know proceed by disintegration into ordinary consciousness or thought.[34]

We are in the state of ignorance, of illusion, "persuaded of the separateness of our individual selves . . . content to *gnaw* off tiny particles, which we call thoughts, from the great Reality".[35] This is man's "rodent" stage: another metaphor with a Lawrentian ring. In *Women in Love*, Loerke, who has no "third consciousness" but is the image of disintegration, of what Lawrence calls "reduction", is likened to "a rat, in the river of corruption".[36]

Finding a Physiological Basis for Cosmic Consciousness

Carpenter is familiar with the fourteenth-century mystics, he quotes Jacob Boehme. But being a man of the late-nineteenth century, he needs, and in this he is not unlike the alchemists, to base his mysticism on some degree of scientific observation. This is why (as will Lawrence in 1918, *after* writing 'The Two Principles') he wants to find in neurology a justification for his beliefs. In 1904, before publishing *The Art of Creation*, he commissioned Henry R. Binns to research for him in the British Museum on this subject. Binns reported his very partial success in a twelve-page letter[37]: "The information obtainable" on "the sympathetic nervous system and its relation to emotions and kindred matters," he wrote, "is neither so clear nor so far-reaching as one could wish." He referred his correspondent to William James, to C. Lange and Ribot, and found for him an article by H. H. Goddard in the *American Journal of Psychology*, Volume 10, October 1898–July 1899, which Carpenter quotes in a Note on the Great Sympathetic in *The Art of Creation*.

But Carpenter's chief authority is *The Ganglionic Nervous System* by J. G. Davey, published in 1858, about which he had heard from Walt Whitman's friend, the alienist and mystic Dr Bucke, the author of *Cosmic Consciousness*.[38] Quoting Davey, William James, Hack Tuke and Féré, he presents the thesis according to which the Great Sympathetic is the seat of the emotions, as well as having "an architectural power, presiding over the formation and life of the body and the organs—a power to which even the brain and the spinal cord were subordinate".[39] Then, having slightly stretched quotations from Goddard and Ribot to suggest that the great sympathetic is "the most primary, and, in a sense, the most independent of the three systems", and "the seat of a primitive sensibility and consciousness", he tries to find in these authors support for his theory that

> . . . the second stage of consciousness, going especially with the evolution of the brain, has in the case of man largely drowned or disguised his earlier sensibilities and intuitions. Is it feasible to suppose that the third stage will correspond with a recovery of these more diffused and general sensibilities and a much closer intimacy and alliance between the three great Nerve Systems, which will make the undue preponderance of any one of them impossible, and consciousness a simultaneous act of them all, pervasive throughout the body?[40]

The question-mark at the end of this question might easily be missed by a passionate reader. Could not this note have started Lawrence on his renewed search for "blood-consciousness" and the psycho-physiological fantasies of 'The Two Principles' and of the booklets on the unconscious? 'The Two Principles' bears the marks of further theosophic reading, J. M. Pryse and Helen Blavatsky; but this took place between the end of 1915 (the letter to Russell on blood-precepts) and 1917. Carpenter might conceivably be at the origin of a search which sent Lawrence headlong on the path of the physiological justification of mystical ideas, and which ultimately leads, through '*Education of the People*', to the *Fantasia of the Unconscious.*

What is in any case common to both men is the reversed psychological hierarchy, by which all that proceeds from feeling, and therefore from the physiological centres, as opposed to what proceeds from abstract thought and "the brain", is considered to be of a higher grade, and nearer to the "Absolute Being". In spite of variations and of many intellectual contortions, Lawrence accepts this creed, and will develop it throughout his later works.

With both men, this inverted hierarchy is linked with their reaction against their social environment, and with their passionate love of and belief in "Life". Their vitalistic creed commands their attribution of pre-eminence to those parts of the body which transmit life, as opposed to those which enable the individual to achieve separate development of his personality: in a way, this contradicts their emphasis on non-generative love, but neither of them seems to have stopped to consider this inconsistency.

* * *

The Body and the Universal Self

Carpenter sees in the cosmic consciousness evidence that "there is a *real universal self*—a one absolute ego and knower, underlying all existences—the *Tat tvam asi*,[41] the essence and life of the whole universe, and the true self of every creature".[42]

Illusive, Separate Selves

But if there is "a real universal self", there is also "an illusive self". "There are millions of selves which are or think themselves separate",[43] an important distinction for whoever wishes to understand the different meanings of "separate" in Lawrence's various contexts.

Thus in '*Study of Thomas Hardy*' and in '*The Crown*', the writer expresses his contempt for the millions who want to preserve their limited, separate selves, their "single separate nullity".[44] But while Lawrence condemns them from his stance of moral mystical superiority, Carpenter on the contrary is at pains to *explain* them: perhaps "illusive" is not the right word, he points out. Using an article of Binet on the 'Psychic Life of Micro-organisms', he shows that the 'Great Self' can also be millions of selves, "just as in the human body, the cells are differentiated, the intelligence of each being an aspect of the intelligence of the whole body. Similarly, the individual selves may very well not know that they are parts of the 'Great Self' ", because "the first form in which the self fairly comes to consciousness is that of separation": this is the "illusion" of separateness. The separate "me" is a necessary stage on the way to the real self, "which must inevitably come":[45] and again we find in *The Art of Creation* the exact description of Ursula Brangwen's progress to the revelation on which *The Rainbow* concludes:

> So for a long time the "Me" goes on growing. Every new thought or experience that is added sinks into the Me; and as long as the ruling idea—of the Me as a separate perishable entity—governs the cluster of organism, so long do greed and fear, hatred and jealousy, sorrow and grief, increase and multiply and hover round, till their presence grows well nigh insupportable. . . . The vision of the True Self at last arises, with wonder and revelation and joy indescribable: the vision of a self that is united to others, that is eternal. . . . The Me-conception (as far as that means isolation, mortality, 'self-seeking') disappears, is broken up, is transformed, and the life is transformed accordingly.[46]

This does not mean that "at once the complete and final Individual is realized"; but this beginning of realization of "universal life and identity" is, in the immense journey of the human being, a landmark "more important even than that which signalled the birth of Self-consciousness. It marks the entrance to an emancipated, glorified, transformed Humanity".[47]

Within Reach of Absolute Being

Ursula, at the end of *The Rainbow*, has reached this beginning: she is ready for a man who "should come from the Infinite", who "would come out of Eternity to which she herself belonged". The optimistic ending of the novel, which some critics have found out of keeping with the preceding chapters, thus corresponds to Lawrence's initial plan, rather than to the mood in which he rewrote those chapters in 1915. Ursula is *not yet* 'the complete and final Individual', but she has begun to see the way to that "universe of life and identity" to which, according to Lawrence's original plan, she was to accede in *Women in Love*. The mood of 1916, however, placed greater emphasis on the satire of society and of mankind than on the discovery of universal life through love. But this satire is not incompatible with the initial design; it only tends to overcloud it and to divert attention from the mystic achievement of Lawrence's hero and heroine.

If Lawrence's 1913 message has thus partly become obscured in the course of execution, it is nevertheless still present in the combined *The Rainbow* and *Women in Love*, an ambitious work of creative imagination which was to show the progress of woman through the necessary individual, separate consciousness and through civilization, to universal life and the return to Paradise. This was to be done, in Lawrence's original scheme, by revivifying art through making it "more the joint work of man and woman":

> I think [Lawrence wrote in 1914] the one thing to do is for men to have courage to draw nearer to women, expose themselves to them, and be altered by them: and for women to admit men. That is the start—by bringing themselves together, men and women—revealing themselves each to the other, gaining great blind knowledge and suffering and joy, which it will take a big further lapse of civilization to exploit and work out. Because the source of all life and knowledge is in man and woman, and the source of all living is in the interchange and the meeting and mingling of these two: man-life and woman-life, man-knowledge and woman-knowledge, man-being and woman-being.[48]

Not many months later, in '*Study of Thomas Hardy*', he announces a new art which "utters the glad embraces and the struggle between" man and woman and "the submission of one": "there shall be the art which knows the struggle between the two conflicting laws, and knows the final reconciliation, where both are equal, two in one, complete".[49]

That is the great idea behind the original design of *The Sisters*, an idea still active in late 1914 when Lawrence began the final rewriting of *The Rainbow*. To what extent was he putting his personal, characteristic, interpretation on this thought of Carpenter?

> We must in the future look to a restoration of the harmony between (roughly speaking) the Mind and the Body, the Brain and the Great Sympathetic, the conscious and the subconscious Man. The *recovery* of the organic consciousness, the realization of the *transparency* of the body and the splendour of its intuitions, is not an impossible feat. The Hindus and other Orientals have in these directions, partly by deliberate practice, come into touch with and command of regions whose existence the Western peoples hardly suspect. In the West, the modern upgrowth of Woman and her influence will ere long make possible a Humanity which shall harmonize even in each individual the masculine and the feminine elements, and bring back at last the Brain and the self-conscious mind into relation with that immense storehouse of age-long knowledge and power which is represented by the physical body of the individual, as it is represented by the communal life and instinct in the mass-people.[50]

Had this last quotation been chosen by Lawrence as the text on which he based his development of his double novel, and as the criterion for selecting what he read while he wrote its second half in 1916, he could not have found a better definition of what he was seeking—the harmony between brain and sympathetic, the recovery of organic consciousness, yoga command of the *chakras*, harmonization of the masculine and feminine elements in each individual, restoration of the relationship of the self with the cosmos, and the luminous transparency of his heroine's body. The pessimism of *Women in Love* alone denies the last sentence and opposes that sense of unity with "the mass-people", in whom Lawrence no longer believed. And yet there is still some hope for the mass of illusive, separate selves, in the last lines of *The Rainbow*.

Perennial Bodily Cells and Race

Carpenter thus seeks for a forgotten knowledge, a lost harmony between conscious and subconscious, between mind and body: and if he does not go quite to the same lengths as Lawrence sometimes does in deifying the body, he takes very long strides in that direction. His conception of the affiliations of the self in the race-life leads straight to his idea of "the Gods as apparitions of the race-life". The concepts of the perennity of the flesh, of race, and of gods and demons as "dwelling in physiological centres", amounting to the attribution of divine, spiritual, or allegoric values to the bodily organs, are inextricably intertwined in his thinking. They are also closely related to a conception of the "self" which leads straight to a theory of the personality very similar to Lawrence's celebrated definition of character as stated in 1914 in an often-quoted letter to Edward Garnett.[51] While this is superficially inspired by Futurism, it responds in depth to a search for "the new human phenomenon", a phrase which may tacitly refer to Carpenter's description of the Mystery of Personality.[52] This, in turn, is founded on an analysis of the religious implications of the cell structure of the body to which we must now give some attention.

Carpenter, although he had read Gustave Le Bon, did not think of crowd-emotions as something which could be engineered at will. He thought they were conditioned by a *race-consciousness*. To use a more modern analogy, his working "model" of the human psyche or self was based on the notion of the cell, and his "model" of the race-consciousness was based on the association of cells in the body—an idea fairly prevalent at the time, which he uses in his assault on the alleged primacy of the brain in the psyche.

The body grows from one cell which splits, the resulting cells multiplying and differentiating; the mind grows according to a similar process, the "total ego" being contained in the original cell, but "necessarily expressed only to a very simple and primitive degree".[53] Consciousness is thus not "limited to the cells in a certain portion of the brain";[54] "the more complex brain-consciousness" has been evolved from "a primitive consciousness" diffused "all through the body".[55] Lawrence in *Psychoanalysis and the Unconscious* will similarly speak of a "pristine consciousness".[56] The "egoes of the body cells" can be thought of as "one with the total Ego which represents the fusion of their separate consciousness".[57]

Similarly a race is "a complex of bodies", and has "all the characteristics of an organic being" . . . "a life of [its] own, inclusive of and superadded to that of [its] individual members".[58] The individual is made of "the same protozoic cells" as his race: "the same cells from which Abraham and his wife Sarah sprung, produced also Solomon and St Paul":

> The conclusion is clear . . . the Jewish race . . . might reasonably be looked upon as the exfoliation of a single Ego which through this long chain, in hundreds of thousands of lives affiliated to it, sought expression and so far succeeded in finding it.[59]

Jesus is thus a "ramification" of a tree produced from a single cell. He might well exclaim: "Before Abraham was, I am":[60]

> His consciousness, the consciousness of his own being, had reached that depth at which it had become united with the consciousness of the race; and in using these words he merely stated a fact which he felt within himself, and knew to be true.[61]

There is no overt anti-Semitism in Carpenter, except an occasional inimical reference to Jewish moneylenders. In the present passage he states clearly that he selects the Jews to illustrate his point merely "because they afford an instance of *a very well-defined race, which, notwithstanding occasional lapses, kept itself very pure and unmixed, and, as a consequence, had the strictest customs and religious ideals and the strongest national consciousness*".[62] [*My italics.*] Nevertheless, the consequences of his complete identification of mind and matter are tangible in this illustration: he believes implicitly in a "consciousness of race", rooted in physical characteristics.[63]

Lawrence shows similar beliefs, reinforced by his reading of the anti-semitic writers H. S. Chamberlain and Otto Weininger: his comments on Mark Gertler's painting *Merry-go-Round*[64] testify to his rooted conviction that there is a physiological and hereditary basis for psychological traits. Like Carpenter's, his psychology is pre-Freudian, unconsciously mechanistic-materialistic, and closer to Krafft-Ebing's view of heriditary neuroses than to the genetic approach of post-Freudian psychology.

Carpenter's spiritualism, grafted on to nineteenth-century science, thus entails a conception of race psychology which, among other consequences, leads him to a clarification of some beliefs which are also found more or less explicit in the writings of Lawrence.

From the idea of the immortality of the protozoic cells, he goes on to underline "the enormous import and sacredness of sex, and its deep association with the religious and communal life of the race";[65] by clear implication, he blames the race mixture of "modern societies and nations" for the loss of the religious idea of sex, which he considers to be both normal and desirable. The sex cells, "passed on with fervent care from generation to generation", are "the most representative of the body and all its facilities, and within them lies the secret and heart of the race".[66] The cult of race and sex-worship are, for him, necessarily associated.

This essentially reactionary belief has to be accommodated with his progressive ideals. The same cells "which produce the first man of the race, produce the last man. But *the last man is not therefore the same as the first man.* [*My italics.*] The first man may be merely a living soul (or psyche), the last man can be a quickening Spirit".

In the last man, the little original cell may attain "at last to Manhood and Deliverance". [67]Here we find the notion of the superman, to which we shall devote a later chapter; here is the mystery of reincarnation, not stated but present behind the whole conception.

Lawrence's mental itinerary from the 'Foreword' to *Sons and Lovers* to the creation of Birkin in *Women in Love*, follows on this point remarkably similar paths:

> "The Flesh is infinite and has no end. . . . The Father is the Flesh, the eternal and unquestionable, the law-giver but not the law", says the 'Foreword'. We, i.e. we individuals, "are the Word, we are not the Flesh. The Flesh is beyond us. . . . This flesh I am is beyond me".[68]

At about the same time, in 1913, in his review of *Georgian Poetry* Lawrence also writes:

> This flesh and blood sitting here writing, the great impersonal flesh and blood, greater than me, which I am proud to belong to, *contains all the future*. What is it but the quick of all growth, the seed of all harvest, this body of mine? . . . We are all love poets. For our religion is loving.[69] [*My italics.*]

Thus he asserts the primacy of the cells, the flesh, over the individual ego, the brain, the word-utterer; and he places the law of the flesh over that of the usurping 'Word'. These concepts will be developed at great length in his '*Study of Thomas Hardy*', as regard his opposition to man-made, artificial laws, both moral and aesthetic; he will also develop *ad nauseam* his image of the flower, "the bit of apple-blossom" representing in the 'Foreword' the everlasting, eternal flesh, beaten thin into "a pink or a purple petal, or a thought or a Word";[70] the rose:

> But what is really 'Rose' is only in that quivering shimmering flesh of flesh which is the same, unchanged for ever, a constant stream, called if you like rodoplasm, the eternal, the unquestionable, the infinite of the Rose, the Flesh, the Father—which were more properly, the Mother.[71]

Lawrence, naturally, adds his own interpretation, his overt purpose being to explain *a posteriori* the idea behind *Sons and Lovers*;

but at a deeper level he is working out the thoughts which will preside over the conception of *The Sisters*, the discovery by Ursula of her superman, one of the '*Sons of God*', whom her experience in *The Rainbow* has prepared her to meet. In an earlier comparison[72] we have shown how the image of the bee fetching and carrying might conceivably echo a passage of *Love's Coming of Age*. It is pursued by Lawrence in what might be another echo, this time of *The Art of Creation:*

> So the man comes home to woman and to God, so God the Father receives his Son again, *a man of the undying flesh*; and so the man goes forth from the house of his woman, so God expels him forth *to waste himself in utterance*, in work, which is only God the Father realizing himself in a moment of forgetfulness. Thus the eternal working. And it is joy enough to see it, without asking why.[73] [*My italics.*]

Not only are the thought and the imagery close to the notion of the permanence of the cells in *The Art of Creation*, but the way in which they lead to an aesthetic conception is the same, as we shall have occasion to show.

In '*Study of Thomas Hardy*', Lawrence further hammers out his idea first stated in the 'Foreword', of the joy of being, expressed in the flower:

> For every petalled flower, which alone is a Flower, is a work of productiveness. It is a moment of joy, of saying 'I am I'. And every table or chair a man makes is a self-same waste of his life, a fixing into stiffness and deadness of a moment of himself, for the sake of the glad cry 'This is I. I am I'.[74]

This idea of artistic creation, and of the flowering of the plant as "waste", as the sudden efflorescence which is the excess of life, the cry "I am I", is also found in *The Drama of Love and Death*[75] and is fundamental to Carpenter's thinking on the beginnings of Love as well as to his aesthetic. It is expounded at length in Lawrence's '*Hardy*' in relation to his ideas both of love and of artistic creation.[76]

It is also closely connected there with the idea of the individual soul detaching itself from the matrix, from the mass-mind, becoming distinct, and creating itself, coming to a second birth,[77] an idea which underlies the whole conception of *The Rainbow* and culminates in the pre-ordained meeting of Birkin and Ursula, who is "referred back" to her lover.[78] The very conception of the character of Birkin, as we have shown elsewhere, is based on the same system of religious thought as Carpenter's "last man", "attaining at last to Manhood and Deliverance"; he is the nearest Lawrence could show in action to the "wonderful, distinct individuals, like angels" forecast by him in '*Study of Thomas Hardy*',[79] who will "move about, each one being himself, perfect as a complete melody or a pure colour". It is not by accident that Carpenter names Jesus in his analysis of the process of the eternal cell of the Jewish race—and then speaks of the "*last man*".[80] [*My italics.*] The mere "living soul" of Carpenter is Lawrence's "unbegotten" man, while the "quickening Spirit" is Lawrence's Birkin, or Ursula, at the moment when they think they may be on the threshold of true life—not *wholly* "born in the process of destructive creation"[81] but partly capable of "entry into pure, single being".[82]

We can now see in the light of Carpenter's conception of man's destiny through the various stages of consciousness, the complete development of Lawrence's ideas from the 'Foreword' to *Sons and Lovers* to the original plan of *The Sisters*. In the details, many parallels could also be drawn between Carpenter's views and Lawrence's pronouncements in that exceptionally creative period of his life which goes from late 1912 to the end of 1916. We shall select a few among the more eloquent.

Value and Limitations of the Brain

Carpenter has a rooted belief in the existence of a "race consciousness"—a belief in which he may have anticipated and possibly influenced, if not Houston S. Chamberlain, at least Carl Gustav Jung, unless his familiarity with German philosophy and psychology merely placed him in the same stream of thought. The ego of the individual, according to him, is "affiliated to that of the race"; indeed he speaks of "the 'I', the Ego, of [the] race", present and existent in the body of each one of us. Because science has to postulate a "subliminal" mind, or "subconscious", or "fringe" which "surrounds the ordinary consciousness", he concludes that there must be "such a thing as a race-consciousness associated with our bodily organization and accessible on occasions to our conscious minds".[83]

This is not in the brain. But the function of the brain is "to be continually making new combinations in which the whole Feeling-nature can find satisfactions—in other words, to be continually extending the area of expression of that nature . . . The Conscious Mind (of the second stage) is the pioneer of progress".[84] The conscious mind, of course, is represented by the brain.

Mindful of the stresses of his own life, Carpenter refers to the existence of discords and discrepancies between the conscious ego and the egoes of all our body cells: "I and my cells fall out to some extent".[85] Such discords are "between the conscious and the sub-conscious minds, between the Brain and the Great Sympathetic. . . . The discord *is* to a certain extent the progress"[86] which the brain pioneers.

In *The Drama of Love and Death* the individual souls are shown "rising each independently" towards "consciousness of the All-Soul", through "all this period of confusion and dismay . . . that we have called the period of Civilization and the Fall of Man . . . But it is in this period that 'divine Souls' are formed, and their feet first set upon the path of splendour".[87]

These passages throw light on the confused, often obscure psychology of Lawrence's '*Study of Thomas Hardy*' and to some extent on that of '*The Crown*', and of '*Education of the People*' and *Fantasia of the Unconscious*, although in these two works traces of J. M. Pryse, and possibly of Lawrence's 1918 reading of Carl G. Jung, can also be detected. First of all, his deep belief, shown in the '*Hardy*', in a race psychology, persisting through the ages and rooted in the body, probably owes as much to Carpenter's idea of race as to Houston Chamberlain's: on this point the two influences undoubtedly converge. Next, Lawrence is almost certainly imbued with the lines of *The Art of Creation* just quoted, when he writes, in a passage which pre-figures and explains the schoolroom discussion on consciousness between Birkin and Hermione in *Women in Love*:

> It seems as if the great aim and purpose in human life were to bring all life into the human consciousness. And this is the final meaning of work: the extension of human consciousness . . . [which is] a necessary condition of life itself. Man is himself the vivid body of life, rolling glimmering against the void. . . .[88]

"The vivid body of life," says Lawrence; "the One endless, boundless, fathomless Self and its myriad affiliations," said Carpenter: "We must now understand, when we look at a man or at a bee . . . that we are looking at a being who stretches . . . into the far backward and abysm of Time".[89]

The Lawrence of 1914 believes that "*The mind itself is one of life's later-developed habits.* [*My italics.*] TO KNOW is a force, like any other force".[90] Life must go on differentiating itself,

> . . . almost as though this differentiation were a Purpose. Life starts crude and unspecified, a great Mass. And it proceeds to evolve out of that mass ever more distinct and definite particular forms, an ever-multiplying number of separate species and orders, as if it were working already to the production of the infinite number of perfect individuals, *the individual so thorough that he should have nothing in common with any other individual.* [*My italics.*]

Consciousness is man's "greater manifestation of individuality".[91]

"The conscious mind," writes Carpenter, "we may . . . regard as the latest outgrowth and expression of the unfolding Ego; and in that sense it is very important." But it would be absurd "to expect our bodies at every moment to transform themselves into expressions of its passing moods". In typically Lawrentian imagery he adds, "It is only the advance guard, as it were, of a moving column; the bud on the branch; the crest of the wave." It needs the subconscious mind, the life of the body, "the great race-Mind behind it":

> It is perhaps the fault of the modern Brain or conscious Mind that it has not perceived this. From the moment when the sense of Self (as a separate being) evolved within primitive man, and entered into distinct consciousness, from that moment an immense stimulus was given to the Brain or the conscious Mind (to devise satisfactions and expressions for the individual self as a part from the race).[92]

The enormous development of brain-power and thought during civilization "has led to a fearful, and for the time being most sinister, divorce between the two parts of man's nature" and "the little self-conscious man has become a very puny creature indeed".[93]

So close to all this runs the argument of '*Study of Thomas Hardy*', that Lawrence develops there at full-length the theme of the "puny creatures" bound up in self-consciousness.[94] But his real concern is with being and not-being, just as Carpenter's is with reaching distinct and creative being.

Thought as Disintegration of Being

Carpenter's aim in *The Art of Creation* is to help his reader recognize in himself the "Creative Thought-source continually in operation" in man, which is "shaping and giving form not only to his body but largely to the world in which he lives";[95] to help him reach it beyond "what we call Civilization", in the midst of which "some of us . . . simply live embedded among the thoughts of other people".

"It would seem as if each soul, detaching itself from the mass, the matrix, should achieve its own knowledge," says Lawrence in '*Study of Thomas Hardy*', and he continues:

> Yet it is not so. Many a soul which we feel should have detached itself and become distinct, remains *embedded, and struggles with knowledge that does not pertain to it.* It reached a point of distinctness and a degree of personal knowledge, and then became confused, lost itself.[96] [*My italics.*]

This, incidentally, describes the fate of Will and Anna Brangwen, who will be "re-enacting some old movement of life's", but fail to be born again;[97] and to a large extent, that of Gerald Crich in *Women in Love*.

For both authors, the second stage of consciousness, that of separate mental existence, if it is a step in the right direction, is not the last step. The third stage is that of

> . . . the only true and absolute knowledge . . . the only true existence . . . for, as we have seen, the world consists of what is known, i.e. of what enters into consciousness. Consciousness *is* existence; and the perfect consciousness is the perfect and true existence. That universal consciousness by and in which the subject knows itself absolutely united to the object is absolute existence, i.e. Being.[98]

In '*Study of Thomas Hardy*', Lawrence follows a similar course of reasoning, and is steeped in the same mysticism of being: but he tends to be side-tracked by an exclusive and obsessive insistence on sex, in his chapter 'Of Being and Not-Being', where "subject and object" become "male and female". With Carpenter, love is one privileged instance of a consciousness of the third kind. In spite of this narrowing of the attention to one type of third consciousness, Lawrence does not vary much from his elder when he develops the concepts of reduction and disintegration: only he carries them one stage further, in his contempt and hatred of common, unregenerate humanity.

Thought, in *The Art of Creation*, is presented as "the last disintegration of knowledge. It is the fact seen from just one most particular and separate point of view".[99] Being *is* universal consciousness, i.e. "the state of absolute Being in which all things *are*, and *from* which the things which we ordinarily see and know proceed by disintegration or ignorance. It is the state *from* which they lapse or fall by disintegration into ordinary consciousness or thought".[100]

"The mind", says Lawrence, "is the dead end of life", it has "all the mechanical force of the non-vital universe".[101] And that of which he disapproves, the struggle for self-preservation, "the little fold of law and order",[102] the "repeating of some old process of life"[103]—all this is reduction, disintegration of being, and belongs to the second stage of consciousness, which in *Psychoanalysis and the Unconscious* he calls by the ambiguous names of "ideal sphere", "ideal consciousness",[104] when he almost quotes Carpenter: "The vast bulk of consciousness is non-cerebral. It is the sap of our life, of all life."[105]

The Temple of the Gods and the Road to Racialism

Combining Platonic ideas with the concept of heredity, in a passage which might have predisposed Lawrence to an understanding of Jung's archetypes, Carpenter asserts that

> . . . external forms built up in any race for the manifestation of Ideas are riveted and emphasized by Heredity (or by the hammering of the race-god through the centuries), and acquire an extraordinary sanctity and transcendent glamour through this process, so that the mere appearance of the form instantly wakes the Idea or deep transcendent feeling which belongs to it.[106]

This modern interpretation of Plato's ideas leads the author of *The Art of Creation* to deification of the body, through a racial conception of the idea of the gods: "What gave to these figures [i.e. the Gods] their intense reality and significance for the people over whom they presided?" he asks at the end of a passage[107] which might be the programme of Lawrence's later search for strange gods. In exalted and beautiful language, Carpenter lists and evokes the deities of Egypt, India, Assyria, Greece, Scandinavia and Mexico, the saints of the Christian church, the Virgin Mary, the Holy Ghost, and Christ. Two letters of Lawrence to Gordon Campbell, written at the same time as the '*Study of Thomas Hardy*' and *The Rainbow*, may be read as a distinct echo of this purple patch of religious interpretation. In one, Lawrence tries to recapture "the tremendous unknown forces of life, coming unseen and unperceived as out of the desert to the Egyptians"; and in the other, to grasp the old symbols "in their whole context, . . . the great satisfying conceptions of the world's greatest periods.[108]

The profound influence of the gods on men is attributed by Carpenter to the fact that "they represent *the life of the race itself* . . . so that through them we reach to *another and more extended order of consciousness*, we partake of a vaster life". [*My italics.*] He does not go quite as far as H. S. Chamberlain in his exaltation of the virtue of race in making the hero. He does not "wish to limit the answer too much, or say that it is *only* through the race-life that we reach a higher order of consciousness".[109] But he does emphasize an idea which might well have found its way even into the key theme of *The Plumed Serpent*, namely the god-making powers of race and heredity, for instance through the transformation of a king into a god:

> Everywhere we see this taking place. The Egyptian Pharaohs were exalted into Gods. To the Roman Caesars temples were built and divine honours paid. The Aztec and Peruvian emperors the same.[110]

From Platonic ideas, through heredity and "the myth-making tendency of races",[111] Carpenter reasons his mystical way to expression of his belief that "the Ideas and enthusiasms which produce myths and legends lie deep down in the very structure and

Illustrations

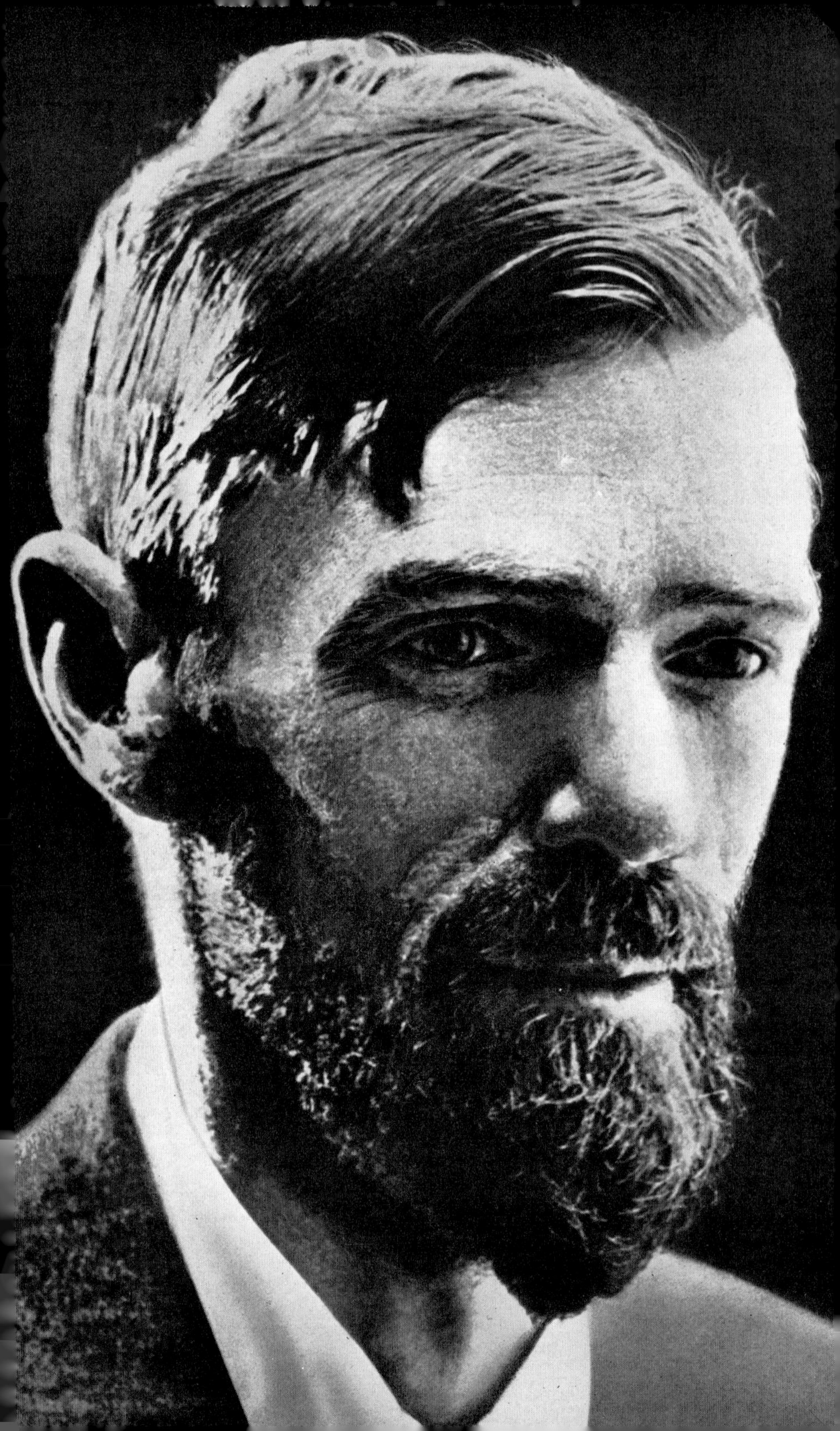

2. Edward Carpenter outside his cottage at Millthorpe
(Photograph by Frank Johnson)

1. D. H. Lawrence (*opposite*)

SIGNATORIES:—

Leonard D. Abbott.
Lucy Adams.
Harry Adams.
Maurice Adams.
Jane Addams.
Hon. & Rev. James Adderley.
Charles Aitken.
Sir P. Arunáchalam.
C. R. Ashbee.
Margaret Ashton.
Roberto Assagioli.
Teresina G. Campani Bagnoli.
Frank Bain.
Mildred Bain.
Granville Bantock.
H. Granville Barker.
George N. Barnes, M.P.
Orlando Barnett.
Count Batthyany.
Countess Batthyany.
Walter Baylis.
Léon Bazalgette.
Edward A. Beck.
Ernest Bell.
Annie Besant.
Henry Bryan Binns.
Katharine Binns.
Rt. Hon. Augustine Birrell, M.P.
Henry Bishop.
Algernon Blackwood.
Robert Blatchford.
Godfrey Blount.
Ethel Blount.
Rutland Boughton.
Harry Brearley.
Helen Brearley.
A. Fenner Brockway.
John Burroughs.
Herbert Burrows.
Sir W. P. Byles, M.P.
Lady Byles.
Alice M. Callow.
I. E. Gasperi Campani.
Micol Gasperi Campani.
Alfred Carpenter, R.N.
Ethel Carpenter.
Francis W. Chapman.
Capt. Lionel Charlton.

H.H. Maharaja Bahadur of Chhatarpur.
Percival Chubb.
Joseph Clayton.
Margaret S. Clayton.
Hariot Clisby, M.D.
Anne Cobden-Sanderson.
Alvin L. Coburn.
Fannie G. Coburn.
Dr. Stanton Coit.
Bessie A. Hardy Collins.
Dr. Alice M. Corthorn.
H. B. Cotterill.
G. Cotterill.
Vera Cotterill.
Sir Henry Cotton, K.C.S.I.
James H. Cousins.
Margaret E. Cousins.
Harold Cox.
C. T. Cramp.
Walter Crane.
R. B. Cunninghame-Graham.
Robert Cust
Eileen de B. Daly.
J. Percival Davies.
Frank Deas.
C. Despard.
Dr. Jas. Devon.
G. Lowes Dickinson.
P. Dimitratos.
J. H. Doncaster.
Harold Dore.
Will Dowson.
Helena B. Dowson.
Platon E. Drakoules.
Alice M. Drakoules.
G. C. Earle.
Dr. Arnold Eiloart.
Havelock Ellis.
Edith O. M. Ellis.
C. Langdon Everard.
H. C. Fairfax-Cholmeley.
Albert Fearnehough.
Guido Ferrando.
Ella Ferrando.
Max Henry Ferrars.
Bessie Ford.
Isabella O. Ford.
Prof. H. S. Foxwell.

Roger E. Fry.
C. G. Gallichan.
Richard Le Gallienne.
John Galsworthy.
Edward Garnett.
Patrick Geddes.
T. Binney Gibbs.
R. Murray Gilchrist.
Isabella Gilchrist.
Frieda A. Girdlestone.
Katharine Bruce Glasier.
G. P. Gooch.
Rev. C. A. Goodhart.
Gerald Gould.
J. Fredk. Green.
G. G. Greenwood, M.P.
Emilie Grigsby.
C. H. Grinling.
Ethel Grinling.
E. Agnes R. Haigh.
J. G. Hamilton.
Lady Isabel Hampden-Margesson.
J. Keir Hardie, M.P.
Isabella B. Hardy.
Wilfred Hargrave.
Austin Harrison.
C. Gasquoine Hartley.
Joseph Haslam.
Richard Hawkin.
E. S. P. Haynes.
Rev. Stewart D. Headlam.
Ellen M. Heath.
Percy Heath.
Carl Heath.
Effie Margaret Heath.
Prof. Chas. H. Herford.
Edwin Herrin.
Prof. Geo. D. Herron.
Mary Higgs.
Marian Hine.
Dr. Magnus Hirschfeld.
Chas. H. Holden.
Margaret Holden.
Laurence Housman.
Geo. Hukin.
Fannie Hukin.
Grace Human.
H. M. Hyndman.

[*Over*

3. The list of signatures to the 1914 Address to Edward Carpenter on the occasion of his seventieth birthday.

Sanshiro Ishikawa.
George Ives.
Holbrook Jackson.
Capt. Arthur St. John.
Gwen John.
J. Johnston, M.D.
Winifred Jones.
W. J. Jupp.
Charles Kains-Jackson.
Robert Kay.
W. Sloane Kennedy.
Alfred Key.
Madame Ellen Key.
Joseph Kirkpatrick.
Peter Kropotkin.
George Lansbury.
Victor Lebrun.
Arrigo Levasti.
Rev. Edward Lewis.
Canon A. L. Lilley.
Bertram Lloyd.
J. Wm. Lloyd.
His Honour Judge B. Fossett Lock.
Major S. L. Lomer.
Jack London.
Hugh F. Luttrell.
Lady Emily Lutyens.
E. W. Lybeck.
Lady Constance Lytton.
J. Ramsay MacDonald, M.P.
A. Mahadeva.
Alf. & Florrie Mattison.
Hugh Mapleton.
Aylmer Maude.
Prof. James Mavor.
Clara Mayers.
Margaret McKillop.
Margaret McMillan.
Austin Meade.
George Merrill.
Jacques Mesnil.
J. F. Mills.
R. H. Minshall.
Alberta V. Montgomery.
Everilda Moore.
Major R. L. Morris.
Margaret Morris.
May Morris.
Robert F. Morse.
R. F. Muirhead.
Ivan Nagivin.
Dr. Anna Nagivin.
Sorofini Naida.
Henry W. Nevinson.
John Gambril Nicholson.
Riccardo Nobili.
Rev. Conrad Noel.
Yone Noguchi.
Alfred Noyes.
Sir Sydney Olivier, K.C.M.G.
Lady Olivier.
Alfred Ollivant.
Biagio di Paola.
M. Sidney Parry.
Ben Iden Payne.
Mona Limerick Payne.
F. Gordon Pearce.
Lionel G. Pearson.
Leonid Perno.
Francis Perrot.
Lisle March Phillips.
Eden Phillpotts.
Elena Pogosky.
Joseph Pointer, M.P.
Arthur Ponsonby, M.P.
Joe Potter.
Florence Potter.
Ernest Radford.
Dollie Radford.
Cecil Reddie.
Robert R. Rentoul, M.D.
Stephen Reynolds.
Ernest Rhys.
Hon. Francis Spring Rice, R.N.
Mary King Roberts.
Lesley Gregory Rose-Innes.
Prof. T. W. Rolleston.
William Rothenstein.
Chas. Roughton.
Chas. Rowley.
Earl Russell.
John Russell.
Elizabeth Russell.
Harry Sacher.
Prof. M. E. Sadler.
Henry S. Salt.
Catherine L. Salt.
Constantine Sarantchoff.
Her Highness Margaret of Sarawak.
Dr. Ettie Sayer.
Marcelle Senard.
Walter Seward.
Olive Schreiner.
Dr. Charles L. Shadwell.
Robert Sharland.
Rose E. Sharland.
G. Bernard Shaw.
Charlotte F. Shaw.
James W. Shortland.
Rev. A. H. Moncur Sime.
Charles F. Sixsmith.
Lucy Sixsmith.
Prof. G. C. Moore Smith.
Adela Constance Smith.
Tom Swan.
H. M. Swanwick.
Rabindranath Tagore.
John Tenney.
Alex. M. Thompson.
J. David Thompson.
Gertrude Toynbee.
Horace Traubel.
G. M. Trevelyan.
Henry S. Tuke, R.A.
Raymond Unwin.
Ethel Unwin.
Francis S. Walkden.
James Walker.
Abraham Wallace, M.D.
Annie I. Wallace.
J. W. Wallace.
Wilfred Walter.
Mary Walter.
The Countess of Warwick.
Robert Weare.
Sidney Webb.
Beatrice Webb.
Sir Wm. Wedderburn, Bart.
Josiah C. Wedgwood, M.P.
Prof. F. E. Weiss.
H. G. Wells.
Prof. Edward Westermarck.
Richard Whiteing.
Rev. Philip H. Wicksteed.
Jean L. Wigglesworth.
Howard Williams, M.A.
Gaylord Wilshire.
Dr. Helen Wilson.
F. L. Woodward.
W. B. Yeats.
William W. Young.
Israel Zangwill.

4. W. E. Hopkin and Florence Potter

5. Alice Dax with her daughter in about 1916

6. Gal's cartoon of W. E. Hopkin in 1929

7. The Naples bas-relief of Paris and Helen which appeared in *Angels' Wings*

(Photograph supplied by Sheffield City Libraries

physical organization of humanity, and in its very *physiology*"; they are "principalities and powers" and belong "to another order of existence". The gods, as his chapter heading puts it, "dwell in the physiological centres".[112]

Mars, Hercules, Hermes, are shapes taken by aspects of "the immense subconscious emotion of the race". So is Aphrodite, whether we call her Venus, Freya or Astarte, "one powerful joint impression" made over the ages upon "some kind of centre or plexus, or group of plexuses, which co-ordinates and dominates the love instinct". Here a footnote points out that, since nerve fibres of the plexus of the sympathetic system are combined in the ramifications of the cerebro-spinal and cerebral systems, we have in each plexus "capacities of immense emotional agitation (the sympathetic), capacities of swift reflex action and response (the cerebro-spinal) and the formation of powerful mental images (the cerebrum). These three elements cannot well be separated from each other, and *working together in any centre they represent a kind of daemonic presence*".[113] [*My italics.*]

Where Havelock Ellis patiently studies the neuro-psychological mechanisms of sexual activity, Carpenter is busily deifying the same processes in a characteristic attempt to go beyond scientific observation, into the realm of metaphysical "explanation" disguised as science.

Thus by degrees, by dint of analysis of religious traditions and myths, Carpenter leads to a demonstration of his idea that

> . . . The body is not vile. It is not only a Temple of God, but it is a collection of temples; . . . we may say [that] the Gods themselves dwell in the centres and sacred places of the body . . . Every organ and centre of the body is the seat of some great emotion, which in its proper activity and due proportion is truly divine. . . . The total physiology of Man is, or should be, the nearest expression of divinity complete, and the replica or image of the physiology of the Cosmos itself.[114]

To what extent, in thus addressing himself to an Edwardian audience, does he pursue educational ends, and to what extent is he caught in the net of his own religious-metaphysical attitudes?

The question is relevant not only to him, but to much of Lawrence's "theoretical" writings.

Beyond the externally rational statement of a mystical belief in the divinity of all bodily organs (a belief which would seem to require this rational treatment largely for the purposes of rhetoric, in reaction against late nineteenth-century prudery), there clearly exists in Carpenter a need to reconcile the rehabilitation of emotions and their corresponding physical needs, with a religious attitude of mind, as well as the Victorian preoccupation with reconciling religion and the observation of science. This continues the familiar debate of the 1870s on science and faith, and records or plays back his own personal mental evolution from Anglican Christianity to a syncretic religious outlook drawing on ancient and primitive creeds. He attaches to rational, outwardly scientific terms, a depth of meaning already charged with the force of vehement, passionate, Lawrentian assertion, partly because the divided man he had been needed to reconcile his codes and his instincts. And he seeks a neuro-physiological explanation, such as will be put forward by many esoteric writers, to justify and explain changes in religion. The appearance of Christianity on the scene "*marked a new growth*. . . . It surely might almost be said that a new centre of organic life was forming—a new plexus among the nerves of Humanity".[115] [*My italics*.] Metaphor is here merging indiscernibly into belief, dignified by a semblance of scientific reasoning.

Even with Carpenter, this notion of religious change based on physical alterations or mutations, is dangerously close to racialism. This can be seen from his references to "a physiological difference between the average Hindu and the average Westerner. . . . His organism seems to be differently keyed from ours".[116] Christianity, he asserts, spread in the Roman Empire when "Oriental ideas and religions and—perhaps more important still—Oriental blood and heredity began to circulate. A new type of human being demanded new gods".[117]

We have traced elsewhere some of Lawrence's ideas on race and religion as well as his anti-humanitarian attitude in the '*Study of Thomas Hardy*' to H. S. Chamberlain's *Foundations of the XIXth Century*.[118] What the passage just quoted suggests very clearly, is that for Lawrence Carpenter's works themselves did nothing to counteract Chamberlain's racial mysticism. The reactionary son-in-law of Wagner and the Fabian had followed parallel mystic paths, and for Lawrence their influences could very easily merge into one powerful adjuvant to his own need for passionate and irrational belief—especially as both were supremely able to cloak their mystical assumptions behind a veil of rational argument which could take in even a George Bernard Shaw, himself of course a potential hero-worshipper.[119]

Jesus of Nazareth, and his representations on canvas or in stone, have "served to waken in the human mind the consciousness of a very real Presence",[120] as real as that of Apollo or Athene for the Greeks, as that of Siva or Vishnu for the Hindu, or of Whitman for Dr Bucke, who appeared to the Canadian alienist "either actually as a God or in some sense clearly and entirely preter-human".[121] The Gods are

> . . . real emanations and expressions of the World-Self. . . . Each unit-mind is an offshoot of the racial mind; each unit-body an offshoot of the racial body; and as far as, for each individual, his mind and body register the Life and Memory of the Race do they form a gate of access to its particular Olympus and group of divinities.[122]

Carpenter's commonsense leads him to put this racialism in perspective in a footnote: "race-life is not by any means the only higher order of life to which we have access . . . in every individual slumbers ever the absolute World-self".[123] He has seen the danger of the exclusive emphasis on race to which his preoccupation with the physiological continuity of the human species might have driven him. But he stands at the parting of the ways between true democratic vistas and the road that leads to racialism and nationalism. Lawrence will also long stand uncertain at this fork, and will be almost decisively tempted to follow the road leading to the dark gods of the body in all their horror.

The Devils, Corruption and Disintegration

The gods being "real powers and centres of vitality" in the body and race, what of the devils? They also are "very real powers and centres of human energy and vitality". While the gods make for life and harmony, the devils make for discord and death; they live in centres of corruption and disease:

> Lust without Love, Desire of food and drink without reverence for Health, love of Power without Pity, love of Gain without Charity, . . . centres of activity which . . . must lead to Corruption and Disintegration. There are similar centres in society at large and in the life of the race . . . these others are the seats of what we call diabolical and daemonic agencies.[124]

Heredity is again enlisted to explain "the strange psychology of passion" and its inner conflicts:

> We bear in our bodies the experience and memory of countless beings, who, having witnessed or embodied the same action from opposite sides, transmit to us on one side an intense and reduplicated magnetism in its favour, and on the other side a multiplied hatred of it; and from both sides the sense of a sinister Agency at work within.

We are then "dealing with centres with contain the elements of strife and disintegration within themselves, and which are therefore leading towards Corruption, Insanity, and Death".[125]

The devils "represent formative ideas, but ideas of a lower grade, which necessarily in time have to be superseded". They are, so to speak, obsolete gods dwelling in centres of activity in the race or the body which "have not always been centres of corruption or degeneration—quite the reverse—though there are various ways in which they become so":[126] either through disproportionate development, or through growth and change in humanity, they have come to "involve the threat of corruption and death to the race or the individual . . . they may have been Angels and Gods . . . they stand for Motives which are being ejected from the bosom of Humanity".[127] Thus Apollo became

Apollyon, Aphrodite "a mere demon and enchantress", and Pan, Satan. The division between Catholic and Protestant and Orthodox Christian is, rather than an intellectual matter, "a difference of instinctive heredity, and *a distinction of race feeling between Latin and Teuton and Slav*".[128] [*My italics.*]

Many ideas and details in this chapter on 'The Devils and the Idols' have their exact parallel in the writings of Lawrence, especially in his 1914 and 1915 efforts in comparative racial psychology in '*Study of Thomas Hardy*' and *Twilight in Italy*. Indeed similarities between the two writers become at this point so numerous as to defy attempts at detailed confrontation. It may be sufficient to draw attention to certain main trends of thought in Lawrence's works of 1914–15, which may be held to have been more directly influenced by *The Art of Creation*.

The insistence by Lawrence on the daemonic, the hidden and suddenly revealed lusts of such characters as Hermione Roddice, when she hits Birkin with a paperweight, may be an artistic illustration of these ideas on devils and idols; the recurrence throughout *Women in Love* of the themes of disintegration and corruption, also relates the novel to this conception of the devils. But an abstract expression of these ideas is to be found in '*Study of Thomas Hardy*' and in '*The Crown*', written at vital moments preceding the rewriting of *The Rainbow* and of *Women in Love* respectively. We shall limit our analysis to some of the guiding thoughts in these works.

If the word "centre" is not defined by Carpenter in *The Art of Creation*, it is used by Lawrence in *Women in Love* with detectable reference to the *chakras* of yoga: an elucidation not in the least contradictory to what is in Carpenter's mind, since many of his ideas proceed from the *Upanishads* and from his conversations with a South Indian *gñani*.[129] But when writing '*The Crown*', Lawrence had not yet read J. M. Pryse and his exposition of the *chakras*. The notions of corruption, disintegration, angels of corruption, are present in that essay, especially in Chapter III, 'The Flux of Corruption', where the serpent is "the god within the flux of corruption", the symbol of "retrogression" and "reduction"

—contrasted with "the golden angels of the Kiss", the angels of "consummation".[130] Lawrence's ideas are less coherently, less rationally ordered than Carpenter's, but in his poetical imagery and symbolization he proceeds to associate, even more specifically than Carpenter, the concepts of disintegration and of mental activity; devils and the mechanical survival of old attitudes. While the two trains of thought are similar, as usual Lawrence carries his further into absolute, passional criticism; he no doubt feels that he is farther down the path of disintegration.

"Assertive egos", lapsing back to "the Beginning . . . through reduction within the closed shell of the Christian conception",[131] enclosed within the rind of "my false absolute self, my self-conscious ego", within "the public form, the civilization, the established consciousness of mankind", are doomed to destruction "by the hands of the angels of separation". The examples given are precisely those of Carpenter's devils, including the evils of disintegrative thought which for Lawrence characterizes all social endeavour:

> The scientist in his laboratory, the artist in his study, the statesman, the artisan, the sensualist obtaining keen gratification, every one of these is reducing down that which is himself to its simpler elements, reducing the compound back to its parts. It is the pure process of corruption in all of us.[132]

Thus Lawrence has synthetized in a powerful imaginative vision of evil Carpenter's objection to analytical thought not redeemed by access to the third stage of consciousness, and his idea of the Devils.

He also remembers Carpenter when he denounces the false attitudes of those who say "I am" when they are not, who are "framed gaps" and not "timeless fountains",[133] who are, like Will Brangwen, "a roomful of old echoes" and are not carried by the creative flow of Life; those who "struggle mechanically, unformed, unbegotten, unborn, repeating some old process of life, unable to become [them]selves, unable to produce anything new".[134]

For him, all gods become devils as time passes: the real god is the flux, the life-stream: "Only perpetuation is sin."[135] "This is evil, this desire for constancy, for fixity in the temporal world. . . . There is no revelation of God in memory. Memory is not truth . . . God is gone, until next time."[136] "To be, and to be different", is Lawrence's comment (and the assertion of his aesthetic) upon Carpenter's distinction between gods and devils: but an assertion very close indeed to the main stream of thought in *The Art of Creation*. Lawrence's imagery is his own, but his thought seems once more to echo Carpenter's when, describing Michelangelo's *Leda and the Swan*, he explicitly assimilates the swan to a God now turned devil: the swan is "one of the symbols of divine corruption" with "its beauty white and terrifying, like the dead beauty of the moon, like the water lily, the sacred lotus, its neck and head like the snake, . . . the phosphorescence of corruption".[137]

Even "the Christ of the early Christians, the Christ who was the Fish", had, according to Lawrence, some of this quality of "cold, white, salty fire of infinite reduction". When Leonardo and Michelangelo

> . . . represent Leda in the embrace of the swan, they are painting mankind in the clasp of the divine flux of corruption, the singing death. Mankind *turned back* to cold, bygone consummations.
>
> When the swan first rose out of the marshes, it was a glory of creation. But when we turn back, to seek its consummation again, it is a fearful flower of corruption.[138]

Corruption, "like growth, is only divine when it is pure, when all is given up to it". Thus Lawrence has given powerful imaginative expression to Carpenter's idea of the devils representing bygone stages of human development.

* * *

The New Conception of Personality

Important aesthetic consequences arise from Carpenter's deification or daemonization of the physiological centres: or rather this rationalization of some of his *a priori* thinking, just like Lawrence's, is integrated into an aesthetic theory which he had expressed as early as 1898, in his remarkable book *Angels' Wings, Essays on Art and its Relation to Life*. Similarly, his rationalization aims at the justification of his ethical views, of which we have seen an earlier expression in 'Defence of Criminals'. His ethic and his aesthetic are closely united in a single interpretation of *Art and Life*, which forebodes the assertion by Lawrence of the unity of art and morals.

The Individual and the 'World-self'

Before exploring this rich field in the next chapter, we shall begin by an analysis of the aesthetic consequences, or deductions, of Carpenter's psychology of the cellular ego, the unit-self made of innumerable selves residing in the cells of his body, he himself a part of the 'World-Self', or 'Great-Self' of the *Upanishads*. It can be advanced, at least as a hypothesis, that Lawrence's conception of the ego of his characters, as expressed in a much-quoted 1914 letter to Edward Garnett, owes more to Carpenter's *Art of Creation* and *Drama of Love and Death* than it does to Marinetti and Futurism, against the pure abstraction and mechanical nature of which, it should be remembered, he was reacting in that letter and in important passages of '*Study of Thomas Hardy*'.[139]

Carpenter's view of human character is antinomian: he constantly opposes the deep natural law of "being" to the artificial law of "civilized man"; and he searches for, and confidently asserts, the superiority of a society in which the individual will be free to follow the law of his own being, i.e. the law of the world-self, or life and love.

We have listened to him showing, through an application of

an evolutionist theory of heredity to the Platonic ideas and archetypes, how the gods and devils dwell in the physiological centres of the human and animal body.

In that evolution, an ego has been formed from the "vast succession of individuals, of generations", and "we are that Ego": "The whole life of the Race from which we have come" . . . is "within us, in our bodies, in our subconscious selves". Every one of our organs is "a habit of thought". Yet, and to this we shall return in the following chapters, there is in us "something more, i.e. that which has not as yet got itself expressed".[140] While we are here and now concerned with his conception of the present ego, not with the ego of the future and of the creative superman, it should be noted that the deep present ego contains the buds or seeds of the superman.

Our bodies are "*mental* legacies from the past". [*My italics.*] If we look at them as such, they "will no longer appear as alien and separate things from our minds, but as our own race-mind made visible, and as essentially continuous with and undivided from that which we more specially call ourselves".[141] They are "the legacies of the immemorial thought of our ancestors . . . they are those thought-forms, habits, prejudices, consolidated into definite shape and function".

New feelings and thought may exercise power "in disturbing or readjusting the organization of the body".[142] This argumentation leads Carpenter to his formulation of *The Art of Creation*, i.e. to his ethic and aesthetic of "non-acting" based on Lao-Tze and the Yoga of the *Upanishads*. This we have to consider in relation to his ideas on art. Nowadays, he thinks, "the Self is entering into relation with the Body":[143] his ethic and aesthetic derive from this idea. Thus and by long practice, may be established "the sense of identity with the universal self". Man can transform himself by transferring his "centre of life" from "unconscious activity in the body to the conscious-self—that is, when the individual self, reaching union with the universal, becomes consciously and willingly the creator and inspirer of the body. That is indeed a Transfiguration".[144]

This last word should be noted: it is the word used by Lawrence of Tom and Lydia Brangwen, when in *The Rainbow* they attain some degree of perfection in consciousness in their love life. While it is not used of Birkin and Ursula, the effect of the chapter '*Excurse*' in *Women in Love* is manifestly intended to be the same; in it Birkin is "awake and potent in that other basic *mind*, the deepest *physical mind*",[145] and Ursula becomes "an essential new being".[146] [*My italics.*] Carpenter once more holds the key to the understanding of Ursula's story: he divides the history of man into three periods, of which the history of the Brangwens, culminating in Ursula, is the epitome:

> The first, an animal period, in which the human being follows his body and its instincts unhesitatingly; the second, or intellect period, in which a half-formed, separate and illusive, self appears; and the third, or period of the Superman (if we like to call it so) in which the self, being identified with the universal being, becomes the centre of absolute recognition and reliance and purpose. The great transformation is that which takes place at the entrance of the third period; and the second period is that of its preparation.[147]

In part, *The Art of Creation* is thus the art of transforming oneself in order to reach the third period: this cannot be done without the pains and chaos of civilization, without the "growth and ascendancy of the self-conscious, analytic, individualizing Brain". The reader will remember Birkin's debate with Hermione on consciousness:[148] "The Brain and Self-Consciousness are the midwives, as it were, of this great birth and transformations—the greatest of all births and transformations—of the soul'.[149]

Then the "real self emerges into consciousness . . . the Brain ceases from its terrified and insatiable quest". "The Man at last lets Thought go . . . and so there comes to him a sense of absolute repose, a consciousness of immense and absolute power, such as completely transforms the world for him." This is "the divine Yoga or union".[150] Man has reached "the sublime Consciousness of simple Being" which "can be seen quite plainly in the look in the eyes of the animals, and in primitive healthy folk and children, deep down unsuspected by the creature itself; and yet there, unmistakable. It is seen by lovers in each other's eyes.[151]

It is seen in Lawrence's characters, not once but many times, simple folk, or lovers, and an illustration of it is to be found in particular in the typical scene of *The Rainbow* in which Ursula in a glance exchanges deep recognition with the impudent blue eyes of a grimy bargee, capable of worship for a woman, "a worship of body and soul together".[152] The same glance is exchanged by the virgin with the gipsy in one of the last novels.[153] While the novelist then exploits the sex implications of this theme, this should not blind us to its wider uses in his theoretical writings, and indeed in his works of imagination, nor to the symbolic and psychological significance of the bargee scene in the basic structure of his double novel.

Carpenter's conception of transfiguration through reaching the third or cosmic consciousness, the Divine Yoga, bases itself on his conception of the individual self and its affiliations in cells of the body, in plexuses, and "centres", and of the perennity in the race of the sex-cells. He develops this in relation both to love and to human character in his *Drama of Love and Death*. This idea, ever present in *The Art of Creation*, finds particularly clear expression in the chapter of the later book entitled 'The Mystery of Personality'.

That volume, published in March 1912, may easily have been one of the determinant influences over Lawrence's general and linked conceptions of the progress of the soul, and of the nature of character, as exemplified in his double novel. In it, Carpenter not only returns "again and again to the question of what we mean by the Self", but he volunteers an important theory of the nature of the human character.

The Main Problem of the Age: a Programme for a Writer

"The general problem of the nature of the ego", he claims, "is *the great main problem which lies before this age for solution.*" [*My italics.*]

Remembering that late 1912 or early 1913 is the time when Lawrence discovers his Messianic vocation, what an invitation and a challenge to a young and ambitious writer we find in this sentence:

> One of the greatest services a man can do is—by psychologic study and manifold experience, by poetical expression, especially in lyrical form, and by philosophic thought and investigation—to make clear to himself and the world what he means by the letter 'I', what he means by his 'self'.[154]

We may compare with this challenge a passage of a letter of Lawrence to Edward Garnett. He had then just written the 'Foreword' to *Sons and Lovers* (January 1913), and a letter to Ernest Collings asserting his belief in "the blood, the flesh, as being wiser than the intellect", in which he also expressed the essence of his antinomianism, of his restrictive interpretation of the role of the intellect, and of his mystical, vitalistic belief in "the mystery of the flame forever flowing, coming God knows how from out of practically nowhere, and being *itself*". [*My italics.*] By the flame, he means "a man's body . . . like a candle flame, forever upright and yet flowing".[155] He now tells Garnett that he has written one hundred pages of *The Sisters.*

> I think, do you know, I have inside me a sort of answer to the *want* of today: to the real deep want of the English people, not just what they fancy they want . . . and this novel is . . . perhaps not such good art, but it is what they want, need, more or less.[156]

That is the novel about which he had just promised Mrs Hopkin to be "a priest of love", "Love Triumphant", the novel which we trust we have shown to be deeply modelled on the pattern of the soul's progress in Carpenter's *Art of Creation* and *Love's Coming of Age*, and in which, as will be shown in a future chapter, these were deep resemblances to other ideas expressed in *The Intermediate Sex*. A novel also wholly related to the conception of '*Study of Thomas Hardy*', whose debt to Carpenter is manifold.

We now propose to show that at the very least a strong case can be made in support of the idea that Lawrence's articulate conception of character, as illustrated in this double novel, and as stated in another letter to Garnett of June 1914, proceeds in a straight line from Carpenter's analysis of the ego.

The Ever-changing Ego

Our ego, according to *The Drama of Love and Death*, assumes many forms according to our age. The question is asked, Is it characterized "by the mind alone, or by the spirit, apart from the body? Or by the clothes? It would be unjust to try to pin it down to a particular one of its many manifestations".[157] There is in us "a very profound self . . . much greater than any one known representation of it"; it exists "perhaps on a different plane of being —underrunning, and therefore in a sense, beyond, Time".[158]

Protozoa split by fission and fuse together; worms, annelids and molluscs divide into two; so may a personality, as when we "talk to ourselves". There is in the psychology of human love, evidence of fusion, similar to that of protozoa, and of "confusion" of personalities. Despite the protests of "the little self-conscious mind" of the civilized man which likes "to think of itself as a separate and definite entity", the whole thing becomes obvious "in the light of the All-self".[159] Consciousness is characterized by its *continual extension*: we may note in this connexion Lawrence's title for two chapters of *The Rainbow*, 'The Widening Circle', which in his sister's copy he had corrected for Chapter XIV as 'The Ever Widening Circle'. "Time is an integral element of consciousness," adds Carpenter, referring his reader for the fourth time in this book to *L'Evolution Créatrice*. "Through memory, it preserves the past, through the present it adds to its stores." But while memory "seems to decide the limits of personalities and their survival", the underlying "All-self" may explain the contradiction between a distinct consciousness existing in time, and the multiform 'One Self': "Is it not possible that the lives of us human beings may go on expanding and growing each according to its own law, and yet the ultimate individual or Being behind them all may remain the same?"[160]

There is no Fixed Personality

This leads Carpenter to a radically new conception of personality, to which the modern English novel, from Carpenter's friend E. M. Forster to Virginia Woolf, possibly owes more than is usually recognized. The Carpenterian ego splits and shimmers like an Impressionist painting, and bears little resemblance to a Cubist or Futurist statue.

> All this seems to suggest to us that our conception of personality must be considerably altered from its ordinary form, and rendered more fluent, in order to tally with the real facts. *There is no such thing as a fixed and limited personality, of definite content and character, which we can credit to our account, or to the account of our friends.* All is in flux and change, the consciousness ever enlarging, the ego which is at the root of that consciousness ever growing in the knowledge of itself as a vital portion of the All-self. That last alone is fixed; that alone as the 'universal witness' is permanent. But the streams of memory and experience, by which from all sides, that central fact and consciousness is reached, are infinite in number and variety.[161]

This important passage, in which the religious thought of the *Upanishads* is associated with cell-biology as known at the beginning of the century, leads Carpenter to a beautiful Whitmanesque image of a tree, each single leaf of which has "a little separate self of its own", these selves being grouped into deeper selves or "personalities" on each twig, then into an "individuality" on the branches, "and so on to the All-self of the tree", all participating in one whole.[162] His purpose is to show the underlying unity, and to lead to his conclusion, namely that "Love and Death are strangely linked and strangely related", both being human passions, and doors through which we pass from one "phase of some far vaster state of being" to another.[163]

The Non-human in Man

These are themes current throughout Lawrence's works, especially at the time of the conception and writing of *The Wedding Ring*, i.e. the first version of the first half of the double novel. But at that time, he is faced with objections from Edward Garnett, about the way his characters behave and are conceived; his highly articulate reaction is that of a man who knows perfectly clearly what he wants to illustrate by the actions of his characters. In demonstration, he quotes not Carpenter, but Marinetti, having just read the *Futurist Manifesto*. But in so doing he marks against Futurism an opposition which he will reassert with force and deep conviction in the '*Study of Thomas Hardy*' and in his objections to Duncan Grant's paintings. Marinetti helps him define what he wants, by providing him with examples taken from physics and chemistry, rather than from cell-biology. But the basic thought in the search for the "non-human, in humanity" is related to his ethic-aesthetic idea, not to its incidental illustration from physics. His new book, he thinks, is "a bit futuristic, quite *unconsciously* so". The psychology is not wrong, only different. To quote Marinetti, he is after "an intuitive physiology of matter":

> I don't care about physiology of matter—but somehow—that which is physic—non-human, in humanity, is more interesting to me than the old-fashioned human element—which causes one to conceive a character *in a certain moral scheme and make him consistent. The certain moral scheme is what I object to.*[164] [*My italics.*]

Like Carpenter, he rejects the law of civilization, the law of the social scheme: he enlarges upon this in '*Study of Thomas Hardy*', when he reproaches Tolstoy (as he does in this letter) for standing, like Hardy, "with the community in condemnation of the aristocrat", i.e. of "a man who, being beyond the average, chooses to rule his own life to his own completion".[165] His conception of character, like Carpenter's, is linked to his antinomianism. And perhaps we may be excused for thinking we detect in the letter to Garnett other echoes of *The Drama of Love and Death*, and of *The Art of Creation*:

> What is interesting in the laugh of the woman is the same as the binding of the molecules of steel or their action in heat. [That is Marinetti's phrase.] It is the inhuman will, call it physiology, or like Marinetti, physiology of matter that fascinates me.

Inhuman is Marinetti's word. Lawrence had said "non-human" just before, and that is much closer to Carpenter's thinking: by "non-human" he means that which is surrendered to his real God, to the flux, the stream of life. "I don't so much care about what the woman feels in the ordinary usage of the word", he continues:

> That presumes an ego to feel with. I only care about what the woman is—what she IS—inhumanly, physiologically, materially—according to the use of the word: but for me, what she is as a phenomenon (or as representing *some greater, inhuman will*), instead of what she feels *according to the human conception*. That is where the *futurists are stupid*. Instead of looking for the *new human phenomenon*, they will only look for the phenomena of the science of physics to be found in human beings. They are crassly stupid . . . You mustn't look in my novel for *the old stable* ego—*of the character*. There is another ego, according to whose action the individual is unrecognizable, and passes through, as it were, allotropic states which it needs a deeper sense than any we've been used to exercise, to discover are states of the same single radically unchanged element.[166] [*Lawrence's underlining, my italics.*]

The introduction of the idea of allotropic states of carbon has perhaps clouded, in the many commentaries made on this text, the similarities of thought with the 'Foreword' to *Sons and Lovers* and with the '*Study of Thomas Hardy*', both of them much closer to Carpenter's idea of character and to his ethics of love and society which the '*Hardy*' echoes in innumerable passages. The fuller implications of these ideas in terms of a general conception of the human soul's progress will appear only later, in the final writing of *Women in Love*, and in the theoretical writings of Lawrence between the autumn of 1914 and the end of 1918. But what is striking in retrospect, is the firmness, the consistency, and the durability of the ideas formed in 1912–13 and followed through in their artistic and esoteric consequences up to the *Fantasia of the Unconscious* and *The Plumed Serpent*. No less striking are the many similarities with the works of Edward Carpenter.

5

THE ART OF LIFE AND INDIVIDUAL EXPRESSION

Angels' Wings, *or Justifying the Ways of God to Men*

In many ways Carpenter's whole literary production may be said to have aimed at justifying the ways of God to himself and to men, i.e. at explaining to men that they were the children of God and should accept themselves as they are, in their endeavour to become more like God who encompasses all. *The Art of Creation* was thus for him the perfect and complete manifestation of man's effort to assert his oneness and unison with divine purpose, that is, with life. Such is the message of the book so entitled, in which the individual is told how he can establish a sense of identity with the universal self: when this is achieved, "strangely obvious is the result and simple the act of Creation".[1] These last words identify Love with "the descent" of the Supreme life and being, and its "partial utterance in the realms of emotion and of thought".[2]

Carpenter's ways to such abstract thought as this are always precise and meticulous: his aesthetic ideas had been subtly and clearly expressed in one of his earlier volumes. Its surprising title, *Angels' Wings*, is completed if not elucidated by the sub-title *a series of Essays on Art and its Relation to Life*. The themes are wholly consistent with those of *Civilization, Its Cause and Cure*, and of all

Carpenter's later volumes. An additional merit is that they explicitly relate his Vedantic ideas, his mysticism of the body and of life, to a theory of art as the expression of the individual, and to a conception of democratic art, in his own special Whitmanesque sense of the word democracy.

* * *

The Art of Democracy

Beethoven, Wagner, Millet, Whitman

After Beethoven, Wagner, Millet and Whitman are for him revolutionaries who accept *everything* in art "provided it is 'in place' ". Whitman discarded "the old verse standards" because they "most distinctly refuse certain words, phrases, effects".[3] His *form* is democratic, like his *feeling*. Wagner followed the example of the Ninth Symphony, abandoning pure music for "the realism of Voice and Speech". Millet, unlike Bastien Lepage, has a sense of "the great unconscious human life (which in Blake one must call God) and of the vast open of Nature stretching eternally beyond".[4] These three herald the coming time when "Art as a *separate* thing from actual life will surely surrender much of its importance".[5] All are distinguished by:

> (1) Strong Realism and acceptance of the Actual—all facts of life, all discords, nothing blinked or concealed, this involving a kind of primitive directness of method and style, the opposite pole of all formalism and artificiality; (2) an intense sense of the whole and acceptance of the universal and unseen, by which alone the brute facts can be redeemed and set 'in place', involving . . . the

> power of making the same motif appear in myriads of forms; and (3) a most intimate prophetic sense of the life of the People, a perception through each individual, even the lowest, of the vast unuttered human heart, the revelation in dim outline of the Gods, carrying with it a sense of sympathy, and even of triumphant, joy and gladness, hardly conceived in Art before.[6]

Points (1) and (2), and the second part of (3), compete with another passage quoted below for the title of the best description of the artistic value and characteristics of Lawrence's early work, both poetry and prose, and in particular of *Sons and Lovers*.

Angels' Wings and Realism in Art

The wings of angels and cupids are a convenient device serving to demonstrate that in art "anything that conflicts very hopelessly and fundamentally with the reasoning faculty cannot be very permanently successful in its influence on the mind".[7] When the artist leaves "the mere ground of actual Nature" in order to express his vision of angels or of the supernatural, to "escape the bounds of definite thought", he must "consider intelligently the problem" he is attacking. Art rejects nothing, but must bear in mind "the time and place of treatment". Thus from a description of Perugino's winged St Michael in armour, we are gently led to a Baudelairean aesthetic.

Discussing 'Art and Realism', Carpenter asserts that "the object of the Fine Arts is to convey an emotion".[8] To this end the artist can draw his materials from three main sources:

> . . . (1) from Nature and the outer world (including in that expression human life and history); (2) from the physiological basis of emotion in the human body; and (3) from the conventional symbols and associations current in the society around him.[9]

He likes to quote Lao-Tze, according to whom "by non-action there is nothing which may not be done". He applies this saying to realist art: you can let nature "do it" for you; the perception of this "immense expressional value of the actual world" has led to the "great modern developments of Realism".[10] But a distinction is drawn between two directions of modern realism: one, which is an error, "tends to an over-elaborate reproduction of Nature" (such as evidenced sometimes even by Zola and Tolstoy, by Burne-Jones, Leighton, and Alma-Tadema); the other aims at "reproduction of those aspects of Nature—the ugly, the obscene, the criminal, and so forth—which are generally ignored or set aside as not available":[11]

> [In] the ruder facts of life, hitherto somewhat untouched, . . . in wounds and death, in physiological facts, in sex, in the common life of the mass-people, in poverty, in criminality, in ignorance, lie huge stores of associations capable of rousing the most keen and complex emotions. . . . The portrayal of the root facts of life, like those of sex, necessarily touches the springs of the most imperative and, in a sense, most important feelings. Any artist must see that these associations, these emotions are there for his use. Yet of course, it does not follow that they are easy to use.[12]

Like discords in music, the obscenities, the criminalities have to be "made to lead to their proper resolutions", to be "burnt up like fuel and rendered transparent, in the great human emotions which are competent to dissolve them".[13] Zola, Ibsen, Sudermann have unearthed "a vast amount of material which, in the hands of future masters, may be available for the most searching effects".[14] And immediately Carpenter, ever a master of gradual exposition, reassures his reader by offering the Parthenon frieze as a perfect example of the best Realism.

The Human Body in Movement

This healthy pause on familiar ground leads on to the next chapter, 'The Human Body in relation to Art', in which the author expresses in terms of aesthetics what he was to say in a more general metaphysical vein in *The Art of Creation* under the title 'The Gods as dwelling in the Physiological Centres'. Each part of the body "relates itself to some emotion or utterance . . . *the heart, the bowels, the lungs,* thrill with feeling". [*My italics.*] "The body is the sign of what man has attained to express so far." Not only the *form* but the *movement,* "every indication of need proceeding from physiological structure",[15] is a lesson about art. Dancing, music produce expression direct from emotion—working at a point where "it is difficult to separate Mind from Body". Painting has "a purely physiological side", and so have prose and poetry, apart from meaning; so have dramatic sequences "a rhythm which must correspond . . . to the natural rhythm of human feeling", such as the "violent and continued knocking at Macbeth's castle door". "The Soul builds the Body; the needs of the Body build the forms of art . . ." And art awakens "far back in the mind a sense of harmony or health of the Soul itself—the striving within us of some divine and universal Being".[16]

The Redemption of the Body

These statements would scarcely be worth reporting were it not for the special significance attributed to them by their author, and their direct relevance to the aesthetic formation and theory of Lawrence. Carpenter is making them in the cause of the vindication of the body against Puritanism. If looking at a perfect body awakes in us "a sense which we endeavour to express by the word beauty"

> . . . how immensely important both for Art and Life, is the redemption and thorough acknowledgement of the Body—that body which Luxury and Puritanism between them have so soiled and desecrated! How important the perfecting of the body on the one hand, and the frank acceptance of it on the other . . . *Yet*

> *the whole group (to take one instance) of the sexual functions, with the emotions which they indicate, has during the modern period suffered this alternate suppression and exaggeration*—a group of course of the very greatest importance. The redemption of Sex, the healthy and natural treatment of it in Art, is one of the greatest works any artist of today has before him to carry out.[17] [*My italics.*]

Tolstoy on Nudity

Not only can the painter achieve what has not been attempted since Michelangelo—but "the poet or novelist" can restore to his palette "one of the primary colours" wiped from it by Milton, Shelley, Wordsworth, Tennyson and Browning:

> . . . notwithstanding the outlines sketched by Whitman, and less healthily by Zola and Ibsen, *the world still waits for anything like a large and artistic treatment of this grand subject.*[18] [*My italics.*]

Indeed "the Sexual lies at the root of Beauty and the Art Sense . . . it cannot and must not be ignored".[19]

After two pages devoted to showing that the sexual is beneath "the supreme sense of Beauty", Carpenter joins issue with Tolstoy's *What is Art?*, the Tolstoy whom Lawrence in so many essays will attack for being "a perverse moralist",[20] and against whom he already measured himself in his 1908 essay 'Art and the Individual'. Carpenter must be quoted here: his own words seem to echo throughout the many Lawrentian references to the author of *Anna Karenina*. Not only the idea but its whole context is the same in *Angels' Wings* as in Lawrence: what is involved is the attack on the law and social convention. One can but wonder how far this could be fortuitous coincidence, even if both men have in fact drawn from common, e.g. Hegelian, sources.

The redemption of sex

> . . . into its true relation to Art is one of the greatest works which awaits us today . . . It seems a pity to think that so great a

man as Tolstoy cannot see this; that he should be so completely dominated *by the fear of the senses;* that he cannot see the blasphemy there is in denying and crippling the human body; that he perceives *no alternative to being a slave to passion, except the killing of it dead.* [*My italics.*] He inveighs, not without reason doubtless, against the modern French novelist in whose pages the word "naked" looms so large, and does not see that to *shun* the word or the fact of nakedness is every bit as indecent, as to revel inordinately in it. It is just in the free sane acceptation of nakedness and grossness as of any other fact or facts that salvation lies. It is just in the facing of all these facts of life and Nature, and in a sense rising out of them into another plane in which they are seen equalized, and their true relation to each other is discerned, that that little word [Beauty] comes in—which to Tolstoy, alas!, comes in only like a guest with a stranger's face, since to him it has no meaning but sensuality.[21]

* * *

Lawrence's 'Art and the Individual'

A Drawing-room Talk to Socialist Friends

A comparison between Carpenter's views on aesthetics and Lawrence's early thoughts on the subject now becomes possible. First of all, certain facts can be usefully recalled. Jessie Chambers, who told us in July 1934 that Lawrence had read all Carpenter's works, relates that he read his juvenile essay 'Art and the Individual', sprawling shyly on the hearthrug, "to a little gathering of the Eastwood intelligentsia at the house of a friend"—the house, indeed, of W. E. Hopkin, who has precisely reported[22] Lawrence's interest at the time in "the experiences of spiritual and bodily awareness", a phrase of special significance coming from a friend of Carpenter. Hopkin is portrayed as Goddard in Lawrence's unfinished novel *Mr Noon*; this elderly socialist sprawls in his armchair reading *The New Age*,[23] to which Carpenter was a frequent contributor between 1906 and 1910.

Jessie Chambers reports in one same paragraph the reading of the essay on art, and the fact that it was Alice Dax who "first showed . . . A. R. Orage's *The New Age* which Lawrence took regularly for a time". We find Orage again, as well as Carpenter and Havelock Ellis, among contributors to *The Occult Review*, which Lawrence certainly read during the war. As early as 1908, Lawrence thus takes his place mentally "inside" a circle of socialists with a penchant for esoteric theories of consciousness and aesthetics. About that time, under the influence of the French realists, he envisages "writing for the French" if the English do not accept his art."[24] The date of the 'Art and the Individual' paper, mistakenly given by Jessie Chambers as Easter 1909, is in fact anterior to 13 May 1908, as appears from Lawrence's *Collected Letters*.[25]

These facts are important; while the internal evidence of Carpenter's aesthetic ideas having influenced Lawrence in his Eastwood days is not in itself overwhelming, there is enough of it to warrant strong presumption, which external circumstances largely corroborate.

Lawrence's youthful paper bears all the marks of personal reflection, and contains many seeds of his later views: delivered before a socialist group (he calls them "communists") whose intentions were to "advance a more perfect social state", it shows, in its effort to synthetize art with socialism, a sense of the difference between the latter, which is "general", and Art, in which "is revealed the individual character".[26] Yet the two are presented as mutually complementary. Lawrence takes a mildly critical and jocular attitude towards repetitive, specialized industrial tasks, and excessively early specialization in education. In this he does not differ from Ruskin, William Morris and Carpenter, nor indeed from Marx. What we are concerned with here is to see whether this lecture reveals any specific similarity between his approach and Carpenter's. He clearly does not yet follow the author of *Angels' Wings* all the way in defining an art of the sexual: but the idea is there, shyly expressed, both positively, and, so to speak, negatively, in the implied criticism of Tolstoy.

Sources, Academic and Otherwise

Lawrence quotes some of his sources; then in his last college year, he has been reading J. Adams's *Herbartian Psychology applied to Education*; he does not name Adams, but he bases his argument on Herbart's classification of interests, to which he significantly adds a sixth, "religious"; this arises from the "social", when the latter form of sympathy "reverentially recognizes the vast scope of the laws of nature, and discovers something of intelligibility and consistent purpose working through the whole natural world and human consciousness".[27]

In this interpretation, "the mystical [Hegelian] and sensual [Darwinian-Spencerian] ideas of art are blended". Aesthetic appreciation is based on approval of harmony, and approval of adaptation to an end.[28] Illustrating this by the image of a swan raising its wings "to attract a mate" (one should always bear in mind the power of such images over Lawrence the poet), he contrasts the bird's winged beauty with the ugliness of its clammy black legs: could this image have been strengthened if not suggested by the contrasts of wings and bodies, discussed by Carpenter in *Angels' Wings*, and illustrated in that book by admirable photographs including one of the Naples bas-relief of Paris and Helen with a swan-winged adult Cupid?

There are more definite signs of possible reminiscence in the young man's choice of examples, especially among English painters (Leighton, Watts); in his references to music and to sexual desire; in his analysis of the three ways in which art is a means of communication; form and colour, sound, and ideas through words—closely similar to Carpenter's Chapter IV, 'The Human Body in its Relation to Art', at the end of which Tolstoy is taken to task. Later on Lawrence also uses the phrase "the physiological aspect of music, of colour". But before this, we come to this paragraph which sounds familiar after Chapters I–III of *Angels' Wings*:

> The essence then of true human art is that it should *convey the emotions of one man to his fellows. It is a form of sympathy,*[29] and sympathy is in some measure harmony and unity, and in harmony and unity there is the idea of consistent purpose, is there not? So it works back to the old definition. But, you will say, *there are emotions desirable and undesirable.* Exactly—then it is bad Art. According to the feeling that has originated it, Art may be bad, weak, good, in all shades. So Tolstoy says that all nude study is bad art—Honi soit qui mal y pense.[30] [*My italics.*]

Young Lawrence seems here to be in "the state of funk" so forcibly described by him in one of his later articles;[31] wrestling with involved problems; aware of his disagreement with Tolstoy, yet not daring to state it openly in public. If, as we believe, he wrote this after reading *The Art of Creation* and *Angels' Wings*, he had taken hints from Carpenter, whose ideas however he did not follow to their logical end. He needed to pursue much further his own mental adventure before the seeds thus sown in his mind could grow. In his 1908 chrysalis state, either he is not yet sure of his own attitude to the "undesirable" in art, or he is feeling his way, shyly testing the reactions of his Eastwood audience.

The Undesirable in Art and Society

The circumstances of the delivery of this juvenile essay perhaps enable one to detect some of the possible reasons for his silence about Carpenter in 1908 and after. To begin with, he probably takes him for granted: speaking on 'Art and Socialism' in the house of Carpenter's friends, palpably using themes and ideas the sources of which his audience would recognize, Lawrence does not need to refer to him by name. Not so Herbart, Hegel, Gorky, Zola and Maupassant, Hood and his *Song of a Shirt*: these are brought in to illustrate one of Carpenter's main ideas on social realism, on the use of the commonplace and the lowly in artistic creation. Their works are instances of "Art transmitting the undesirable". The reason for naming them is to stress how their works "express their deep, real feelings", how their works are "art", because they "express a true emotion".

The lesson of *Angels' Wings* has penetrated, more deeply than is suggested by the outer shell of 'Art and the Individual'; Lawrence's silence as to his source is intelligible both on account of what he takes for granted, and of the internal struggle going on within him at the time of the second writing of *The White Peacock*. The "undesirable" character of Annable is then being first worked into the idyll: he will be further integrated into it after Lawrence reads George Moore in Croydon. In Eastwood in 1908, the young novelist does not know how far he dare go; perhaps he has not yet discovered how far he *wishes* to go, in depicting the undesirable.

But if he knows Carpenter's personal background well—as he must have done through Hopkin, sentences such as the following may also have for him and some of his audience a special significance. They may even respond in his mind to a precise idea of the compiler of *Ioläus: an Anthology of Friendship*, in which are recounted all the great stories of love between young men. One of the members of the group addressed was Jessie Chambers's brother Alan, whose friendship with the novelist is described in the chapter entitled 'A Poem of Friendship' in *The White Peacock*:

> We too can love and suffer at parting. We still count the story of David and Jonathan one of the finest in the world. There are

> *other tales incomprehensible to us*—and only a few can recognize the ideal, the noble emotion which many mediaeval artists expressed so perfectly in their Madonnas . . .[32] [*My italics.*]

The critic who searches below the surface, and the psychologist, will read these three sentences again after taking another look at the relevant chapter devoted to friendship in *The White Peacock* and at the suppressed 'Prologue' to *Women in Love*. They will not reach any conclusion, but they may think they understand why Lawrence delivered his lecture sprawling on the hearthrug, avoiding facing his audience, and refrained from naming the main source of the aesthetic ideas he was trying to formulate.

From the Drawing-room Table to the Language of the Masses

During Lawrence's early formative years, a paper by Carpenter on 'The Drawing-room Table in Literature'[33] in *The New Age* can scarcely have escaped his attention at the very time he was putting the last touches to *The White Peacock*, and contrasting the gamekeeper's coarse dialect with the drawing-room language of the other characters.

Regretting with Havelock Ellis that English literature had been confined since the nineteenth century "within the stifling atmosphere of the drawing-room", Carpenter foreshadows in English literary usage developments which in fact lead straight to the vocabulary of *Lady Chatterley's Lover*:

> A thousand words which were in common parlance in the earlier time, and which were available for the use of Shakespeare or the translators of the Bible have now been dropped out of class-current speech, and more decisively still out of literary use. And the consequence is that the language is not only poorer by so many words, but *is poorer by a whole group* of words—that group, namely, which

represents the coarse, the concrete, the vulgar and the physiological side in human life and passion.[34] [*My italics.*]

He imagines the effects upon musical composition, of a decision that "the bass notes in music were vulgar and impossible":

> We don't *want* the lights in a picture without the shadows. We must and will have contrast. The spiritual must have the material to give it body; the material has no meaning without the spiritual.

"Today" the author "is like a bird with one wing tied". There shall come a day when *Ann Veronica* will not be banned from the drawing-room table. "The Twentieth Century is on us, and a new world is preparing." "The commercial system" of the nineteenth, with its "intellectual and spiritual life unfed and unnourished from the breasts of the common humanity", will make room for a better social and literary atmosphere:

> The only road back to sanity is through the remingling of classes and masses, and the large readoption of the modes of life, thought and speech still current among the latter.[35]

A little more than a year later, Lawrence was to sign a collective letter to *The New Age*[36] protesting against an attack by *The Spectator* against *The English Review* for publishing serially parts of *The New Machiavelli*: his sympathies with the literary theory of class and language upheld by Carpenter and others were then evident, and the ideas expressed in *The New Age* by the veteran Fabian at the least were part of the very climate of his literary formation.

* * *

Creation of the Individual

In what we may call the second phase of Carpenter's influence on Lawrence, the 1913–16 period, culminating in *Women in Love* among the works of imagination, and in theoretical writings such as '*The Crown*' and '*Reality of Peace*', there are found other signs of deep consonance between Lawrence's aesthetic position and those of the author of *Angels' Wings*. The aesthetic theories in that book, combined with some of the expositions in *The Art of Creation* and *The Drama of Love and Death*, are relevant to that phase. The key-themes are summed up by the older writer "To be absolutely oneself"; and by Lawrence as "To be, and to be different".[37]

Incompatibility of Expression and Conventions

Art is expression: and so in his chapter 'Tradition, Convention and the Gods', Carpenter analyses the tendency of artistic representation to crystallize and conventionalize. From the *totems* adopted by the early races (Carpenter was among the first to exploit *The Golden Bough* in literature) mankind rises to the gods, "the noblest work of man"; amongst them he does not omit to refer to "Siva, two-sexed" and the evil Gods, Kali, Priapus, Pan, etc.; and then to symbols: the cross, the lingam, the unicorn or the phoenix, the palm or the cypress. To use those gods or their attendant symbols in art, involves a danger: traditions and conventions are constantly withering:

> It seems to me [he sums up] that the only way in which an artist can make his work durable and great is by seeking to arrive at the most direct expression of something actually felt by himself as a part of his own, and so part of all human experience. He must go to the root of all Art, namely the conveyance of an emotion or impression with the utmost force and directness, from himself to another person.[38]

To do this, the artist must dominate, must "volatilize" the conventions: "Expression is continually tending to die, to become external, mechanical, inhuman": the artist must conquer this tendency, and yet remain in touch with "the Collective Consciousness of the race, which is in fact Religion . . .":[39] we see why perhaps Lawrence added Religious Interest to Herbart's classification, although he was speaking before an assembly of so-called Eastwood "Pagans".

'The Individual Impression' is the title of the next chapter, reinforced by a quotation from Verlaine: "*L'art, mes enfans, c'est d'être absolument soi-même.*"[40] The true artist labours like a Titan, in suffering. He is an angel come down from heaven, he is like a "woman in travail till he is delivered". The romantic theory of the artist's destiny is here fully expressed, with its Verlaine credentials.

Impressionism, Symbolism and Social Life

There is a feud between the individual and tradition, and this extends to social affairs: "No one can well refuse to see Beethoven's relation to the social changes of his time": the artist's "most intimate personality" must be

> . . . grafted on and rooted in the Mind of the Age, and yet growing out of and actually in the end transforming it . . . 'To be absolutely oneself'—and to be oneself through the profoundest sympathy with one's subject—that seems to be the secret.[41]

Having exalted the individual, the socialist, the scientist, and since the believer in him sees in science an instinctive recognition of Nature's underlying *unity*, Carpenter deduces that what matters in art is "the new feeling which comes to a man". The effect of art will be profound "because the sensation expressed is profound, reaching back to the great bases of Humanity, which lie at the root of every individual". There is no such thing as exact realism:

every scene is inexhaustible.[42] What matters is the impression of the artist. In a definition which is by anticipation one of the best ever given of what is most characteristic in the art of the younger Lawrence, he says:

> In the best work Impressionism and Realism simply blend and become parts of one whole.[43]

Impressionism has "made the all enclosed harmonies of the atmosphere and the wonder-world of movement the main subjects of its portrayal".[44] It was "an advance towards a subtler Realism". The reader who remembers in *Women in Love* the word-picture of the late-arriving bridegroom pursuing the bride towards the church, and who in an instant "had caught the angle of the silent stone with his hand and had swung himself out of sight, his supple, strong loins vanishing in pursuit", may detect a relationship between this form of Lawrence's visual imagination and Carpenter's definition of the new realism, especially if he turns to the passage in *Angels' Wings* describing the Etruscans' preoccupation with the "huge thighs and loins" of their pottery figures. Here is "the wonder-world of movement". Memories of such passages read in youth possibly have their role in the slow gestation of the creative flashes of an artist's imagination.

As for the aesthetic of *light*, and its importance to the Impressionists, to which Carpenter devotes some paragraphs, a considerable part of Chapter VIII ('The Light of the World') in the '*Study of Thomas Hardy*' bears upon its role in painting, and elaborates Lawrence's views on the marriage of body and spirit, of light and darkness.

Carpenter cannot conceive history without prophecy: after reviewing cases in history when art died down, to be resuscitated again only "by the advent of a new Religion", he seeks the religion of the future, which

> . . . must come from the bosom itself of the modern people; it must be the recognition by Humanity as a whole of that Common Life which has really underlain all the various religions of the past;

> it must be the certainty of all the organic unity of mankind, of the brotherhood of all sentient creatures, freeing itself from all local doctrine and prejudice, and expressing itself in every available form. The seal and sanction of the Art of the future, call it Impressionism, or Symbolism, or Realism, will be its dedication to the service of this Religion.[45]

Is there in 'Art and the Individual', apart from the emphasis on religion, a timid and half-convinced, but similar, attempt to associate the artist's individualism with socialism?

> What then is the mission of Art? To bring us into sympathy with as many men, as many objects, as many phenomena as possible. To be in sympathy with things is to some extent to acquiesce in their purpose, to help on that purpose. We want, we are for ever trying to unite ourselves with the whole universe, to carry out some ultimate purpose—evolution, we call one phase of the carrying out.[46]

Art and Life: to Create Oneself

After two chapters devoted to detailed discussion of Beethoven's sonatas and symphonies, Carpenter concludes his treatise on aesthetics with a chapter called 'The Art of Life', which already contained in 1898 the central message of *The Art of Creation*. Its essence is that Life is the greatest of the arts; the socialist, altruistic nature of Carpenter's thinking is immediately manifested when he adds that to discuss this theme adequately would "lead into the question of the reconstruction of Industry, into the programmes of Socialism and Anarchism".[47] "Life is Expression", and to be an art it must be "an expression of one's self", not by the pursuit of pleasure but "by going your own way and letting the pleasure pursue you".

With the deep social insight which marks many of his pronouncements, Carpenter sees through the accidental effects of the

Industrial Revolution, to the potentialities of its humanized evolution: the ideals of Marxism and aesthetic socialism are clearly united in his vision:

> We are approaching a great culmination in the history of the human race . . . a period when mankind will rise to something like a true understanding of Life and to a subjugation of Materials to the need of Expression.[48]

Following the scramble for existence, which made men "slaves to materials, barely able to satisfy their hunger", the present era "must rise above materials to the conception of making use of them all indifferently—the only purpose for which they exist". The "marvellous development of mechanical powers" should enable the coming age to "free the human race at last from its long bondage to earth and give Wings to Man, so to speak, by which he may rise into something like his true life".[49] Materials are "the symbols of the Soul-life" and when the mass of men no longer work "to please their masters" but "to create", not from fear but from love, "Life will become an Art". The simplification of life, the return to nature, heralded by John the Baptist and Rousseau, represent the preparations for mastery, they clear the ground for expression which is *union with others*, in which man "must use all his motives to express himself", in spite of the division of labour and of Mrs Grundy:

> The key to the expression of one's true self is boldness. William Blake said the true artist should always err in the direction of excess. Boldness and loving Acceptance.

Faithful to the ethic of 'The Marriage of Heaven and Hell', Carpenter concludes that "these so-called evil motives" must be allowed to "have their expression":

> To your own Self be true and it will follow 'as the night the day' you will be in touch with all other Selves: you will have the Angel-wings which will carry you in an instant from one end of heaven to another.[50]

This analysis of *Angels' Wings* and its comparison with 'Art and the Individual' seems conclusive: Lawrence's essay is a timid, hesitating, but faithful, and to a large degree original, adaptation of Carpenter's book; it shows that the main ideas of that book had been faced, if not fully assimilated, by him as early as 1908.

Aesthetic Theory in '*Study of Thomas Hardy*'

We do not now propose to do more than point out briefly how in '*Study of Thomas Hardy*', '*The Crown*', and '*The Reality of Peace*', the three major formative theoretical expositions of his aesthetic, Lawrence works upon themes developed by Carpenter in *Angels' Wings* and *The Art of Creation*, and upon some of the ideas contained in *Drama of Love and Death*, enriched of course by his own experience as a creative artist and by his other reading, and so thoroughly assimilated that almost all traces of "sources" of "influence" have disappeared.

The theme of life as an art is fundamental with Lawrence, to such an extent that it underlies all his conceptions of ethics and aesthetics during his later formative years and even after. The neatest expression of this idea is perhaps to be found in a letter of March 1915 to Lady Ottoline Morrell:

> I see Van Gogh so sadly. If he could only have set the angel of himself clear in relation to the animal of himself, clear and distinct but always truly related, in harmony and union, he need not have cut off his ear and gone mad . . . . He should either have resigned himself and lived his animal 'other horses'[51]—and have seen if his art would come out of that—or he should have resisted, like Fra Angelico. But best of all if he could have known a *great humanity*, where to *live* one's animal would be *to create oneself*, in fact, *be the artist creating a man in living fact*—and where the art was the final expression of the created animal or man—not the be-all and being of man—but the end, the climax. And some men would end in

artistic utterance, and some would not. But each one would create the work of art, the living man, *achieve that piece of supreme art, a man's life.*[52] [*Lawrence's underlining, my italics*].

In our book on the formative years of D. H. Lawrence[53] we have analysed at full length the ideas contained in '*Study of Thomas Hardy*' and the two series of essays, '*The Crown*' and '*The Reality of Peace*', abridged versions of this long attempt by Lawrence to formulate for himself a "philosophy". How derivative the '*Hardy*' is, we had not fully grasped before making the more detailed comparisons attempted in the present study. It may be enough to recall briefly the essential themes, arising from that particular association of ethics and aesthetics which is not exclusive to Carpenter, which is indeed often derived from Baudelaire, and from Coleridge through him, and Poe, and in part from Hegel.

Lawrence thus had many opportunities to absorb and make his own an aesthetic theory which proceeds from the identification of the human spirit with the divine, and thus unites ethics and aesthetics in one single whole. But the combination of ethical and aesthetic views, the conception of the progress of the soul through a second birth to the creation of the Self, the implicit esoteric lore which is behind many passages of the '*Hardy*', suggests that in 1914, when writing it, he was trying to assimilate into a system of thought of his own, ideas and images widely and deeply absorbed in earlier years, of which Carpenter produced the nearest and most readily accessible synthesis.

Women's suffrage, laws and antinomianism, the money-sickness or cash-nexus, the war, are subjects inextricably mixed in some of these chapters, to which is added a new subject, hitherto unknown or rather scarcely mentioned at all in Lawrence's writings: sex-perversion, and the laws which punish "the sex-degraded" with prison.[54] One might say that all the themes implicit or hinted in 'Art and the Individual' began to exfoliate and were budding all over the '*Hardy*'. Other influences also had been brought to bear on Lawrence, among which are prominent those of Houston Chamberlain and of Weininger, and of Jane

Harrison's *Art and Ritual*. The main stream of thoughts and images, which develops that of the 'Foreword' to *Sons and Lovers*, also owes much to Blake (in particular this idea of *excess* in procreation and in art, which had been singled out in *Angels' Wings*) and to Carpenter himself. *The Intermediate Sex*, which we discuss in the next chapter, had by then become a new and vital inspiration to Lawrence's attempts at the psychology of sexual union and maladjustment.

But his leading idea, the one on which he concludes, is that the only possible "re-sourcing" of art, after Hardy, Dostoievsky, "the symbolist poetry of Mallarmé and the others", and the music of Debussy, is to be found in "the final knowledge" of the "Great Peace" of the union in joy of male and female.[55] That is Lawrence's, and probably Frieda's, temporary and personal contribution to an aesthetic debate which had dimly begun at W. E. Hopkin's house in March 1908 with the reading of 'Art and the Individual'.

The Point of Divergence: Contempt of Men

But apart from this characteristic specialization of the artistic creative function in the direction of sex, which follows, but going a little further, the same course as Carpenter's aesthetic, there are other and already significant differences in the '*Study of Thomas Hardy*' between the younger writer and his Victorian forerunner. They can be briefly stated, and their origins can be dated with some degree of accuracy.

At the time of writing a 'Foreword' to *Sons and Lovers*, Lawrence has discovered the mystical significance of the blood, and in the same letter to Ernest Collings,[56] in which he states this belief (merely adding "the blood" to the more Carpenterian concept of "the flesh"), he also, for the first time, takes up an anti-English and anti-humanitarian point of view:

> 'To be or not to be'—it is the question with us now, by Jove—
> And *nearly every Englishman says 'Not to be'*. So he *goes in for Humanitarianism and such like forms of not being*. [*My italics.*]

The letter goes on in the antinomian spirit of the 'Foreword': in this we detect not only ideas and images derived from Carpenter, but a beginning of personal rancour against England and its laws, combined with what may be the first signs of the influence not only of Nietzsche but of the anti-humanitarian and reactionary creed of Houston Chamberlain. This will manifest itself more clearly, in words containing direct evidence of contamination, in the '*Study of Thomas Hardy*', that boiling cauldron of all the ideas fermenting in Lawrence's mind between 1912 and 1915.

In the '*Hardy*', the anti-humanitarian assertion of his self by the true, twice-born hero, contrasted with the false "unbegotten hero", follows the line of thought of the 'Foreword': there is no law for the twice-born; no *word*, no mere repetition of other words, can bind the word-utterer; our neighbour is but an echoed old word, a lie, a deformity. The supreme artist, be he the creator of his own life or of works of imagination, is above the law and above the common people. He may kill; the victim then is to blame: "If in my passion I slay my neighbour, it is no sin of mine but his sin, for he should not have permitted me".[57] The Blakean images of the cabbage rotting at the heart, of the tiger and the lamb, of different laws for the lion and the ox, have replaced the earlier vision of harmony and unity with the common people.

The '*Hardy*' marks the dividing line, outlined in the 'Foreword' and the letters of early 1913, between Carpenter's romantic humanism, with its profound nineteenth-century socialist optimism, and the potential totalitarianism of a Nietzschean Lawrence. Yet the two trends of thought will co-exist for a time; perhaps indeed Lawrence was never any more able than were many of his contemporaries until the Second World War, to discern without that bitter test of experience, the choice which had to be made between the doctrines of contempt and those of love and of hope in mankind. It is a sobering thought when looking at the past, that Bernard Shaw could write in *Fabian News* that

The Foundations of the XIXth Century was a book that "should be read by every good Fabian", calling it "a message of really scientific history".[58] The dividing-line between the Victorian and the late Edwardian is drawn through contempt, egotism and despair.

It is perhaps significant to note that this evolution also roughly coincided in time with the increasing influence of T. E. Hulme in *The New Age*, in the days when Orage was moving towards his later creeds, guild socialism, and later social credit, and occultism: the *New Age* review of Carpenter's *Drama of Love and Death* was decidedly cool, if not contemptuous.[59]

The Aesthetic of Loneliness

'*The Crown*' brings a more original, more poetical, also more personal expression to Lawrence's aesthetic theories and to his doctrine or at least his attitude of contempt. It marks an important stage towards the development of his personal mythology, which found after 1919 its full theoretical expression in *Fantasia of the Unconscious* and its poetical form in *Birds, Beasts and Flowers*. In it, the memories of Carpenter's religion of life and of life as an art remain vivid, but deeply fused in Lawrence's own imaginative processes.

Predominant is the contempt of the "myriads of human lives that are not absolute nor timeless", that "never become more than relative, never come into being".[60] Predominant also the dualism of "the End and the Beginning", of creation and corruption, the obsession with an unnamed Siva,[61] the thought of Brahma, also unnamed but present as "The Beginning". Most characteristic of Lawrence's current thinking is his belief in what he called the Holy Ghost, the unrevealed god, "the utter relation between the two eternities" of the source and the goal, of creation and destruction. To achieve consummate being is to achieve immortality, through submission to the divine grace, *and* through conquering by divine grace: to the aesthetic and ethic of non-action, the Lawrence of 1915 adds the ethics of the creative but spontaneous violence of the tiger, of the great terrible conquerors, the male warriors.

This, in a way, is a natural development of Carpenter's aesthetic of the art of life, of the expression by man of "all his motives", also of his pluralist Hinduist faith in Brahma and Siva: but the late-Victorian writer's belief that evil motives "are only evil because they have not yet found their place, their balance"[62] finds much more violent expression in the 1915 essay '*The Crown*', where Blake's notion of *excess* has become predominant in guiding Lawrence's ethics, if not quite his aesthetics. The work of art becomes a solitary, timeless, momentary but eternal achievement in a wilderness: the artist, who is "God created where before God was uncreate", effects "a sheer fusion in himself of all the manifest creation, a pure relation, a sheer gleam of oneness out of manyness".[63] He is the mediator, the flash of timeless revelation of the one and the eternal in the flux of time and plurality.

The aesthetic of timelessness, perfectly expressed by Lawrence in 1919 with its Whitman associations in 'Poetry of the Present',[64] has here become the aesthetic of the loneliness of the artist, as opposed to Carpenter's aesthetic of the common people. The aesthetic of the Marxist and Fourierist thinker working towards social integration and harmony of all men with the universe, has given way to the solitary song of the alienated superman. Yet in that, as we shall soon discover, Lawrence, distracted by the war and personal unhappiness, still follows to their bitter consequences some ideas which in all probability stem from Carpenter and from Whitman, those two singers of a very special brand of democracy.

Non-action, and how to Accept Evil in the Self

In the 1917 essays, '*The Reality of Peace*', many of the ideas of '*The Crown*' find new expression, sometimes in slightly less allegoric form. The essays are rather more directly inspired by the ethic and aesthetic of "non-action", closer to an almost Gandhian conception of peace by non-violence; they contain, however, a characteristic invocation to death, and they harp on the familiar image of the tiger pouncing on its willing prey—the killer provoked by his victim's nature.

Acceptance of the evil and the loathsome in ourselves, of the flux of darkness and decomposition, is a recurrent theme: we should "admit with simplicity" any "loathsome thought or suggestion" in ourselves; "we are angels and we are devils . . . We are whole beings, gifted with understanding . . . complete beyond the angels and the devils". "There is nothing to be ashamed of." "I shall accept all my desires and repudiate none."[65]

But where Carpenter hoped that the devils would become subdued and the tigers lie down with the lambs, Lawrence hesitates between such a conception of peace, and that of peace by conquest and free play for the tigers and conquerors. Nietzsche's blond beasts must triumph over the slaves before peace can reign. The '*Reality of Peace*' essays remain irresolutely suspended between these conflicting beliefs, the need of peace, and the conviction that the wild beasts must have their day.

In spite of this, the 1917 Lawrence seems to have attained greater peace of mind in reconciliation with himself and his desires—as if the lesson of Carpenter's balance and spirit of union with the universe had partially triumphed. Is this the result of an initiation into the lessons of Freudian psychology, or the fruit of a period of personal reflection? Possibly both; in the meantime Lawrence had read J. M. Pryse and Helen Blavatsky, and achieved some additional although limited knowledge of yoga. When he says "we must yield our ultimate will to the unknown impulse or remain . . . outside the river of life", it is permissible to think that he expresses a full synthesis of personal and vicarious experience, of his reflexion and his reading.[66]

But the acceptance of oneself, angel and devil, includes giving oneself wholly both to love and to hate, to "fellowship and communion" and also to "resistance and isolation". The idea of the polarity of opposites is already formed, which will lead to

Lawrence's vehement denunciation of Whitman's 'One Identity', i.e. of Carpenter's sense of solidarity with men and of universal sympathy between the self and the other selves, exfoliations of the 'All-self'. This idea goes further than Carpenter's attempt at a synthesis of good and evil by the ultimate triumph of good; Lawrence accepts the terrible conquerors, "Jehovah, Egypt and Sennacherib", the "terrible and grand" God of the Psalms in preference to "Democracy, En-masse, One Identity".

6

THE ANDROGYNOUS SUPERMAN

From Victorian Optimism to Georgian Pessimism

We have seen the themes of love and sex, ethics and aesthetics, art and society, art and the fulfilment of the individual, inextricably associated in the writings of Carpenter. We have noted the mingling of the same themes in the younger Lawrence. With both men, religion tends to fall into two categories, my own and that of others, just as ethics tend to subdivide into mine and Mrs Grundy's. But Carpenter the Victorian is in this respect more restrained than his Edwardian follower. Whether or not there is between them a fundamental, or an accidental and temporal, difference is a matter for consideration. As we reach the climax of the similarities between the late-Victorian and the Edwardian, a short retrospect on the sources of Carpenter's religious outlook may help us to gain perspective.

When he was a minister of the Established Church in that most Anglican of institutions, the Cambridge of the eighteen-seventies, three, or rather four, determinant forces were brought to bear on his faith and conduct: Whitman's poetry, Greek and Roman Art, Max Müller's *Sacred Books of the East*, and a sense of personal inadaptation to his environment, closely associated with what must be called, in spite of his own assertions, a sexual deviation.

Carpenter had the good fortune of learning relatively early to accept his exceptional nature, to compose with it, and to overcome the sense of shame and abnormality which was frequently associated with such a disposition even in enlightened circles, e.g. among the medical observers of that time. It should be remembered that even a Krafft-Ebing as well as his contemporaries believed in "heredity" (with all that it then implied by way of derogatory undertones) as the main explanation of neuroses and of sexual anomalies.

His artistic nature, his almost feminine gifts of human sympathy, his intensity of religious experience and craving for communion with other human beings, his deep and almost Buddhist awareness of the essential equality not only of humans but of all living beings, were fused together in an original and, by all contemporary accounts, ascetic and saintly synthesis, largely through meditation on the wisdom of the *Bhagavad-Gita* and the *Upanishads*.

His experience in the presentation of unfamiliar ideas to popular audiences as a university extension lecturer, developed the masterly skill of exposition and gradual revelation of the ultimate goal of his writings which marks such books as *Angels' Wings* and *The Art of Creation*. With illustrations from Christian symbolism, from the most traditionally accepted and revered works of art—Perugino and Michelangelo, the Parthenon frieze, and Dying Gaul and the Naples bas-relief of Paris and Helen, he knew how to gain from a Nonconformist or anglican reader, acceptance of his most unorthodox views on art and self-expression.

This goes deeper than mere rhetoric: there is, underlying all his work, a profound conviction that all religions correspond to an intense and sincere experience of mankind at a given moment. There is a firm belief in the advent, as a human need and an essential form of human expression, of a new religion which will embrace the whole of mankind: a typically late-Victorian view, which few would share in the Britain of the nineteen-twenties and after.

Faith in Organization

There are more than suggestions of a similar attitude in the younger Lawrence; but with a significant difference, which lies in the sense of despair characterizing his attitude towards mankind; in the rift between the Lawrentian artist and hero, and the common man. Carpenter's book of poems is entitled *Towards Democracy*, and by democracy, as Edward Lewis has rightly pointed out, he means "a perpetual will to new incarnations, new creation", a shaping, creative consciousness which "shall become, in the course of time, organization in the world".[1] Carpenter never deviated from the nineteenth-century conviction that all human effort led to better and more humane organization. His ideas on the superman, strange though they seem, should be viewed in the light of this Victorian conviction. But take away this important difference, namely Lawrence's despair and his disbelief in the common man, his intolerance and haunted fear of the effects of an unjust civilization, and the basic creeds, the forms of expression of those beliefs are essentially the same, as will appear from their attitudes to the superman and his role.

* * *

Carpenter and Esoteric Tradition

Carpenter's Hinduism goes back to 1881 and to his first reading of the *Bhagavad-Gita*. Later experience fortified it: *From Adam's Peak to Elephanta*, relating his 1890 voyage to Ceylon and India, contains four important chapters on his visit and talks with a *gñani*, or teacher, of the South Indian school of Brahminical thought.

Particularly important is the description of methods of attainment of another order of consciousness used by the *gñana-yogis*, intense concentration of the thoughts on a fixed object leading to effacement of thought altogether.

There is no direct and specific evidence anywhere of Lawrence having been familiar with those chapters, and indeed until he read J. M. Pryse's *Apocalypse Unsealed* in or around 1916, he may have obtained such knowledge of Hindu esoteric traditions, as he shows in his 1913–15 writings, mainly from *The Art of Creation* and *The Drama of Love and Death*, as well as from other more general literature, including the Vedas with which a letter from him to Earl Brewster suggests he had some sort of familiarity.[2] On the other hand, if Lawrence had read in early youth *From Adam's Peak to Elephanta*, or heard Carpenter lecture on Hindu thought as he frequently did, he would be well prepared by such initiation for his later interest in oriental religion.

A Cautious Approach

In his chapter 'Traditions of the ancient wisdom-religion', Carpenter relates, with all due precautions in warning his reader against "accepting anything I say, except with care and reserve", the cosmogonic and other traditions of the Hindu sages. He does so not without some criticism, e.g. to express surprise "when I found a man of so subtle intelligence and varied capacity calmly asserting that the earth was the centre of the physical universe and that the sun revolved about it!"[3]

He duly reports that his *gñani* did not mention any "modern theories of submerged continents and lower races in the far past", thus probably correcting some of the wilder statements and racialist theories of Helen Blavatsky and even of Annie Besant. He makes a remarkable contribution to his own and perhaps to Lawrence's anti-intellectualism, by relating that his Hindu friend quoted the sacred books to the effect that "everything which can be thought is untrue".[4] In the old doctrines of "Astronomy, Astrology, Philology, Physiology, etc. . . ." handed down from time immemorial to the *gñanis*, he sees "an element of cosmic-consciousness . . . which has given them their vitality and seal of authority so to speak".[5]

Mediaeval alchemy also receives some sort of blessing *en passant* from his tolerant interest in the primaeval traditions of India. But at no time does he assert an organized system of thought which might compete with modern science; he marks the limitations of science but does not contest its practical results.

Lawrence and Esoteric Lore

Lawrence, by the time he committed to paper the cosmogony of the 'Two Principles', and later of *Fantasia of the Unconscious*, had read other books on Hindu tradition and esoteric lore, and followed them much further. If he had read these pages of Carpenter in his youth or in 1914–15, they might have awakened or deepened his interest in occult traditions. But the essential relationship of his mental universe with Carpenter's is not there. His occultism of 1916 onwards is closer to that of Annie Besant and Helen Blavatsky, and is less restrained by a sense of the basic Western tradition of analytical thought.

The Attraction of the Superman

But through occultism, through the idea of an esoteric knowledge handed over by wise men from a unique source and a "universal mystic language",[6] he is pursuing his old idea of the superman, the utterer, a mystic justification of his Messianic view of himself. Between 1912 and 1918 it is difficult to determine what with him is mental play and literature, and what is belief, incantation,mental auto-intoxication; where the man of letter, ends, and the Messiah begins. The creation of Birkin in *Women in Love*, and Lawrence's statements on Whitman in 1918–20 relate to this tortured, and sometimes almost insane, period of his mental life; and in that period we find many signs of a new climax of activity in his mind, of ideas traceable to Carpenter. Lawrence's views on sex and the superman are strangely and uniquely linked with his occultism, and, as we shall see, with the implications of some of Carpenter's more daring opinions.

How closely Lawrence's Messianic tendencies and Carpenter's idea of the superman are related, appears from the underlying ideas on sex and the hero, physiological and mystical concepts, mainly but not only expressed in '*Study of Thomas Hardy*' and in *The Symbolic Meaning*. In those works ideas are more or less explicit which are hidden in the novels. A study of Carpenter's thought on sex and the superman will help at the same time to show the similarities of the explicit statements and to clarify the intentions of the more obscure imaginative creations. The great difference between the two writers is not in *what* they think, but in the course which they take either to present their thinking—(this applies more to the Victorian), or to discover their own thoughts and follow them to their consequences (and this refers to Lawrence's painfully gradual, incomplete and often obscure confession, as well as to his velleities of political action). Carpenter's works may be read as a skilful, controlled *apologia pro vita sua*. Lawrence's writings until the end of the war are an involved, tormented and sometimes horrified self-exploration haunted by the ambition of leadership, of Messianic redemption of men; while this is well-known, the probable role of Carpenter's writings in this exploration has not so far been examined.

* * *

What is meant by Superman?

Love's Aim is Religious

If we accept the view that Carpenter, in such essays as 'Defence of Criminals',[7] 'The Art of Life',[8] 'The Free Society'[9] and even 'Love as an Art',[10] and in the whole small volume *The Intermediate Sex*, is trying to establish a permissive morality which will liberate the homosexual from social and legal reprobation, the motivation underlying his ethic and even his aesthetic of love becomes apparent. He is attacking the conventional morality at the very base of all ethical thought on sex, by refuting the argument that in the divine or natural scheme love is intended to ensure procreation. While he does not accept love for love's sake, synonymous with art for art's sake, which he rejects as passionately as does William Morris, the aim and purpose of love is not for him generation or pleasure. The object of sex is religion: this he repeats in many places, beginning with *Love's Coming of Age*:

> Taking all together I think it may fairly be said that the prime object of sex is *union*, the physical union as the allegory and expression of the real union, and that generation is a secondary object or result of this union.[11]

Union means yoga, and "absolute union can only be found at the centre of existence".[12] His Hinduism permeates his notions of sex, in a deeply religious spirit, so that when he refers in 'Love as an Art' to Ovid's *Art of Love* and to the *Kama-Sutra* of Vatsayana, he expresses the wish that others may "proceed much further into the deep realms of psychology, biological science and ultimately of religion"[13] in the treatment of such a subject.

Writing on 'The Homogenic Attachment' in *The Intermediate Sex*, he points out that "the popular opinion" concerning it "has probably been largely influenced by the arbitrary notion that the function of love is limited to child-breeding; and that any love not concerned in the propagation of the race must necessarily be of dubious character".

He sees in the Hebraic and Christian tradition on this subject a vestige from "far-back times when the multiplication of the tribe was one of the first duties of its members, and one of the first necessities of corporate life". And he supposes that "nowadays when the need has swung round all the other way" "a similar revolution" may take place "in peoples' views of the place and purpose of the non-childbearing love".[14]

Not only the needs of the tribe, but "the dominant Christian attitude", is to be blamed: it has "converted love, from being an expression and activity of the deepest human life and joy, into being simply *a vulgar* necessity for the propagation of the species. A violent effort was made to wrench apart the Spiritual and corporeal aspects of it".[15]

As we have seen, Lawrence, although in the 'Foreword' to *Sons and Lovers* he does not seem to rule out the thought of having offspring,[16] soon made his own the theory that love is for regeneration, not generation: 'Rose of All the World' expresses this briefly in poetry, and the '*Study of Thomas Hardy*' in abundant prose, with a superfluity of botanical and floral metaphor. "The latent seeds [are] secondary", within the "fire" that is the flower of the poppy.[17] "Seed and fruit are produced, they are a minor aim: children and good works are a minor aim. . . . The final aim of every living creature, or being is the full achievement of itself."[18] And by this, Lawrence does mean "itself", not the next generation.

The Physiology of Love and Reincarnation

It is difficult with Carpenter to know which came first, the physiology or the psychology of love: so persistent and systematic is his effort, answering a genuine need, to unite body and psyche in one single act of comprehension. In all his works, but more particularly in his two last books on love and art, *The Art of Creation* and *The Drama of Love and Death*, he endeavours to base all his arguments on an understanding of the physiological processes.

But while a Havelock Ellis, to whose 'Art of Love' he refers several times in *The Drama of Love and Death*, centres his attention on the physiological and nervous mechanisms of love in the individual, Carpenter for metaphysical reasons is more concerned with the cellular prehistory of sex physiology, and with the light which it seems to him to throw on sex psychology and the religion of love.

Love is "primarily, (and perhaps ultimately) an interchange of essences",[19] which "leads to Regeneration first, and so collaterally, and at a later period, to generation".[20] Apart from reproduction by budding or division, protozoa also reproduce by union of two cells, exchange of fluids, and parting: "It is a new form of nourishment; it is the earliest form of Love."[21] The two cells are "regenerated". At this stage there is "but little differentiation between Hunger and Love". Love is only a special hunger. "And so far there is no distinction of sex."[22]

The reader familiar with the detail of *Women in Love* will probably recognize here a parallel with Birkin's meditation on love at the beginning of Chapter XVI, although other elements, from *The Secret Doctrine*, from Weininger's *Sex and Character*, and from *The Intermediate Sex*, are no doubt mixed with memories of this analysis of 'The Beginnings of Love'. This passage may have originated Lawrence's quest for mystic explanations of the physiology of love; while the chapter from which it is quoted was only included after 1923 in *Love's Coming of Age*, Lawrence could have read it in 1912, when it first appeared in *The Drama of Love and Death*.

Sex comes in "at a later period", and Carpenter describes the specialization between male and female: pursuit and capture of food activity on one side, digestion, assimilation of food, quiescence, on the other. He discusses the elaborate system of sex-cells, the chromosomes in the genetic cells, and insists on the significance of the fact that "the entire creature, in all its form and feature . . . *is* indeed that original cell with its latent powers and virtue made manifest"; the original cell was itself "the fusion of two parent cells".[23]

With the haste of the philosopher trying to bend scientific observation to his system, he then imagines that in the fusion of the parent cells, when the total number of parent chromosomes is reduced by half, it is possible that in the one case "certain male elements are expelled, and in the other case certain female elements"; he finds support for this idea in Plato's notion of "male and female being only the two halves of a complete original being",[24] a comforting corroboration for a regular reader of the *Upanishads*, who thus remains on familiar ground. The evolutions and affinities of the infinitely small remind him of those "of the unimaginable stars" and he supposes that they are "an allegory or symbolic expression of some other plane of being".[25]

This transposition or *transference* from the material or cellular to "some other" plane of being, is indeed highly characteristic of both writers; and Lawrence's realism, if it is to be properly understood, has to be seen and interpreted in the light of his search for that "other plane of being", both in love and in sex, that is to say his quest for what he calls sometimes the *Crown*, sometimes the *Holy Ghost*, sometimes "giving oneself up" triumphantly to "a quick, new desire to have new heaven and earth",[26] "a dual understanding", "death understood and life understood".[27] The relationship between material explanations of biological phenomena, and metaphysical explanations based on a vitalistic belief in the "life impulse", or, as Lawrence calls it, "the quick of life", is of mystical nature with both writers, and naturally centres on the facts of sex reproduction and physiological exchanges in sexual union.

They have this common feature, that both view those physiological exchanges apart from the fact of generation, and from the angle of regeneration of the individual: Carpenter, as we shall see, mainly without woman; Lawrence at first, in 1913–14, with woman; but after 1915 he has occasional and important reservations about woman. The main difference is to be found in Lawrence's variations on this point; the main resemblance in his exaltation of male comradeship, not only in his earlier essay on Whitman, but in other works of the same inspiration. Indeed, coinciding with the probable reading of Carpenter's *The Drama of Love and Death* by Lawrence sometime after its publication in

March 1912, there appears to have begun in his mind a train of thought which slowly leads to the Whitman essay of 1921,[28] to *Aaron's Rod*, and to *The Plumed Serpent* through *Kangaroo*, via the androgynous hero Birkin in *Women in Love*, Lawrence's first attempt to draw the portrait of the superman-hero. This train of thought related to theosophy, and maybe also to a gnostic interpretation of early Christianity which had currency in certain esoteric circles close to Carpenter.[29]

In describing 'Love as an Art', Carpenter takes up a position based on his earlier analysis of "the love affairs of the protozoa" and on criticism of the "negative Christian dispensation" on love, which is rapidly approaching to its close as "the necessity of love *in its various forms*, as part and parcel of a healthy life, is compelling our attention".[30] [*My italics.*] It is in the behaviour of the cells seeking regeneration that he looks for the reunion of profane and sacred love, "corporeal intercourse" and "true affection". Love and sexual union ensure a "fusion of complementaries" not only "in respect of their sex-cells, but probably also to a considerable degree in respect of their body-cells", and also on the spiritual plane since it fills lovers "with mad and immortal seeming ecstasies".[31] He even quotes Weininger's *Sex and Character* on this subject of complementariness and exchange of essences, but in moderate terms,[32] his friend Havelock Ellis having possibly dissuaded him from making much of the work of that "youthful genius", more noticeable for his Wagnerian outpourings than for the soundness of his physiology.[33]

The '*Study of Thomas Hardy*', as we have shown in detail elsewhere,[34] owes much to this physiological theory of the exchange of essences or plasmas. So does Birkin's meditation on love in Chapter XVI of *Women in Love*, with the important difference, relevant to what follows in the present chapter, that in the '*Hardy*' Lawrence believes in the profound virtue of the plasmic exchanges between male and female, whereas in *Women in Love* Birkin the superman seems to fear woman's desires, is weary of "fusion", of "merging", and seeks a state of being in which he would be "single in himself, the woman single in herself", when sex would "revert to the level of the other appetites" and cease to be a "fulfilment".[35]

But the 1913 Lawrence, when he conceived *The Sisters*, in spite of the early storms and stresses of his love for Frieda, was still aiming at joyously "sticking up for" and illustrating "love between man and woman",[36] and not the comradeship of males which sometimes attracts Birkin almost as strongly as does Ursula.[37] Any contradictions between the 1913 conception and the 1916 achievement are probably to be interpreted in the two-fold light of Lawrence's marital experience of love and sex in the interval, and of his meditation and probable re-reading of Carpenter's and of other works at the same time, coinciding with his insistence, which both biographical and literary facts corroborate, on the problems and theory of male friendship, to use the form of understatement still prevalent among the majority of Lawrence critics.

The physiological explanation of the nature of sexual characteristics, such as Carpenter presents in *The Intermediate Sex*, is clearly related in his mind, and indeed in his exposition, to an attempt to show that homosexual tendencies are neither degenerate nor hereditary: his doctrine on this point, essentially modern in its ethical aspect, also marks progress as compared with the earlier view that homosexuality derived from a degenerate heredity. Yet it appears quite old-fashioned compared with the genetic concepts of Freudian and behaviourist psychology. It is at the same time remarkably enlightened and tolerant, and conspicuously obsolete as far as it draws on a fanciful psycho-physiology of love, marked with all the symptoms of the philosopher's interest in the *why* of things when the *how* is imperfectly known.

The Origin of the Individual Soul

The theory of the origin of the individual soul or ego, which Carpenter shares with Lawrence, is basic to the understanding of his explanation of the mixture of male and female characteristics in the individual. Love frees the souls of lovers, disengages them from "the race-matrix": "It breeds souls out of the Race-self, and finally brings them away to an independent life." The stirrings and convulsions of love dig up the soul "from its roots in the race and plant it out in the great Eden garden of emancipate humanity—the beginning of a new career".[38]

If souls are thus born once, only to be born again through the experience of love, how did they come into bodies in the first instance? And what is the relationship between love and this first birth? "Those who are truly married on earth are in heaven one Angel", says Swedenborg. Thus,

> . . . by love a new soul is sometimes generated which takes possession of both persons. . . . And by love, we may also think, between man and wife, a new soul or soul-bud is sometimes created, which *may descend into and vivify the physical germ* of their child.[39] [*My italics.*]

Thus there may happen on the *psycho-physical* level what always happens on the spiritual level:

> Does it not seem likely that . . . at the same moment that the germ of a bodily child is being fertilized, there is formed in the race-soul a soul-bud corresponding, which consequently descends into the physical germ and becomes its organizing life—the soul-bud thus being related to the souls of the parents, somewhat as the physical germ is related to their bodies?

In other cases, Carpenter supposes, "some older and more developed soul-bud—which has perhaps already had some earth experiences" takes possession of the germ. And "if deep love be absent", some other passing soul-bud "may enter in and possess the developing organism". This may lead to strife, conflict and doubt, possibly to "heroic developments" and tragedy.[40]

Thus in one stroke is reincarnation "explained", together with strife and conflict, neurosis and tragedy, and the birth of a hero. And also "soul-alliances and even soul-fusions, by which we humans in our turn build up the very life of the Gods". Reincarnation explains the godlike presences of the great men, such as Walt Whitman.[41]

That this or a very similar train of thought is a familiar one for Lawrence, one could show by numerous examples. Might he not have in mind something of the sort when in 1912 he writes to Edward Garnett about his son David: "By Jove, I reckon his parents have done joyously well for that young man", referring to young Garnett's fine physique and gay nature contrasted with his own "unlucky and lugubrious self".[42] In 1918, in 'The Two Principles', the idea is followed through to its mystic consequences:

> The coming together of the sexes may be the soft, delicate union of pure creation, or it may be the tremendous conjunction of opposition, a vivid struggle, as fire struggles with water in the sun. From either of these consummations birth takes place. But in the first case it is the birth of a *softly rising and budding soul*, wherein the two principles commune *in gentle union*, so that the soul is harmonious and at one with itself. In the second case it is the birth of a disintegrated soul, wherein the two principles wrestle in their eternal opposition: a soul finite, momentous, active in the universe as a unit of sundering.[43] The first kind of birth takes place in the youth of an era, in the mystery of accord; the second kind preponderates in the times of disintegration, the crumbling of an era. But at all times, beings are born from the two ways and life is made up of the duality.[44] [*My italics.*]

And the next few lines show that Lawrence, like Carpenter, is thinking of the "continual process of sundering and reduction", of "mechanical" action of the soul—in fact of civilization: "reduction" is his favourite word to describe the mental processes of analysis which he finds destructive of "the spiritual being", of "that blissful consciousness which glows upon the flowers and trees and sky, so that I am sky and flowers; I who am myself",[45] i.e. Carpenter's third stage of consciousness.

But what does he say of the birth of the human soul? In his pamphlet against Freud and idealism, *Psychoanalysis and the Unconscious*, he adopts exactly the same theory as Carpenter: "The vast bulk of consciousness is non-cerebral."[46] There is, "beneath the navel", "a centre of consciousness in the tiny foetus".[47] What is it and where does it come from? It is a "pristine consciousness", a "sap-consciousness", which Lawrence also calls "the unconscious" and which "begins where life begins"[48]: "the term unconscious is another word for life . . . it is the active self-evolving soul bringing forth its own incarnation and self-manifestation", which is its "whole goal . . . the whole goal of life".[49]

The absolute parallelism of these beliefs with those of Carpenter or of his ancient Indian sources, will appear when we see that for Lawrence also "a new unit of life, of consciousness," arises "in the universe" at the moment of conception, life and individuality being "inseparable".[50] *Psychoanalysis and the Unconscious* does not, however, refer to this grafting of soul-buds on to the foetus in which Carpenter sees the explanation of geniuses, heroes and neuroses: but Lawrence rarely discloses all his esoteric beliefs at one go, and we have to turn to *Fantasia of the Unconscious* to learn that the souls of the dead

> . . . decompose into some psychic reality, and into some potential will. They re-enter into the psyche of living individuals. The living soul partakes of the dead souls, as the living breast partakes of the outer air, and the blood partakes of the sun. . . . The dead soul remains always soul, and always retains its individual quality. And it does not disappear, but re-enters into the soul of the living, of some living individual or individuals. And there it continues its part in life, as a death-witness and a life-agent.[51]

By the time Lawrence wrote *Fantasia of the Unconscious* in the Black Forest in 1921, he had widened his knowledge of theosophy and Indian sacred literature; he was in touch with the Brewsters, and with Mabel Luhan who was some years later to make him read Ouspensky; the early sources of his beliefs were merging with those later streams from a common fountainhead in ancient Eastern traditions. At that point the trace of a definite influence from Carpenter becomes lost in the wider tide of esoteric interests of the mature writer.

Male and Female: the Mixture and the Balance

The mystic physiology of sex, as seen by both writers, serves to explain, for the one his homogenic attachments, for the other, his inability to find complete fulfilment and accede to "being" through the love of women.

This excessively brief summary of a complex and evolving Lawrentian problem is necessary at this stage; the reader should remember that the Lawrence of early 1913 ('Foreword' to *Sons and Lovers*) is not exactly the Lawrence of 1914 ('*Study of Thomas Hardy*') nor the same as the Lawrence of 1918 (first essay on Whitman and the beginning of *Aaron's Rod*). The continuous link between these different characters is the search for a satisfactory explanation of the "mixture" of male and female in the individual, the idea of such "mixture" being itself forced on the writer by his own sense of a deficiency in his love life. Lawrence's changes of attitude become intelligible if we start from the hypothesis that his ideas as attempts to understand himself originally stem from Carpenter's own explanations, and that his conception of himself in relation to sex and love varies from late 1912 to late 1918. We are comparing a stable phenomenon, Carpenter's ideas on male and female, with a variable one, i.e. Lawrence's views which evolve as a result of his experience and his need to explain it to his own satisfaction.

The mystic physiology of sex, in so far as it provides a link and a mediator between an ill-adapted earthly life and the deep conviction of both writers that they have a "message" and a "mission" on earth, also serves to complete their conception of the role and nature of the superman, the hero, or Messiah. It is essential to the understanding of their conception of the predestined creative artist or leader of men.

Melville and Michelangelo

The first appearance in Carpenter's works of the idea of a "mixture" of ingredients—"the two groups of ingredients which represent the two sexes"—is to be found in *The Intermediate Sex*. There are no external clues enabling us to state that Lawrence had read this book before the moment when he first conceived the theories of sex expressed in the '*Study of Thomas Hardy*'. But there are very strong indications that he read it attentively and perhaps repeatedly between the beginning of the war and the end of 1916.

The idea that sex ingredients are unequally and irregularly mixed in each individual is essential to the understanding of the main and highly personal interpretation by Lawrence of Hardy's characters; it is explicit in several passages of the '*Study of Thomas Hardy*', where it is accompanied by evidence of direct borrowings from Weininger's *Sex and Character*, as well as from Carpenter's 1914 study *Intermediate Types among Primitive Folk*. These will be singled out later where appropriate. There are also definite suggestions that the character of Birkin owes much to the description by Carpenter of the "Urning", or man of homogenic nature.

We know from Robert Nichols's memorial of his friend Philip Heseltine that when at Oxford the latter had been greatly impressed by Carpenter's works; Heseltine was Lawrence's constant companion at Porthcothan and Zennor in the early months of 1916. They cannot have failed to discuss Carpenter since they shared at that time many interests including one in the occult and in the mediaeval mystics. While all this pleads in favour of a *renewal* of Lawrence's interest in Carpenter in 1916, it is also clear that when he wrote the '*Study of Thomas Hardy*' in late 1914 he had already read *The Intermediate Sex* and probably *Intermediate Types*. It is also possible that he had read Carpenter's 'Story of my books' in *The English Review* of February 1916 or that W. E. Hopkin may have sent Lawrence the 2/6d offprint which Carpenter had given him on 4 April 1916 in exchange for the loan of *The Rainbow*. All this points to the probability of repeated reading and discussion of Carpenter's books between late 1914 and the summer of 1916, a period during which Lawrence is keenly interested in writing his "philosophy", i.e. in explaining his own nature to himself as well as his relation to the cosmos.

A striking coincidence is to be found in his sudden absorption in Melville in 1916. It is true that he had, according to Aldington, found a copy of *Moby Dick* among Beresford's books at Porthcothan, and "loved it",[52] as he tells Barbara Low in a letter of May 1916. In this same letter, he asks her for *Omoo* and *Typee*. It so happens that both books are quoted by Carpenter in *The Intermediate Sex*,[53] *à propos* of "the most romantic male friendships" in vogue among Polynesian islanders. This passage is highly significant in relation to the Lawrence of May 1916, who in the same letter was telling Barbara Low (a psychoanalyst whom he occasionally consulted on his physical health) that Middleton Murry and Katherine Mansfield had decided to leave their Cornish group of cottages, with effects on Lawrence's feelings which Barbara Low remembered clearly enough to mention them in conversation with the present author in 1934. One of Lawrence's haunting preoccupations was then the failure of his friendship with Middleton Murry: "Though little inclined to jealousy in ordinary love matters, the Tahitian will hear of no rivals in his friendship": thus Carpenter, quoting Melville.[54]

Are we to find in this passage both a motivation and a source for this sudden curiosity, three full months after reading *Moby Dick*? At the time, Lawrence is writing the final version of *Women in Love*. He shows Birkin tempted by an obscene "African way", an "awful African process", obsessed by the problem of "eternal union with a man".[55] In the first American edition of *Women in Love*, the "African way" is replaced by a "Polynesian way".[55a] While on page 42 of *The Intermediate Sex*, Carpenter refers to *Omoo* and *Typee* and to 'Polynesian male friendships', on page 43 he mentions betrothal ceremonies between comrades among "the Balonda and other African tribes", an enlightening juxtaposition, if considered together with Lawrence's variants of a particularly obscure and oblique passage, in which, as Eliseo Vivas has noted, he tries to obfuscate rather than explain.

Another clue may be related to this Melville coincidence.

Lawrence's interest in Michelangelo's homosexuality was already marked in the '*Hardy*', where he had discussed him at length (in 1914) as an artist not interested in the female form, and as "containing too much of the female in his body ever to reach the geometric abstraction" of Raphael: "for his own body is both male and female".[56] In *The Intermediate Sex*, Carpenter refers with admiration to Michelangelo a few pages after his references to Melville and to the Balonda. He discusses the painter's lack of "romantic" sentiment for his female figures, which mostly represent women as "mother, or sufferer, or Prophetess, or poetess". "His pure beauty of expression", he writes, "lifts the enthusiasm into the highest region as the direct perception of the divine mortal form".[57]

On 7 April 1916, i.e. at the very moment when he starts the final rewriting of *Women in Love*,[58] Lawrence writes to Lady Ottoline Morrell a letter about Romain Rolland's *Life of Michelangelo*,[59] which he then has just finished reading. He sees the painter's eyes turned "to the Great God of Power and Might, whose sons we are", and he looks in vain for a way out of the present "Christian-democratic epoch", out of "our old mire of 'Love thy Neighbour'":[60] here Carpenter appears both as a guide, and as someone to argue with, as the author from whom hints are taken, while strong marks of dissent are perceived from his belief in democracy and his identification with his fellow-men. This dissent will find definitive expression in the final version of Lawrence's paper on Whitman in *Studies in Classic American Literature*.

It thus would seem that in April and May 1916, while writing *Women in Love*, Lawrence was very probably "documenting" his conception of Birkin's character in *Omoo*, *Typee*, in the *Life of Michelangelo*, and, in all likelihood, also in *The Intermediate Sex*. The 'Prologue' to *Women in Love*[61] contains passages which are clearly and unmistakably inspired by the life of Buonarotti, and by Carpenter's comments on it,[62] as well as by its author's own tortured state of mind of the moment, after Middleton Murry's rejection of his offer of *Blutbrüderschaft*.

Characteristics and Role of the Intermediate Sex

Carpenter's description of the intermediate sex, compiled for the general public in 1908 out of essays written and privately published from 1894 on, is less outspoken than some of his later papers on the hermaphrodite as superman.[63] It bears the marks of careful editing, it very often suggests rather than stating outright. A summary of its views may thus tend to overstress what is only hinted in it. Yet only a summary is possible here.

The Introduction strikes an important keynote: there are increasing numbers of men and women "of an intermediate or mixed temperament"; there exist "distinctions and gradations of soul-material in relation to Sex". Can it be that some important change in Nature is now in progress?

> We do not know, in fact, what possible evolutions are to come, or what new forms, of permanent place and value, are being already slowly differentiated from the surrounding mass of humanity.[64]

The Messianic element immediately follows this mystic idea of the mutation of the species; and the analogy is striking with Birkin's character and his conception of his role in relation to a society doomed to destruction:

> Just as worker bees have differentiated from others, it may be that at the present time certain new types of human kind may be emerging, which will have an important part to play in the societies of the future.[65]

The Urnings were so named by an Austrian, K. H. Ulrichs, from Uranos, heaven. Carpenter's familiarity with astrology more than suggests that he accepts the hint of a theosophic significance to the name. This new human type will probably become "in affairs of the heart, to a large extent *the teachers of future Society*", thanks to their "immense capacity of emotional love".[66] [*My italics.*]

As in his own case-history written for Havelock Ellis, Carpenter is at pains to refute any suggestion of morbidity in the intermediate type: for this he draws upon the evidence of Havelock

Ellis and even of Krafft-Ebing, whose degeneracy or neurosis theories of homosexuality he briefly refutes.[67] He takes the view that nervous troubles are an effect, not a cause, of sexual inversion. A passing and slightly scornful reference to the Oscar Wilde case leads him to assert that the homogenic manifestation of the sex instinct is normal and healthy, constituting "a distinct variety of the sexual passion", due to "a mixture of male and female elements in the same person".[68] It is "instinctive and congenital", and "can be detected in childhood".[69] Popular opinion in these matters has been influenced "by the arbitrary notion that the function of love is limited to child-bearing", an idea enforced with the help of the "Hebraic and Christian tradition".[70]

Urnings are endowed with special psychological powers; with them "intuition is always strong", and "like women they read characters at a glance, and know, without knowing how, what is passing in the minds of others".[71] If Lawrence knew what others said of him, he would recognize in this description not only himself but also, among characters of his creation, Paul Morel and Birkin. Urnings are excellent sick nurses:[72] again this almost describes Lawrence's cure of Middleton Murry's illness in 1915, and Lilly's skilful nursing of Aaron in *Aaron's Rod*.

Although they are not inclined to fall in love with women, they do not despise them, they are "by their nature drawn rather near to women, and it would seem that they often feel a singular appreciation and understanding of the emotional needs and destinies of the other sex".[73]

Could anything be nearer to a description of Birkin, who

> . . . was always drawn to women, feeling more at home with a woman than with a man, yet it was for men that he felt the hot, flushing, roused attraction which a man is supposed to feel for the other sex. . . . He studied the women as sisters, knowing their meaning and their intents. . . . The women he seemed to be kin to, he looked for the soul in them. . . .[74]

Thus placed "on the dividing line between the sexes", Carpenter's Urning, *anima muliebris in corpore virili inclusa*, has a special role to play as "the interpreter of men and women to each other".[75] He and his likes have an exquisitely delicate and complicated nerve-system, and form "the continual counterpoise to the sheer masculine portion of society" which is after "mere restless greed of gain and material sensual pleasures".[76] They are in possession of "a certain freemasonry of the secrets of both sexes which may well favour their function as reconcilers and interpreters".[77] There are few situations "in courtship or marriage which the Uranian does not instinctively understand".[78] His role will be important:

> . . . when love is at last to take its rightful place as the binding and directing force of society (instead of the cash-nexus) and society is to be transmuted in consequence to a higher form.[79]

Not only Birkin, the superman, is thus described very much as his creator made him—so too is Paul Morel reconciling Clara and Baxter Dawes. If one were tempted to see in Birkin a deliberate *invention* rather than a combination of systematic literary creation *and* of a projection of Lawrence's psyche, one should remember that particular scene of *Sons and Lovers*, and the long discussion of art and painters in the '*Study of Thomas Hardy*': this ends with an artistic programme which consists in seeking "the Reconciler" between man and woman, love and the law:[80] the mediator, that is for Lawrence The Holy Ghost, which is both male and female. Such is the programme out of which came the last writing of *The Rainbow* and *Women in Love*, except for an important shift of emphasis towards the attraction of the male in the latter novel.

This change concerns the writer's attitude to woman and to love. The '*Study of Thomas Hardy*' marks the continuation of the 1913 spirit of love triumphant between man and woman—but also the beginning of some questionings. These relate to the mixture of male and female in the individual, and to the first indications of a doubt in Lawrence's mind about his exclusive or dominant maleness. He first applies to races the concept of greater or lesser femininity or maleness,[81] using for this purpose indications most probably borrowed from *The Intermediate Sex* concerning the sex-mixture in such men as Goethe, Shakespeare, Shelley, Byron, Darwin, on the "feminine side", and Alexander, Socrates, Plato, Caesar, Michelangelo, Charles II, William of Orange, on the "supervirile" side.[82]

When he does apply this idea to individuals, it is to stress how in the act of love there is an exchange of essences which purifies the lovers: "that which is female in me is given to the female" and vice versa, so that each becomes "singled out unto ourselves".[83] In other words, Lawrence at that time believed in "singling out" through merging, fusion, and exchange of complementaries. He builds on this process his explanation of Hardy's characters, and in particular of Jude, Sue and Arabella—strangely reminiscent as it is of his own love problems in late adolescence and early manhood.[84]

Vaticinatory Role of Intermediate Types

Both Tess of the d'Urbervilles and Sue Brideshead are described as types of women who are deficient in femaleness. And here one is compelled to accept the view that Lawrence had read *Intermediate Types among Primitive Folk* either just before or while writing his '*Hardy*': the book had been reviewed in July 1914 in *The Occult Review*, by such an eminent authority as Havelock Ellis,[85] who emphasized that according to its author "there really is an organic connection between the homosexual temperament and unusual psychic or divinatory powers".[86] Carpenter indeed describes the religious role of the intermediate "as Prophet or Priest", "as Wizard or Witch", as inventor of arts and crafts. Quoting Westermarck, he associates change of sex, a man "imagining" himself to be a woman, with shamanism, and he describes the cult of Apollo at Delphi. He again refers to the feminine traits noticed in certain geniuses, naming Shelley and Byron, St Francis of Assisi and Jesus. He advances the view that the visionary faculty of homosexuals may be due to their considerable degree of continence. He refers to the church ceremonial attending the brotherhood union of men in Albania, quoting a case of two men making incisions in each other's fingers, sucking drops of each other's blood: "Henceforth, one must stand by the other in life and death."[87]

Lawrence, in the autumn of 1914 and early 1915, is full of the theme of the "prophetess", priestess of Apollo, Cassandra: assimilating Ottoline Morrell, Sue Brideshead, and Jessie Chambers into one same type, he writes to Lady Ottoline that she is not, and should give up all idea of being, "an ordinary physical woman —wife, mother, mistress".

Like the Hermione of the 'Prologue' to *Women in Love*, she belongs primarily "to a special type, a special race of women; like Cassandra in Greece, and some of the great women saints. They were the great *media* of truth, of the deepest truth". This type has to "reassert itself on the face of the earth . . . the priestess, the medium, the prophetess", who will trust to "that fundamental pathetic faculty for receiving the hidden waves that come from the depths of life, and for transferring them to the unreceptive world".[88] Hermione "seemed like a prophetess violated"; to Birkin she was "like a priestess", while he himself is compared to "a god who would do nothing if his worship were neglected"; she feeds on, and finds fulfilment in, their disembodied love and consuming ecstasies, which leave his body "grey and consumed" and his soul ill.[89] In the same way, Sue Brideshead "belonged, with Tess, to the old woman-type of witch or prophetess, which adhered to the male principle, and destroyed the female. But in the true prophetess, Cassandra, for example, the denial of the female cost a strong and almost maddening effect. But in Sue it was done before she was born."[90] Sue is the Cassandra and Aspasia of the North, "the witch type, which has no sex": the whole analysis by Lawrence of *Jude the Obscure* seems full of echoes of *Intermediate Types*, as well as of Lawrence's passionate return to his early love experience, which he endeavours to reinterpret in the light of new ideas. The description by Carpenter of the cult of Apollo at Delphi[91] would seem to have been his guide, for when he wrote the '*Hardy*' he had not yet read *The Golden Bough*.

Some Additional Clues

There are other incidental reasons to think that Lawrence drew extensively from *Intermediate Types* in the '*Study of Thomas Hardy*', a long essay in which the notion of a bisexual god is more nearly explicit than in any of his previous writings.[92] Carpenter refers to it in his fourth chapter, 'Hermaphroditism among Gods and mortals', where he refers not only to Brahma as the "two-sexed" God of Hindu mythology, the original "sole being" who "fell in twain" because he wished for the existence of another, but also to Baal as being double-sexed in combination with Astarte; this is precisely mentioned within a few pages of the reference to feminine traits in artists, geniuses, priests, prophets and gods.[93]

In another chapter, Carpenter refutes a German author, Adolf Bastian,[94] who supposed that "the priests among early peoples, as representatives of the bi-sexual principle in Nature, encouraged homosexual rites in the temples on the same footing as heterosexuality". Quoting his friend Lowes Dickinson, he shows that with the Greeks the low estimation of the female sex was not directly related to the high estimation of "manly love".[95] Lawrence in his '*Hardy*' makes more than passing reference to "Greece, in whom the female was overridden and neglected" and to the male influence of the "Greek stimulus" on the Renaissance after the "female", Jewish-inspired faith of the Middle Ages.[96] It is quite possible that not so much these ideas themselves, as their association and combination, owe something to *Intermediate Types*. In that case Lawrence's revulsion against supporters of the Women's Suffrage Movement, and preoccupation in the same breath with "sex-perversion",[97] may also have reference in his mind to Carpenter's assertion that "It is the Uranian classes of men; or those at least who are touched with the Uranian temperament, who chiefly support the modern Woman's movement".[98] He shows himself in such passages both attracted and repelled by ideas which in his Eastwood advanced circles were both current, and related to Carpenter's personal environment. In view of innumerable similarities, there can be little doubt that both *The Intermediate Sex* and *Intermediate Types* were simultaneous and complementary sources of Lawrence's ideas between the summer of 1914 and the time of his rewriting of *Women in Love*. Further evidence of this could be adduced from comparisons between the chapter 'Affection in Education"[99] and the lesbian episode in Ursula's sentimental education in *The Rainbow*.

But a major and very significant difference between Lawrence's two novels is that in *The Rainbow* homosexuality is presented in an unfavourable light, in the characters of Winifred Inger, of the younger Tom Brangwen, whom Winifred ultimately marries, and of Skrebensky whose friendship with Tom is slightly shadowy; whereas in *Women in Love*, especially in its suppressed 'Prologue', homosexuality is endowed with a power of fascination which suggests a marked change in outlook between March 1915 and the summer of the following year. While this conversion may be due to reasons other than literary,[100] it is not unconnected with the persistent influence of *The Intermediate Sex*, both on *Women in Love* and on later works.

* * *

The Superman as Artist-hero and Leader

Birkin's Secret: the Way to Permissiveness

This evolution of Lawrence is expressed in two revealing sentences of the suppressed 'Prologue'. Birkin is here shown, just as

Carpenter describes himself in his troubled Cambridge days, as sexually indifferent to women, whereas it was men whom "he apprehended intoxicatingly in his blood"[101]; he was assailed by shameful desires which he wanted to "cast out":

> This was the one and only secret he kept to himself, this secret of his passionate and sudden, spasmodic affinity for men he saw. He kept this secret even from himself.[102]

In exactly the same manner, Ursula had kept hidden from her best friends, even from herself, as a "secret side-show to her life, never to be opened"[103] the memory of her love affair with her schoolteacher Winifred.

Women in Love, with its 'Prologue', may thus be read as a first step by Lawrence towards a widening of his sexual ethic, and as an effort in self-understanding. The alternative to that interpretation would be that in it he was attempting to describe a "case"; that Birkin was not intended to represent his creator, but was a sort of clinical study. We do not think this interpretation can be supported by conclusive evidence; but in either hypothesis, *The Intermediate Sex* would seem to have played an important role in helping the novelist to come to terms with the problem.

After the significant scene of the wrestling match between Birkin and Gerald, the school-inspector makes a statement of importance in view of what the 'Prologue' reveals about his "secret": "The wrestling had some deep meaning to them—an unfinished meaning. . . . We are mentally, spiritually intimate, therefore we should be more or less physically intimate too—it is more whole", said Birkin, who promptly added: "I don't know why one should have to justify oneself." And a little later, after commenting on Gerald's beauty and "plastic form", he concluded, "We should enjoy everything".[104]

This might be construed as the literary presentation, in concrete novel form, of a passage of *The Intermediate Sex* justifying homogenic attachments against those who only think of "the debaucheries of a Nero or a Tiberius" or of the "scandals of the Police Courts". Such people, to whom "physical intimacies of *any* kind seem inexcusable", make "no distinction between a genuine heart-attachment and a mere carnal curiosity", they do not see the "interior love-feeling which when it exists does legitimately demand *some* expression".[105]

Just as Birkin is hesitant between Gerald and Ursula, between the "African" or "Polynesian" way and the road to Paradise, Carpenter offers Lawrence a pattern (and, in an autobiographical construction of his novel, a way of escape):

> There are all possible grades of sexual inversion . . . from that in which the instinct is *quite exclusively* directed towards the same sex, to the other extreme in which it is normally towards the opposite sex but capable, occasionally and under exceptional attractions, of inversion towards its own—this last condition being probably among some peoples very widespread, if not universal.[106] [*My italics.*]

Carpenter's exposition of his permissive ethic of sexual relations develops slowly but surely, very much on the same lines as will Birkin's: science has "destroyed the dogmatic attitude" of public opinion; homogenic attachments, in spite of "those instances which stand most prominently perhaps in the eye of the modern public" (another allusion to Oscar Wilde) are recognized as "a distinct variety of the sexual passion". The whole subject is freed from misunderstanding by the invoking of science in justification of practice as well as of feeling: science not only "recognizes the deeply beneficial influence of an intimate love-relation of the usual kind on those concerned, it also allows that there are some persons for whom these necessary relations can only come from one of the same sex as themselves".[107]

If we consider the autobiographical, not the strictly literary, interpretation of *Women in Love*, a passage such as this may indeed have been one of the means used by Lawrence's friends to help Lawrence face up to his psychological problems of 1916. We tentatively suggest that Barbara Low, in her double capacity as friend and medical adviser, was one of those friends: the one whom he asked for *Omoo* and *Typee* just after the bitter disappointment of Murry's departure from Zennor. We are admittedly entering the realm of conjecture; the merit of such an interpretation is that it helps to understand the changes which took place in Lawrence's attitudes between the "Love Triumphant" letters of 1912, and the 'Prologue' to *Women in Love*, which we have reasons to date in the summer of 1916.[108]

Its opening lines contain allusions to events of the early summer of 1914: the mountain-climbing tour in the Tyrol during which Birkin met Gerald, is reminiscent both of a walking tour through Switzerland with a Vickers engineer from La Spezia, and of Lawrence's trip to the Lake district in late July with Koteliansky and two other men. In view of the strange attraction exercised over Somers by Ben Cooley (*Kangaroo*, a physical portrait of Koteliansky), it does not seem altogether impossible that the "trembling nearness" felt by Birkin for Gerald, might be in some way reminiscent of that Westmorland experience. Gerald and Birkin are shown as "vividly aware of each other's presence, and each was just as vividly aware of himself, in the presence of the other".[108a]

But another element makes the dating even more certain: the allusion to another type of man which exercised a powerful fascination over Lawrence, and vividly recalls William Henry Hocking, the Cornish farmer:

> There would come into a restaurant a strange Cornish type of man, with dark eyes like holes in his head, or like the eyes of a rat, and with dark, fine, rather stiff hair, and full, heavy, strong limbs. Then again Birkin would feel the desire spring up in him, the desire to know this man, to have him, as it were to eat him, to take the very substance of him. And watching the strange, rather furtive, rabbit-like way in which the strong, softly-built man ate, Birkin would feel the rousedness burning in his own breast, as if this were what he wanted, as if the satisfaction of his desire lay in the body of the young, strong man opposite.
>
> And then in his soul would succeed a sort of despair, because this passion for a man had recurred in him. It was a deep misery to him. And it would seem as if he had always loved men, always and only loved men. And this was the greatest suffering to him.[108b]

Such passages, taken together with the descriptions of Hermione as "a prophetess violated", "a priestess", which echo not only 1915 letters to Ottoline Morrell, but also passages from *Intermediate Types among Primitive Folk*, definitely place the 'Prologue' in the period of time when Lawrence, having finished *The Rainbow*, began to work again on its sequel *Women in Love*, i.e. the spring and summer of 1916.

The suggestion made above, that Barbara Low (or possibly Dr Eder) might have drawn Lawrence's attention to an undercurrent of homosexual tendencies in his own nature, might indeed be one of several concurrent explanations of Lawrence's renewed interest in *The Intermediate Sex* which does not seem to have attracted his attention before 1914, when he started the '*Study of Thomas Hardy*'. He called the '*Hardy*' "a sort of Confessions of my Heart".[109] His use of *The Intermediate Sex* in late 1914 certainly antedates his friendship with Heseltine. The reading of *The Intermediate Sex* would thus be related to the great ferment which led to those 'Confessions'.

"It is the ultimate mark of my own deficiency, that I feel like this", thought Birkin, refusing to "face the question" of his desires for men.[110] With his usual insight and sincerity, Lawrence in the '*Study of Thomas Hardy*' states peremptorily *à propos* of Tolstoy that "a sense of fault or failure is the usual cause of a man's making himself a metaphysic, to justify himself".[111] That is exactly what he was himself doing, especially in his elaboration of the theme of the mixture of male and female in each individual. This metaphysic or "philosophy" leads, if not to the invention, at least to the execution of the character of Birkin, the would-be superman. We have shown in *D. H. Lawrence: l'homme et la genèse de son œuvre*,[112] Lawrence's debt to the theosophist idea of a news race of men, of which Birkin is the forerunner and the herald, a "fifth-rounder", one of the Sons of God. We may now see what he owes to Carpenter.

Indeed this indebtedness helps to solve a minor Lawrence mystery: his knowledge of certain aspects of esoteric tradition seems to antedate his reading of Helen Blavatsky's *Secret Doctrine*. The essential, and less intellectually repulsive, aspects of this teaching in relation to the superman are to be found in Carpenter, and in particular in a few pages of *The Intermediate Sex*, which are summarized below.

From Permissiveness to Glorification

If Lawrence, as we think is highly probable, deliberately created in Birkin a type of Messianic forerunner of a new heaven and new earth, one of the hopes of mankind after the cataclysm of "decay and decomposition" in the autumn of a dying world,[113] he had also intended him to be a "priest of love". Carpenter's Uranian, as we have seen, is not only the forerunner of the "new types of human kind"; he has a special role to play in this respect as the heaven-sent reconciler of the sexes. He is also exceptionally endowed, being "mostly of refined, sensitive nature", and the type includes a great number of individuals "highly gifted in the fine arts, especially music and poetry".[114] Some of the very greatest names "are also noted for their homogenic attachments, as well as the greatest artists".[115] By degrees Carpenter thus leads his reader to the idea that "the other" love "has its special function in social and heroic work, and in the generation . . . of those children of the mind, the philosophical conceptions which transform our lives and those of society".[116] The modern version of the idea of the hermaphrodite priest and prophet is thus formed.

From then on, as he crosses the invisible boundary between the aesthetic and philosophical on one side, and the social and political on the other, Carpenter's ideas on the heroic role of the Uranian take a turn of which certain implications were made clearer to us by the hindsight of sixty years of history. We can but see them in that light; and yet we should remember that his own contemporaries, or a man of such political naïvety as D. H. Lawrence, may have accepted them as he did himself as innocent speculations. The swastika was then only an Indian religious symbol.

An inveterate optimism, Platonic memories, and the "democratic" glamour of the story of Harmodius and Aristogiton, colour Carpenter's speculations. Perhaps there is also in his mind a hint of Fourier's conception of the specific social function of all different human types; this makes it tempting to argue that Harmodius, if his love had been for a wife and children, or if he had not had the benefit of "a close affectionate tie of some kind", might not have slain the tyrant!

> It is easy to see that while on the one hand marriage is of indispensable importance to the State as providing the workshop as it were for the breeding and rearing of children, another form of union is almost indispensable to supply the basis for social activities of other kinds.[117]
>
> . . .
>
> It is difficult to believe that anything can supply the force and liberate the energies required for social and mental activities of the most necessary kind so well as a comrade-union which yet leaves the two lovers free from the responsibilities and impediments of family life.[118]

Such rhetoric could serve a good lawyer in defence of almost anything from celibacy of priests to various less-defensible causes. Many are the new tasks offered to the modern celibate heroes: there are "hydra-headed monsters" to be slaughtered instead of tyrants, new forms of society to be built up, "new orders of thought and new institutions of human solidarity" to be established" all of which need a "comradeship as true and valiant" as that of the Dorian warriors. This leads Carpenter to the exaltation of Walt Whitman as the great apostle of male comradeship.

Walt Whitman as Preter-human Hero

Before we go further into a sequence of ideas which culminates in Lawrence's 1921 article on Whitman, it is necessary to return to earlier pronouncements of Carpenter on the American poet. Whitman had been one of his favourite themes for essays and lectures since his visits to America in 1877 and 1884.

He was for Carpenter the guide and the master, the beacon showing the way to the accomplishment of his own destiny. There is not one of his books in which he does not name him, quote him, describe his personal magnetism, and invest him with the attributes of divinity. In *The Art of Creation* he cites at some length their mutual friend Dr Bucke, relating how "it became impossible" for the Canadian alienist "*to believe that Walt Whitman was a mere man*" [*My italics*]: "It seemed to be at that time certain", Dr Bucke wrote, "that he was either *actually a God or in some sense clearly and entirely preter-human.*"[119] [*Carpenter's italics.*]

Carpenter's careful, gradual methods of exposition, ever aware as he is of his reader's possible reactions, should be borne in mind here: by quoting another, by cautious approach, he suggests rather than states. But he knows where he is going. In his *Days with Walt Whitman*, he is already quite definite: Whitman, he says, "gave you that good sense of *nowness*, that faith that the present is enjoyable, which imparts colour and life to the thousand and one dry details of existence".[120]

Not only does he find in Whitman's person and, like Lawrence, in his poetry, that mystic sense of the present, of the now, but he volunteers the thought that the poet, somewhere within himself, could see "the typical man of a new era", and "gave himself to the utterance of what he saw". In many ways Whitman

> . . . marks a stage of evolution not yet reached, and hardly suspected, by humanity at large, but in no respect is this more true than in respect of his capacity of Love. If you consider Whitman's life you will see that Love ruled it, that he gave his life for Love.[121]

Whitman thus appears as the living synthesis of Carpenter's idea of love, of his aesthetic, and of his belief in the superman. This becomes even more apparent in the essay 'Walt Whitman's

Children'. In it Carpenter asserts that "after the age of forty-five or so" Whitman had no attachments with the other sex:

> . . . whether this large attitude towards sex, this embrace which seems to reach equally to the male and female, indicates a higher development of humanity than we are accustomed to—a type supervirile, and so far above the ordinary man and woman that it looks upon both with equal eyes; or whether it indicates a personal peculiarity, this . . . I have not touched upon.[122]

Perhaps Carpenter felt it wiser in 1906 not to touch upon this delicate subject. He was however to speak his mind very clearly, in a lecture which he read in 1922 before the British Society for the Study of Sex Psychology. These outspoken views on Whitman were felt to be safe for private publication in 1924. There is no reason to think that they were not formed and either privately or semi-publicly expressed to sympathetic audiences, many years previously. It is true that Lawrence may not, that he could not, at any time relevant to the present study, have known the text of this lecture. But it can be assumed that Carpenter's views were familiar to his immediate circle of friends, and may have been known to W. E. Hopkin, among others. Could this be the meaning of Lawrence's statement in a letter to Sallie Hopkin, "the Whitman essay [which he was writing] reminds me of Willie"?[123] In his 1921 essay Lawrence shows much clearer awareness of Whitman's real attitude to women than he does in the later *Studies in Classic American Literature*, when he has partially recovered from his 1918 enthusiasm. In those, he equivocates on Whitman's women.

In the 1922 lecture, Carpenter refutes the biographers and critics who had accepted at its face value Whitman's "pose", presenting him falsely as possessing a "capacity for flirtation and carrying on with the girls": the poet's denial, in a letter to J. A. Symonds, of the "morbid inferences" drawn from '*Calamus*' and the "gospel of comradeship", was, he asserts, a lie, due to "the atmosphere on all these matters" at the time. Léon Bazalgette (a friend and correspondent of Carpenter's, who had sent him his translations of Whitman's poems, and his *Whitman, sa vie et son œuvre*, from among his publications) was unduly influenced by a sentimental French opinion "inclined towards adoration of the Female".

Carpenter's final and sincere statement, based on his talks with the Good Gray Poet, is that Whitman "was before all a lover of the Male".[124] This leads him to formulate, with at last complete frankness, his long-concealed idea of the superman:

> In fact we see plainly enough that if ever there is to be evolved a higher type of humanity of such a nature as to include male and female characteristics, it is pretty certain that on the way to that ideal will occur lop-sided and unbalanced types straying far in one or the other direction, but that we need not on that account abandon our faith in an ultimate and admirable result. . . . After all the continuation of the race is not the main object of love and sex intercourse. . . . The main thing is the actual establishment of and consolidation of a new form of life—the double life.[125]

Exactly what thoughts were current in Carpenter's circle of friends in the British Society for the Study of Sex Psychology will be appreciated from the following quotation from Dr Cecil Reddie, who incidentally was the founder, with Carpenter, R. F. Muirhead, C. R. Ashbee, G. Lowes Dickinson, etc., of Abbotsholme School in 1889. Dr Reddie, having stated that "the homogenic varieties of psychology are more numerous than most people suppose", continues:

> These types have an especial importance as mediators between the other types: which perhaps explains somewhat their considerable influence throughout history. It is indeed probable that the symbolic figure of Jesus depicts this type of mediator. At any rate it can hardly be disputed that some of the greatest men that ever lived were of this type, including Michelangelo, Shakespeare, Walt Whitman, and Edward Carpenter himself.[126]

The Love of Comrades and the Mystic Circuit of Death

We are concerned here with the implications of such beliefs only in so far as they may assist in understanding the climate in which Lawrence's writing developed mainly in the years between 1915 and 1920; even when he modified in part his earlier admiration for Whitman, and forcibly asserted his opposition to him as a believer in a political democracy of the American type,[127] he continued up to the writing of *The Plumed Serpent* to place his hopes in mystic leadership. The fact that he detached himself from, and reacted forcibly against, expressions by Carpenter and Whitman of belief in "democracy" does not mean that he did not follow some of their thoughts on leadership to their logical consequences, but simply that he was no longer satisfied with Carpenter's late-Victorian compromise with political democracy and with ambiguities which remained tolerable in Edwardian days but ceased to be acceptable after 1920.

Quoting from *Democratic Vistas*, Carpenter shows Whitman continually insisting on the social function of "intense and loving comradeships, the personal and passionate attachment of man to man".[128] "The love of comrades", "fervid comradeship", "adhesive love"—a phrase used by Whitman, as well as "adhesiveness", to express "a personal attachment between men that is stronger than ordinary friendship"[129]—these are means of counterbalancing "materialistic and vulgar American Democracy"; without "loving comradeship", democracy will be incomplete, in vain, and incapable of perpetuating itself.[130]

These statements, which Carpenter finds to have been made "with a kind of authority on the subject", lead him to note "widely through all modern society" the hidden ramifications of "the homogenic passion":

> . . . among the masses of the people as among the classes, even below the stolid surface and reserve of British manners, letters pass and enduring attachments are formed, differing in no obvious respect from those correspondences which persons of opposite sex knit with each other under similar circumstances.[131]

These unrecognized "sane and spiritual" manifestations of the love of comrades, are "really a moving force in the body politic"; as Whitman says, they have "deepest relation to general politics": an instance of this is the development of the homogenic passion in the female sex which, according to Carpenter, accompanies "the movement among women towards their own liberation and emancipation".[132]

The world would indeed be astonished "if it became widely known *who are* the Uranians". "Eros is a great leveller", and the true democracy may rest "on a sentiment which easily passes the bounds of class and caste".[133] Some "very permanent alliances grow up in this way", and who knows but "something like the guilds and fraternities of the Middle Ages might thus be reconstructed, but on a more intimate and personal basis than in those days: and indeed there are not wanting signs that such a reconstruction is actually taking place".[134]

With his characteristic optimism, Carpenter, having thus evoked in all but name the creation of secret societies of inverts—for what else does he mean, unless he is more woolly-minded than one is justified in thinking him?—foresees that

> . . . the Uranian spirit may lead to something like a general enthusiasm of Humanity, and that the Uranian people may be destined to form the advance guard of that great movement which will one day transform the common life by substituting the bond of personal affection and compassion for the monetary, legal and other external ties which now control and confine society.[135]

A German, E. Bertz, having pointed out that Whitman's gospel "derives from an abnormality" in its author, Carpenter protests that Whitman by his own confession "represents the average man"—a complete and surprising reversal of his superman theory—and that Whitman's idea of comradeship "may in course of time become a general enthusiasm".[136]

The intellectual weakness of this wishful thinking underlines the very point where Lawrence will ultimately separate himself not so much from the superman idea, as from the concepts of democracy and the average man.[137] But the Lawrence of 1917–18 is still feeling his way to his own formulations, and even if democracy and the aspects of comradeship which it implies already repel him, we find him fascinated by Whitman, and most probably by Carpenter's conception of the American poet. Indeed between Lawrence and Whitman, a dialogue has been going on since early youth. Even the strident tones of some of Lawrence's later pronouncements allow expression of the admiration which the American has inspired: "Whitman, the great poet, has meant so much to me." That is the cry from the heart.[138] In between the early readings of Whitman to Jessie Chambers and Louie Burrows,[139] and the denunciation of 'One Identity' and 'En-Masse' in the *Studies in Classic American Literature*, Lawrence often sees Whitman sanely: now he refers to the "self-revelation of a man who could not live, and so had to write himself . . . really false as hell . . . but . . . fine too";[140] later, in 'Democracy', he tries to reduce to its essence the concept of democracy which Whitman shares with Carpenter.[141]

But in 1918, and in the 1921 essay, a different view prevails, one which, we hope to show, owes much to the presentation of Whitman by Carpenter in *The Intermediate Sex*. This is the time for Lawrence of the great esoteric temptation, and of the wholehearted exaltation of male comradeship, on which he will nervously, shamefacedly, go back later.

His real feeling is expressed in a private letter:

> You are a great admirer of Whitman, R. said. So am I. But I find in his '*Calamus*' and Comrades one of the clues to a real solution—the new adjustment. I believe in what he calls "manly love", the real implicit reliance of one man on another: as sacred a unison as marriage: only it must be deeper, more ultimate than emotion and personality, cool separateness and yet the ultimate reliance.[142]

"What a great poet Whitman is: great like a great Greek," he exclaims in his Whitman essay of 1921. He is "on the shore of the last sea", at "the extreme of time; so near to death"; he is responsible "for the *great new era of mankind*", which will be established on "*the sheer friendship, the love between comrades,* the manly love which alone can create a new era of life".[143] [*My italics.*]

Who is speaking here, the author of *The Intermediate Sex* or that of *Women in Love*? Carpenter had presented the Gray Poet as "the inauguration of a new world of democratic ideals and literature and . . . the most Greek in spirit and performance of modern writers".[144]

Lawrence of course is a poet, and as such finds in Whitman a model of his aesthetic, of his conception of form as coming "new each time from within"; he does not need a model to express his admiration. But is it possible that in this appreciation of Whitman he echoes John Burroughs's *Flight of the Eagle,* quoted in Carpenter's *Days with Walt Whitman*?

Form, with Whitman, is not "a thing apart" according to Burroughs; it "vanishes in the meaning" like our bodies after death. The emotions which he expresses could not "be caged in a symmetrical verse or stanza". When he is

> . . . thus soaring in freedom and the fulness of power . . . he finds a rhythm and a music of his own. . . . His lines are pulsations, thrills, waves of force, indefinite dynamics, formless, constantly emanating from the living centre, and they carry the quality of the author's personal presence with them in a way that is unprecedented in literature.[145]

In infinitely better prose Lawrence says much the same:

> Whitman, at his best, is purely himself. His verse springs sheer from the spontaneous sources of his being. Hence its lovely, lovely form and rhythm: at the best it is sheer, perfect *human* spontaneity, undecorated, unclothed. The whole being is there, sensually throbbing, spiritually quivering, mentally, ideally speaking. . . . It is perfect and whole. The whole soul speaks at once, and it is too pure for mechanical assistance of rhyme and measure.[146]

Such resemblance as there is does not enable one to assert that this passage is a "source": what matters however is the essential resemblance, namely the belief, which in 1919 he still shared with Carpenter, that the love of comrades could change the world, inaugurate the mutation which would "establish the new, perfect circuit of our being", "link up the mystic circuit".[147]

The difference is in the perception that "the love of comrades", if it leads to identification of the individual with the mass, with democracy, to "merging", will result in "only a half truth". "The other half is Jehovah, and Egypt, and Sennacherib: the other form of Allness, terrible and grand, even as in the Psalms."[148] Lawrence had seen through the contradiction between superman and average man, and in so far as he still believed in the superman, he then opted for his leadership and authoritarian rule, not for democracy. '*Education of the People*', written and rewritten during the same months as the various Whitman essays, testifies to this.

In 1920, when he revised in Sicily his 1918 'Whitman', and presumably *a fortiori* in 1918 when he first wrote it, the thought of the male superman still predominated over all other concerns: his sympathy then went out to Whitman, not as the advocate and prophet of democracy, but as the superman for whom, as for Michelangelo,

> . . . the woman is reduced, really, to a submissive function. She is no longer an individual being with a living soul. She must fold her arms and bend her head and submit to her functioning capacity. Function of sex, function of birth.[149]

He found in the Whitman of '*Calamus*' the glorification of the warrior:

> Acting from the last and profoundest centres, man acts womanless. It is no longer a question of race continuance. It is a question of sheer, ultimate being, the perfection of life, nearest to death. Acting from these centres, man is an extreme being, the unthinkable warrior, creator, mover, and maker.[150]

Whitman has known "positively" that "the polarity is between man and man" not "negatively" like others who have wished to "*épater le bourgeois*"—perhaps a passing contemptuous allusion to Oscar Wilde.[151] Lawrence expresses special admiration for the '*Calamus*' poems, with their sense of death, the poems in which Whitman abandons his pose as a womanizer, and proclaims that he will "sound [himself] and comrades only . . . never again utter a call, only their call".

In his praise of '*Calamus*', can anyone really think that Lawrence, as his 1923 essay tries to suggest, was ignorant of the real meaning and intention of that sequence? His images and thoughts are identical when he speaks of Whitman and of Sappho: "Sappho leaped off into the sea of death."[152] Whitman, "great like a great Greek", finds himself "on the shore of the last sea. The extremes of life: so near to death", at the point of responsibility for "the new great era of mankind", which will be established "on the perfect circuits of vital flow between human beings". What was meant by those "circuits", and how they relate to death, the reader of the poem 'Manifesto' and of the chapter 'Excurse' in *Women in Love* may understand with the help of J. M. Pryse's chart of the *chakras*, some of which Lawrence finds he cannot refer to in print in *Psychoanalysis and the Unconscious*.[153] Indeed "creative life must come near to death, to link up the mystic circuit" that of "the manly love which alone can create a new era of life" and which will "surpass" marriage, having "no ulterior motive whatever, like procreation": "the great life-circuit which borders on death in all its round".[154]

Whitman and Lawrence

Whitman's influence on Lawrence has been deep and prolonged: the 1921 essay marks its climax. Does it owe anything directly to Carpenter as a poet and disciple of Whitman? It is not possible to answer this question categorically. Carpenter himself was too deeply steeped in Whitman's thoughts and images for the two influences to be separable. But Lawrence's permanent debate with Whitman begins with his study of *The Intermediate Sex*; it throws light on his own divided self, on his debate with himself and with the man he had been. 'Art and the Individual' had shown him torn, in 1908, between his nascent aesthetic, and his allegiance to socialist friends, trying to find his way between the two, between "the individual character" and "what is general in the human character". Divided as was indeed Carpenter, whose contradictions are aptly described by E. M. Forster:

> Like most mystics, he wanted both to merge in the universe and to retain his identity, and since he was neither a strong nor a wary thinker he brought forward no plausible solution of the contradiction.[155]
>
> * * *
>
> It was the socialism of Shelley and Blake. He strove to destroy existing abuses such as landlordism, and capitalism, and all he offered in their place was love. He was not interested in efficiency or organization, or party discipline, nor industrialism, though he tried to be. He believed in Liberty, Fraternity and Equality—words now confined to platforms and perorations. He saw the New Jerusalem from afar, from the ignoble slough of his century, and there is no doubt that it does look more beautiful from a distance.[156]

Sometimes Lawrence defines with clarity a point on which he differs from both Whitman and Carpenter, although he does not name the latter: he sees that "spiritual and mystical needs" have "nothing to do with the average"—as if his 'Democracy' essay[157] were an answer to Carpenter's ineffectual rejoinder to E. Bertz. But he also sees clearly, with genuine sympathy and insight, what democracy meant for Whitman and for Carpenter. It is not a political or social system:

> It is an attempt to conceive a new way of life, to establish new values. It is a struggle to liberate human beings from the fixed, arbitrary control of ideals, into free spontaneity.[158]

Here is the meeting ground of all three poets, the reconciliation of their separate quests. Lawrence, however, because he is a man of the twentieth century, an Edwardian trying his best to understand Georgian Europe, Mussolini's Italy, and the America of

Harding and Coolidge, is attracted by the marching in step of comrades after the war: in that, he is closer to the poet of the War of Secession, than to the 'New Life' perfectionist and Fabian socialist. His idea of the love of comrades leads more consciously, more dangerously than it did with Carpenter, to secret societies and esoteric action groups:

> Let [men] realize that they must go beyond their women, projected into a region of greater abstraction, more inhuman activity . . . There, in these womenless regions of fight and pure thought and abstracted instrumentality, let men have a new attitude to one another. Let them have a new reverence for their heroes, a new regard for their comrades: deep, deep as life and death . . . and the extreme bond of deathless friendship supports them over the edge of the known and into the unknown.[159]

The marching of storm-troopers and the strains of the *Horst Wessel* song already echo through those sentences. And yet how close, how faithful they are in spirit to some of the implications of *The Intermediate Sex* and of '*Calamus*'! When the shrill accents of opposition and anger against the disappointing New World democracy of machines calm down, when a more balanced Lawrence thinks calmly and serenely of the positive development of man, how close he is again to the best of Whitman and the best of Carpenter in their approach to a definition of democracy. His anger against the misuses of the world *love* and its Christian connotations of self-sacrifice subsides, and he offers *sympathy* as the term defining his own and Whitman's positive conception of the accomplishment of the soul in communion with others:

> The love of man and woman: a recognition of souls, and a communion of worship. The love of comrades: a recognition of souls, and a communion of worship. Democracy: a recognition of souls, all down the open road, and a great soul seen in its greatness, as it travels on foot among the rest, down the common way of living. A glad recognition of souls, and a gladder worship of great and greater souls, because they are the only riches.[160]

"Recognition of souls", this exactly defines the many instances in Lawrence's novels and short stories when eyes meet casually and two people exchange a deeper and eternal knowledge, just as when the poet of *Towards Democracy* encounters in the crowd a little ragged boy, and "in an instant" clearly sees in his eyes "the lie . . . and the truth, the false dreams and the awakening . . . the joy of free open life under the sun . . . sweet comradeship, few needs and common pleasures".[161] The climate is the same, it is that of the sudden revelation to a young and eager Eastwood boy of the beauty of life and friendship.

This 1923 essay on Whitman is not the end of Lawrence's continued dialogue with himself, with the Good Gray Poet and with the spirit of Carpenter's *Towards Democracy*: but it is one of the moments where his deeper, his more permanent feelings express themselves without opposition or discord, defining the best of himself and of his need for human recognition and communion. It is permissible to think that this instant of unison with Whitman is also a momentary return to his old adolescent self, free from the stresses of unresolved psychological problems.

The passages quoted from E. M. Forster exactly situate the temperamental resemblances between Lawrence and Carpenter: superficial divergences on politics are of minor importance, compared with their deep affinities as mystics. How would Carpenter's socialism have developed had he known the nineteen-thirties, how would Lawrence's hatred of democracy and equality have evolved had he witnessed the rise of national socialism in Germany and the nineteen-forties? These are speculative questions. The fact that the mystic ideas of both men potentially contained seeds of sinister historical developments does not constitute a judgment on either. Robust good sense was mixed with the maddest speculations in both; inadaptation to an ordinary social life, sexual anomalies or frustrations, led both to try to forge for themselves a total explanation of human nature embracing their own problems into a norm; they could not but fail as soon as this endeavour tried to encompass the social side of individual lives.

The temptation of leadership, however, linked with a

fundamental mysticism, lasted with Lawrence almost to the end, as is suggested by his associating in the same thought, in 1928, Annie Besant, Gandhi and Mussolini, as being among the rare true leaders left.[162] To what extent Carpenter's mysticism had contributed to the development of that idea of leadership is a subject on which this study may have thrown some light.

Frustration and Withdrawal

Any divergences between the political attitudes of the two men during and after the First World War appear, in the light of what we have seen of the relationship of their modes of thought, as being of secondary importance. Their differences are mainly those between generations. Like many of his Labour friends, Carpenter as early as 1916 placed his hopes in the idea of the League of Nations, of which he became an ardent supporter. Lawrence pooh-poohed the idea and scorned the institution almost as derisively as did Mussolini. He scoffed at political democracy, while retaining his faith in a democracy of his own dreaming, which did not differ much from Carpenter's own conception of the free and spontaneous individual. Both tended to make a limited idea of civilization the scapegoat of their frustration in a man-made environment.

Both were in fact dreamers in love with a Golden Age. For the Victorian it was still easy to see the millenium just round the corner. As England emerged from the Edwardian transition it became difficult for Lawrence to believe in that millenium. The 1914–18 deluge fostered in his mind the politics of frustration and despair; it increased his disgust with "the dream-helplessness of the mass-psyche"[163] and encouraged him in the vain quest for "life-submission" to the "heroic soul of a greater man".[164] Fortunately for him and others it did not lead him into action, only into a dream-world of mystic and heroic fulfilment in the form of the cruel fantasy of *The Plumed Serpent*.

Faced with the post-war world, the receptive Edwardian became an echo of the new movements agitating that period. His dreams reveal how sensitive he was to currents which stronger and equally frustrated men exploited ruthlessly for their own ends: movements leading away from "a theoretical socialism started by Jews like Marx, and appealing only to the will-power of the masses, making money the whole crux".[165] Movements seeking "a new tie between men", a "new democracy", based on Whitman's "love of comrades",[166] "a new recognition of the life mystery".[167] Yet the essence of Carpenter's criticism and faith is found among the last words of *Kangaroo* in which Lawrence states his intention to withdraw from the world of men: Somers, who is Lawrence, declares himself "the enemy of machine-civilization and this ideal civilization"; but he is in favour of "the deep, self-responsible consciousness in man, which is what I mean by civilization".[168]

Outward forms and circumstances have altered, the pace of civilization has accelerated and the places where a man can be alone with his contemplation of nature have shrunk, but the dream and the thought remain identical. Somers wished to go into the Australian bush "to have a house and a cow of my own—and—damn everything":[169] a solution, except for the important last words, just one step further from the social world of men than the Victorian compromise between nature and civilization illustrated by Carpenter's life at Millthorpe.

7

CONCLUSIONS

What began many years ago as a chance observation of similarities between two authors—one already famous, the other slowly receding into near oblivion after being keenly present in the minds of most English and American literary men and women of his day—has now led us to a close comparison of their ideas, their favourite themes, and some of their familiar images. This comparison has stopped at the close of the formative years of the younger writer. It might also have led to a more detailed analysis of their personalities; but that analysis belongs to the fields of psychology and perhaps social pathology more than to literary studies; we have therefore not directly attempted it, while sketching out some of the more visible similarities in those domains.

We have seen how, after 1919, certain themes absorbed and meditated in youth had become such an integral part of Lawrence's personality, that further comparison would have tended to become both artificial and futile, as the preceding chapter suggests; we may note that our remarks in the first chapter on Ouspensky's *Tertium Organum* do not contradict that suggestion. That is not to say that Carpenter's influence had lapsed: but it had become so thoroughly assimilated that it had ceased to be distinguishable from Lawrence's own mental universe.

This study therefore comes to its natural close with Lawrence's passage into his mature years, during which his characteristic attitudes and ideas found their full and highly personal expression in his novels and short stories. Those attitudes did not change much after 1920, when, except for the *Fantasia of the Unconscious*, he stopped writing "theoretical" works and devoted himself to more artistically rewarding writings. At no time however did he depart from his preference for some form of Eros over Civilization, from his denunciation of the "mental" and the "ideal", from his passionate quest for communion with and faithfulness to the life force, to what he calls "the quick of life". He will remain rooted in his conviction that life *is* the individual, a fairly self-evident truth, related, in his psyche, in the very vehemence of its assertion, to his inability to see or conceive the social, except perhaps in the mystical form of the "love of comrades" and of a type of leadership illustrated by *The Plumed Serpent*.

From this social and religious fantasy, he will pass on to withdrawal into the acceptance of death. But before he achieved that relative peace, violence and cruelty, those characteristics of our age—which in spite of his call to "freedom and Savagery", would have revolted such a gentle nature as Carpenter's—had become part of Lawrence's later religion, as indeed they were already inherent in his very earliest works. *The Plumed Serpent* belongs to the twentieth century, by this insistence on violence in the name of inhuman gods. Its violence is that of hopelessness before the social problems of man. If in it civilization is submerged, can anyone pretend that Eros triumphs?

After *Aaron's Rod* and *Kangaroo*, is not *The Plumed Serpent* the logical translation into an action-fantasy of the theme of the superman as we have seen it gradually emerging from Carpenter's ethic and aesthetic and from his religion of reincarnation and of the race-self?

The present study could most probably not answer those questions, even if it had been thought advisable to follow through those later works the meanderings of currents of thought which have been traced in the earlier Lawrence in their relation to Carpenter's views. But it does invite further thought concerning the consequences of ideas prevalent in the atmosphere of the early years of this century—ideas on the relationship of the individual and social organization, whether the individual be considered as genius, e.g. Nietzsche, Wagner, Lawrence, or as the anonymous everybody suffering from a vague sense of alienation. In fact this study raises the problem of mental health in relation to the creative values and the normative or therapeutic merits of art, in so far as mental health includes ability, acquired in family life, to adjust to a social environment. The Lawrence critic is sooner or later faced with the problem of catharsis in literary creation, and our analysis faintly suggests that Lawrence's social trauma, whatever its spontaneous psychological sources, might well have been aggravated by the writings of Carpenter, because of a profound and long-unconscious similarity of their personalities.

* * *

Our factual study has established that Lawrence had read Carpenter's works, and indeed that he was not once but repeatedly subjected to their action. First of all in early youth at Eastwood, where autographed copies of Carpenter's works, including *Angels' Wings*, were among the treasured possessions of Willie Hopkin; most probably during 1912, certainly again in late 1914 and in 1916, and up to 1918 if not later. To say the least, over a period ranging perhaps from before 1906 to 1918, Carpenter was consistently present in Lawrence's mental environment: through his Eastwood friends up to 1912, and through a community of spiritual interests, as a member of a wide literary and philosophical or occultist circle during the war years. *The New Age*, *The English Review*, and *The Occult Review*, help define that circle. Common friends, common interests, common oppositions, were numerous enough to provide a solid base of facts to comparative studies.

While internal evidence cannot categorically prove definite borrowings, it strongly suggests them, and it testifies to the existence of whole similar courses of thinking, in late 1912 and early 1913, in late 1914, and between the end of 1915 and the drafting in Sicily of the second version of the Whitman essay. After that date, the debate continues between Lawrence and Whitman, inseparable from, but greater than, Carpenter: just as the debate endlessly goes on between Lawrence and himself, between the exile of Taormina, of Taos or of Florence, and the boy from the Midlands mining village and the country of Robin Hood.

Taken together with the results of our factual contribution, textual comparisons at the very least reveal a remarkable similarity of ideas, of vocabulary and imagery, between *Love's Coming of Age*, *The Art of Creation*, *The Drama of Love and Death*, and the writings of Lawrence between 1912 and 1914. From late 1914 to 1918 *Intermediate Types among Primitive Folk* and *The Intermediate Sex* are more prominent among probable sources of much of Lawrence's work, from the '*Study of Thomas Hardy*' to the final writing of *Women in Love* and of its suppressed 'Prologue', as well as to '*The Reality of Peace*' essays and the early versions of the American Literature papers, notably 'The Two Principles' and the second 'Whitman'.

The tentative chronological sequence offered in our first chapter is thus confirmed, and gains in precision through textual study. This textual analysis also tends to enhance the role of Carpenter's influence on Lawrence's reading of Melville, as it tends to show that *The Intermediate Sex* and *Intermediate Types* played a vital part in forming or modifying Lawrence's judgments on homosexuality. Those ideas in turn, as manifested in the 'Prologue' to *Women in Love*, in the 1921 'Whitman', in '*Education of the People*', and in various other writings of the same period, throw a much needed light on Lawrence's intentions, and on the views underlying his creative writings of that time, as well as on the variations, nature and value of his interest in and "teaching" on love between man and woman. They raise serious doubts as to the so-called "normative" values of *Women in Love*.

* * *

Such thinkers as Bergson and Freud are freely named by critics as early influences on Lawrence's works. We hope to have shown conclusively that the ideas which were in his mind when he wrote his two most ambitious novels, the two most definitely structured on a system of ideas, owed very little to Bergson and next to nothing to Freud. He did not have to look so far from home for his psychology, and he had found it ready-made in his Midlands as a complement to the more orthodox teaching at Nottingham University College. Even his interest in yoga, in the Vedas, in Asia, even his determination to go to America via India and Ceylon, might be imputed to Carpenter and to very early and durable impressions. As for his aesthetic, deeply indebted as it is to English romantic tradition, and influenced by late nineteenth-century realism, it seems based on a synthesis of ideas which is found in Carpenter as much as in symbolism and post-realist literature and art.

An idiosyncratic process of Lawrence's creative writing is the unceasing return to the mystery of his own character and ego, the need to discover a satisfactory explanation for the failures of his youth, and most of all for the failure of "the great experiment of sex" with Jessie Chambers. From *Sons and Lovers* to *Women in Love*, and still, although in a different mood, in *Lady Chatterley's Lover*, Lawrence harks back to that searing experience. For some year, from the time of his legal marriage to Frieda until he finally accepted his dependence upon "the Queen Bee", he pursued the attempt to understand the reasons of his failure to combine the love of the flesh and that of the spirit.

And somehow, the realization that he loved men as much or more than he did women, appears to have dawned upon him between the summer of 1914 and the writing of the revelatory 'Prologue' to *Women in Love* in Cornwall in 1916. The internal evidence from his works which suggests this is definitely linked with the influence and use of Carpenter's books on the intermediate sex: we feel that it is safe to conclude that Lawrence's interest in those books contains a decisive confirmation of the nature of his change of attitude to love, and helps towards an understanding of a troubled and obscure period of his life and some well-identified obscurities in his novels.

* * *

However important these discoveries may be from the biographical angle, it should be remembered that Lawrence is first of all a poet and a novelist, who will continue to interest and attract readers independently of any incidents in his life. How does the influence of Carpenter affect the understanding and appreciation of his works of imagination?

Let us first of all dispose of any suggestion of common plagiarism. There are, it is true, definite resemblances between whole passages of Carpenter (for instance on marriage) and scenes in *Women in Love*. The novel may be considered as an illustration in action of ideas received from the author of *Love's Coming of Age*. But there is no question of plagiarism or of copying; this is part of the normal process of imaginative creation, which Lawrence understood perfectly when he wrote "One can only build a great abstraction out of concrete units":[1] he was constructing the concrete units out of the abstractions of Carpenter, and this is fair play in literature.

His poetry and his aesthetics of poetry owe much to Whitman. The influence of the great American, as we have seen, is often indistinguishable from that of his English disciple Carpenter. We have produced evidence of the interest of Lawrence in *Towards Democracy*: the two influences merge, and yet both are perceptible. Both are of historical and biographical rather than poetic interest. Lawrence's poetry is his own, being the lyrical expression of what he was, irrespective of how he became what he was.

The White Peacock and *Sons and Lovers* are novels largely based on the writer's personal, immediate environment: descriptive and narrative works in which realism is the starting-point, followed by the attempt to extract from scenes taken from life, a deeper, hidden, secret meaning. This method is close to the aesthetics of *Angels' Wings*, a book which appears to have exercised a potent effect upon the early aesthetic conceptions of the young novelist. Not only themes and images, but the mystic attitude inspiring *The Art of Creation* and *The Drama of Love and Death*, can be traced down to the final chapters of *Sons and Lovers*, and to the 'Foreword' written after the final revision of the novel.

That 'Foreword' opens a period of intense ferment and proliferation of themes and ideas in Lawrence's mind. For the first time not only does he then conceive a vast new work not directly dependent on environment and autobiography, or, like *The Trespasser*, on the relation of an incident in another person's life, but upon a general conception of human character, of the Fall and Redemption, of the soul's pilgrimage through generations, from Golden Age back to Paradise. *The Rainbow* and *Women in Love*, but for accidents on the way, rest upon this conception. Their unity, the links between the generation of Brangwens, between Ursula as a child and young girl, and the different Ursula of *Women in Love* (a difference much commented on, and now perhaps intelligible), the very nature of the contrasts between generations and between couples, to some extent obscured by the vicissitudes of drafting and changes of emphasis due to Lawrence's shifting moods—all these none the less appear when one compares the novels with Carpenter's idea of the soul's evolution through the three stages of consciousness, of redemption through cosmic union. New, and we hope definitive, light is thus thrown on the intentions of the artist at the vital creative moment.

The birth of the much-discussed Lawrentian idea of the character in the modern novel, free from "a certain moral scheme" and from the artificial obligation of internal consistency; the origin of the formulation of the quest for the "physical" in the human being; these too fall into an English perspective, as being part of an integrated system of ethical and aesthetic interpretation, closely allied to a religious attitude which Lawrence was at pains to assert at the same time of his life. The Lawrence of 1913 becomes more comprehensible, the links between his old Eastwood self and his new creations appear more clearly, and this in turn makes his later return to his origins, his passionate retrospective self-analysis in the *Study of Thomas Hardy*, more intelligible and more revealing.

Women in Love and its 'Prologue', following soon after the '*Hardy*', also become more intelligible as a partial confession, when viewed in the light of Lawrence's study of *The Intermediate Sex* in 1916. It becomes clear that by then Carpenter's works had assumed a special significance for Lawrence in his search for a clue to his own nature. "Passionate experience" indeed is the key, as he points out,[2] to the poems and novels: but experience relived, re-examined in relation to what must have seemed to him then a "philosophy" containing the clues to his passions and his failures.

The love of comrades, the praise of Whitman, the lassitude with woman whom he too wished to reduce to her "functions", following the examples of Whitman and Michelangelo, and of Carpenter up to a point, also fall into place. So does the later revulsion from Whitman, the stridency and almost double-faced denial of past enthusiasm and temptations in *Studies in Classic American Literature*:

> Walt was really too superhuman. The danger of the Superman is that he is mechanical.
>
> . . .
>
> If I'd been one of his women I'd have given him Female, with a flea in his ear.[3]

Here the Lawrence of 1923 goes back on his 1918–19 self, still recognizable in the 1921 Whitman essay; he has renounced the love of comrades, he no longer thinks that "out of this manly love will come the inspiration of the future".[4] "It slides over into death. David and Jonathan. And the death of Jonathan. It always slides into death. The love of comrades."[5] His waking self has given up the temptation of Jonathan's love, at which he had shyly hinted in *Art and the Individual*.

This was the end of the overt dialogue, and this perhaps answers our earlier question: why did Lawrence remain completely silent on the meaning of Carpenter to him? The retort to Whitman "with a flea in his ear" rings like one of Frieda's rejoinders, and also like an echo from the voice of the poet's dead mother. The female is triumphant, the Great Mother has won the battle against the superman and the love of comrades.

Did Lawrence and Frieda, after 1921, think that it was better for his public image to delete all traces of the intellectual and emotional temptations of his darker years, as Frieda certainly did after his death? Were the reasons for his silence the same that led him to suppress the 'Prologue' to *Women in Love*? That is, a mixture of legal and social precautions, and a general wish to safeguard his fragile reputation?

While it cannot answer this question finally, our comparative study does bring some corroboration to scanty biographical data, and we hope it may enable the reader of Lawrence's wartime and later novels to assess their moral and aesthetic values, and after measuring the distance between original intentions and ultimate achievement, still to appreciate that which is best and most durable in Lawrence's art.

NOTES

ABBREVIATIONS OCCURRING IN THE NOTES

A. of C.	*The Art of Creation* (E C)
A.W.	*Angels' Wings* (E C)
C.C.C.	*Civilization, Its Cause and Cure* (E C)
C.L.	*The Collected Letters of D H L*
C.P.	*Complete Poems* (D H L)
C.S.St.	*The Complete Short Stories* (D H L)
D.H.L.	D H Lawrence
D.H.L. etc.	Delavenay: *D. H. Lawrence: l'homme et la genèse de son œuvre*
D.L.D.	*The Drama of Love and Death* (E C)
D.W.W.W.	*Days with Walt Whitman* (E C)
E.C.	Edward Carpenter
E.T.	Jessie Chambers: *D H Lawrence, A Personal Record*
Fantasia	*Fantasia of the Unconscious* (D H L)
F.A.P.E.	*From Adam's Peak to Elephanta* (E C)
H.E.	Havelock Ellis
Int.H.	Harry T Moore, *The Intelligent Heart*
I.S.	*The Intermediate Sex* (E C)
I.T.A.P.F.	*Intermediate Types among Primitive Folk* (E C)
L.	*The Letters of D H Lawrence*
L.C.A.	*Love's Coming of Age* (E C)
M.D.D.	*My Days and Dreams* (E C)
Nehls	Edward Nehls: *D H Lawrence, A Composite Biography*
Ph.	*Phoenix* (D H L)
Ph.II	*Phoenix* II (D H L)
Ps.U.	*Psychoanalysis and the Unconscious* (D H L)
R.D.P.	'Reflections on the Death of a Porcupine' (D H L)
Rw.	*The Rainbow* (D H L)
S. & L.	*Sons and Lovers* (D H L)
S.C.A.L.	*Studies in Classic American Literature* (D H L)
S.F. of W.W.	*Some Friends of Walt Whitman* (E C)
S.M.	*The Symbolic Meaning* (D H L)
S. of T.H.	'Study of Thomas Hardy' (D H L)

T.D.	*Towards Democracy* (E C)
T.I.	*Twilight in Italy* (D H L)
Wh.P.	*The White Peacock* (D H L)
W.L.	*Women in Love* (D H L)

Introduction

1. Thomas Mann, *Lotte in Weimar*, translated by H. T. Lowe-Porter: Harmondsworth, Penguin, 1968, p. 62.

2. *Ibid.*, p. 61.

3. Leonard Woolf, *Downhill all the Way*: London, Hogarth Press, p. 59.

4. Pierre Auger, "Le Régime des Castes dans les Populations d'Idées", *Diogène* No 22, Gallimard, 1958.

5. *Fantasia of the Unconscious*, pp. 7–8.

6. *Ibid.*, p. 9

7. M.D.D., p. 208.

8. *The Savage Pilgrimage*, p. 63; *Lorenzo in Taos*, p. 59.

Chapter 1

1. T. D., 1949 edition, p. 11.

2. M.D.D., p. 14.

3. Irene Clephane, *Towards Sex Freedom*: London, John Lane, The Bodley Head, 1935, pp. 183–4.

4. M.D.D., p. 42.

5. M.D.D., p. 35.

6. Charles Kingsmith in *Edward Carpenter: In Appreciation*, p. 226; Hugh Dalton, *Call Back Yesterday*, 1887–1931, 1953.

7. M.D.D., p. 77. One cannot but be struck by the similarity between this passage, published in June 1916, and a few lines in the 'Prologue' to *Women in Love, Phoenix II*, pp. 104–5.

8. I.S. pp. 64–6.

9. Arthur Calder-Marshall, *Havelock Ellis, a biography*: London, Rupert Hart-Davis, 1959, p. 86.

10. Professor William Knight, *Thomas Davidson*, 1840–1900. *Memorials of Thomas Davidson, the Wandering Scholar*, p. 7.

11. St John Ervine, *Bernard Shaw, His Life, Works and Friends*, p. 120.

12. Lord Elton, *The Life of James Ramsay MacDonald* (1866–1939), pp. 61, 64–5.

13. A. Calder-Marshall, *loc. cit.*, p. 152. "After his introduction, he reviewed previous writers on the subject and then analyzed the development of sexual inversion in men and women, illustrating his points from the case histories

provided by Symonds, Carpenter and his wife from their own experience and that of their friends. What distinguished Ellis's histories from those published previously was that they were not drawn from police and alienist records but from members of society at large and people of more than normal intelligence." Carpenter's case history is case No VI in Ellis's *Studies*, beginning with the words: "My parentage is very sound and healthy".

14. Archibald Henderson, *George Bernard Shaw, Man of the Century*, p. 544.

15. M.D.D., p. 135.

16. M.D.D., p. 144. "*A Visit to a Gñani*", extracted from *Adam's Peak to Elephanta*, relates the visit to the Eastern Sage".

17. M.D.D., p. 164.

18. See below, Chapter III, p. 86.

19. Philip Snowden, *An Autobiography*, p. 61.

20. M.D.D., p. 134.

21. F. M. Ford quoted in Nehls, I, p. 152, from pp. 176–8 of *Return to Yesterday*.

22. E.T., *D. H. Lawrence, A Personal Record*, p. 120. In a letter quoted below Mrs Enid Hilton states: "Alice Dax was a great admirer of Carpenter. She had all his books and *I think* that she and Lawrence argued a great deal about him." (18 January 1969).

23. Delavenay, *D.H.L., etc.*, Appendice IV.

24. Enid Hilton, quoted by Harry T. Moore, *Int, H.*, p. 134. For 'Simplification of Life' see Carpenter's *England's Ideal*, 1887, and *Angels' Wings*, 1898.

25. Letter from Alice Dax to Frieda Lawrence, in the latter's *Memoirs and Correspondence*, p. 217.

26. Moore, *loc. cit.*, pp. 134–5. See above on Carpenter's friendship with Ramsay MacDonald from the latter's early youth and Bristol days.

27. C.L., p. 227, 18 Sept. 1913.

28. Letter to the author from Olive Hopkin, 6 April 1967.

28a. Letter to the author from Mrs Enid Hilton, 18 January 1969.

29. 'The Schoolmaster', *cf. Complete Poems*, pp. 894–904; 'Dreams Old and Nascent,' *cf. ibid*, pp. 905–9; in particular 'Nascent,' pp. 908–9, a poem much rewritten between its first publication in *The English Review* (November 1909) and *Collected Poems*, 1928. These lines are sheer imitation of 'Towards Democracy':

Through the wakened afternoon, riding down my dreams
Fluent active figures of men pass along the railway.
There is something stirs in me from the flow of their limbs as they move
Out of the distance, nearer.
Here in the subtle, rounded flesh
Beats the active ecstasy, suddenly lifting my eyes
Into quick response.

The fascination of the restless Creator, through the mesh of men
Moving, vibrating endlessly in the rounded flesh
Challenges me, and is answered.

The reader may compare this with the 'Prologue' to *Women in Love* (*Phoenix II*) and draw his own conclusions. He will also compare '*Virgin Youth*' (C.P., p. 893) and '*The Wild Common*' (*ibid*., p. 891) as being of the same vein.

30. From a letter from Helen Corke to the author, 9 October 1968.

31. C.L., pp. 170–1. For the enduring memory of Alice Dax, *cf*. 'Prologue' to *Women in Love*, *loc. cit*., p. 106: "He went into violent excess with a mistress whom, in a rather anti-social, ashamed spirit, he loved. And so for a long time he forgot about the attraction that man had for him."

32. C.L., pp. 172–3.

33. C.L., p. 307. For American sources to Lawrence's Rananim idea, *cf*. Delavenay, *D. H. L., etc*., Livre II, Ch. IV

34. C.L., p. 368.

35. C.L., pp. 360–3; Lady Cynthia Asquith, *Diaries* 1915–18: London, Hutchinson, 1968 p. 70.

36. Sir Stanley Unwin, *The Truth about Publishing*.

37. *Cf* Delavenay, *D.H.L., etc*., Livre II, Ch. III.

38. C.L., p. 316. The rumour was reported by E. M. Forster. The publisher, Duckworth, has no records of that period.

39. Lady Cynthia Asquith, *loc. cit*., p. 85. "They take such an exalted point of view about the war—calling it blasphemy, etc.—that I am not at all sure that technically it doesn't amount to treason. Certainly it might be said to discourage recruiting. Poor fools, it's not a good moment in which to hope to found a new religion." The "poor fools" are Lawrence and Middleton Murry.

40. For facsimiles of relevant Home Office documents see Delavenay, *loc. cit*., pp. 305–8.

41. *The English Review*, September 1914 to January 1915.

41a. On the manipulation to which the senior staff of Methuen were subjected on the part of Detective-Inspector Draper, very probably on the advice of the solicitor acting for the Commissioner of Metropolitan Police, see *The Times Literary Supplement*, 27 February 1969, John Carter, "The Rainbow Prosecution", and 17 April 1969, letter from the present author.

42. Letters communicated by Mrs Olive Hopkin.

43. E. Carpenter to Helen Corke, 24 August 1916, quoted in a letter from Helen Corke to the author, 9 October 1968.

44. C.L., pp. 404–5.

45. The review in *The New Age*, 4 April 1912, of *The Drama of Love and Death*, is definitely chilly.

46. C.L., pp. 354 and 385.

47. Cecil Gray, *Musical Chairs*, p. 129.

48. C.L., p. 511.
49. C.L., p. 562.
50. C.L., p. 491.
51. *The Symbolic Meaning*, 253*ff*.
52. C.L., p. 556, June 1918.
53. Cecil Gray, *Peter Warlock, p.* 67
53a. Letter to the author, 18 January 1969.
54. Lady Cynthia Asquith, *Diaries* 1915–18, 9 March 1918, etc.
55. Concerning D. H. Lawrence's fears on this score, *cf.* Delavenay, *loc. cit.*, Livre II, Ch. IX and n. 113.
56. *Cf.* Delavenay, "Le Phénix et ses Cendres," *Etudes Anglaises*, XXI–4, 1968.
57. *John Bull*, 17 September 1921.
57a. Letter to the author, 7 February 1969.
58. E. W. Tedlock, Jr., "D. H. Lawrence's Annotations of Ouspensky's *Tertium Organum*", in *Texas Studies in Literature and Language*, Vol. II, No. 2, Summer 1960, pp. 206–18.
59. Cecil Reddie, *Edward Carpenter, 1844–1929.*
60. P. D. Ouspensky, *Tertium Organum, A Key to the Enigmas of the World.*
61. Tedlock, *loc. cit.*, p. 207.
62. *Ibid.*, p. 207.
63. *Ibid.*, p. 217.
64. *Ibid.*, p. 218.

Chapter II

1. Edith Ellis, *Three Modern Seers*, p. 8.
2. M.D.D., p. 209.
3. M.D.D., p. 106.
4. T.D., VI. p. 18.
5. Edward Lewis, *Edward Carpenter, etc.*, p. 37.
6. A of C., p. 91.
7. T.D., III, p. 14.
8. T.D., XI p. 25. Compare D.H.L's Croydon poem of the Helen cycle, 'A Spiritual Woman' (*Amores* 106) and its cruder 1928 version 'These Clever Women', C.P., pp. 118–9.
9. T.D., pp. 312–13.
10. *Amores*, p. 106; C.P., p. 893; *cf* C.P., p. 38 for the 1928 version.
11. T.D., XLVI, p. 64.
12. M.D.D., p. 107.
13. T.D., p. 13.
14. M.D.D., pp. 139–40.
15. M.D.D., p. 141.
16. M.D.D., p. 142.

17. M.D.D., pp. 134, 218.
18. M.D.D., p. 222.
19. T.D., p. 64: "The young printer (but he has a wife and family at home) with large projecting eyes, going absent, miles away, over his work—thinking of Swedenborg and the dance of atoms and angels." On Swedenborg and the Fellowship of the New Life see also above, Chapter I, p. 17.
20. Walt Whitman, 'Song of Myself', 39, lines 1–2.
21. C.C.C., p. 1.
22. C.C.C., p. 160.
23. C.C.C., p. 5.
24. C.C.C., p. 6.
25. C.C.C., p. 13.
26. Wh.P., p. 224.
27. Archibald Henderson, *George Bernard Shaw, Man of the Century*, p.803.
28. Wh. P., p. 199.
29. C.C.C., p. 15.
30. C.C.C., pp. 20, 22.
31. C.C.C., p. 25.
32. C.C.C., p. 25.
33. *Cf.* C.L., pp. 160–61.
34. W.L., p. 129.
35. C.C.C., p. 27.
36. C.C.C., p. 27.
37. Delavenay, *D.H.L., etc.*, Livre II, Chaps. VI, VII, etc.
38. C.L., p. 273.
39. C.C.C., p. 29.
40. C.C.C., p. 30.
41. C.C.C., p. 30.
42. T.D., LIII, p. 75.
43. W.L., p. 44.
44. C.C.C., pp. 32–3.
45. Wh.P., p. 131.
46. C.C.C., p. 38
47. C.C.C., p. 39.
48. T.I., pp. 97–103.
49. C.C.C., p. 41.
50. C.C.C., p. 41.
51. W. L., pp. 109–10. The reader who is curious to relate this scene to other Lawrence themes will compare it with the poem 'Restlessness' (*Amores* 52, C.P., p. 179), and with this line by Carpenter: "Benedict plunges his midnight lust in nettles and briars." T.D., VII, p. 18.
52. C.C.C., pp. 44–5.

53. C.C.C., p. 57.
54. C.C.C., p. 60.
55. M.D.D., pp. 141–2.
56. C.C.C., p. 64.
57. C.C.C., pp. 64, 66. Houston Chamberlain takes a closely similar view of species: *Cf.* p. 251, Real, *The Third Reich*, London, Weidenfeld and Nicolson, 1955, published under the auspices of the International Council for Philosophy and Humanistic Studies and with the assistance of Unesco (pp. xvii + 910). Here, as in other respects, he may have followed in Carpenter's footsteps.
58. C.C.C., p. 70.
59. C.C.C., p. 84.
60. C.C.C., pp. 93–4.
61. C.C.C., p. 100.
62. C.C.C., p. 104. 'The Science of the Future: a Forecast.'
63. C.C.C., p. 105.
64. C.C.C., pp. 106–7.
65. C.L., p. 393, 8 Dec. 1915. See also above, p. 33 and *n.* 53a.
66. C.L., p. 553.
67. C.C.C., pp. 182–3.
68. C.C.C., p. 108.
69. Rw., p. 464.
70. C.C.C., p. 108.
71. C.C.C., pp. 108–9. The reader may compare with the sense of the Sun's mystic reality in Lawrence's *Fantasia of the Unconscious* and '*The Two Principles*' (*Phoenix II*).
72. *Fantasia*, etc., pp. 7–8.
73. C.C.C., p. 110.
74. C.C.C., p. 112.
75. *Phoenix*, Ch. VII, *Of Being and Not Being*.
76. C.C.C., pp. 198–9.
77. C.C.C., p. 216.
78. C.C.C., p. 162.
79. Teleological : C.C.C., p. 180: "Perhaps, if we are to use the word Cause at all, we should do well to use it in the old sense in which the *final* cause and the *efficient* cause are one (the *eidos* of Aristotle). . ." Vitalist: *Cf.* C.C.C., p. 165:

> The two forces are in constant play upon one another; but in some ways that would appear to be the more important which proceeds from the Man (or creature) himself, since this is obviously vital and organic to him, and therefore the most consistent and reliable factor in his modification, while the external force—arising from various and remote causes—must rather be regarded as continuous and accidental.

80. C.C.C., p. 175.

81. C.C.C., p. 172.
82. C.C.C., pp. 165–6.
83. C.C.C., pp. 177–8.
84. '*Education of the People*', *Phoenix*, p. 609.
85. C.C.C., pp. 183–4.
86. *Cf.* below, Ch. VI.
87. "Creation's incessant unrest, exfoliation." C.C.C., p. 161.
88. C.C.C., p. 193.
89. C.C.C., pp. 194–5.
90. C.C.C., p. 126.
91. C.C.C., p. 131.
92. C.C.C., p. 131–1.
93. C.C.C., p. 137.
94. C.C.C., p. 139.
95. C.C.C., p. 145.
96. C.C.C., pp. 146–7.
97. He says " The Widening Circle". But in his sister's copy of *The* Rainbow he corrected the title of Chapter XLV to "The Ever-Widening Circle".
98. C.L., p. 263: "In the scheme of the novel. . . I must have Ella get some experience before she meets her Mr Birkin." Ella is the first name of the heroine, who became Ursula.
99. C.C.C., p. 148.
100. C.C.C., p. 150.
101. C.C.C., p. 152.
102. C.C.C., p. 153.
103. C.C.C., pp. 155–6.
104. C.C.C., p. 157.
105. C.C.C., p. 160.
106. C.C.C., p. 224.
107. C.C.C., p. 226.
108. C.C.C., p. 230.
109. C.C.C., p. 220.

Chapter 3

1. See below, Ch. VI, *The Intermediate Sex*, pp. 209 *ff.*
2. M.D.D., p. 196.
3. M.D.D., pp. 196–7.
4. Havelock Ellis, *My Life*, p. 294.
5. A. Calder-Marshall, *Havelock Ellis, a biography*.
6. Havelock Ellis, *op. cit.*, p. 297.
7. L.C.A., p. 99.

8. L.C.A., p. 5.
9. W.L., p. 208.
10. L.C.A., pp. 11–12. The reader may wish to compare this with Lawrence's important poem 'Manifesto', C.P., pp. 262–8.
11. W.L., p. 153.
12. W.L., p. 157.
13. W.L., p. 158.
14. W.L., p. 216.
15. L.C.A., p. 106.
16. L.C.A., pp. 106, 120; *Cf.* W.L., p. 372: "I tell you . . . on earth" (see below, p. 111, *n.* 64).
17. L.C.A., 121.
18. L.C.A., p. 122.
19. L.C.A., pp. 14–15.
20. L.C.A., p. 15.
21. L.C.A., pp. 20–1.
22. L.C.A., p. 22. *Cf.* W. L., Ch. III, p. 42: Birkin to Hermione: "Even your animalism, you want in the head."
23. L.C.A., pp. 27–8. One hesitates to compare with this passage, the following words from Lawrence's 'New Eve and Old Adam' (C.S.St., I. p. 91): ". . . he felt himself growing dim, fusing into something soft and plastic between her hands. *And this connection with her was bigger than life or death.*" [*My italics.*] If these words, as they may, echo Carpenter, then his influence is indeed deeply pervasive.
24. L.C.A., pp. 28–9. The question of generation versus regeneration is further discussed in Chapter VI below.
25. W.L., pp. 59–60.
26. C.P., pp. 218–19.
27. W.Y. Tindall in *D. H. Lawrence and Susan His Cow*. There was at Croydon a theosophic church at which Carpenter certainly spoke on the 'All-Self' in late 1912 or shortly after. Helen Corke does not think (1968) Lawrence knew of it or was interested in theosophy in 1911. On the other hand, Enid Hilton (see above p. 38) remembers Lawrence's early interest in theosophy, which she associates with Carpenter's lectures.
28. Delavenay, *D. H. Lawrence*, etc., Livre II, Chapitre VII, p. 493, *n.* 20, p. 510.
29. Delavenay, *loc. cit.*, p. 510 and *n.* 78, and fig. 10.
30. L.C.A., p. 129.
31. C.L., pp. 170–3.
32. C.L., p. 161. On the theme of impotence *cf.* Delavenay, *loc. cit.*, Livre II, Chaps. I and II.
33. D.L.D., p. 51 (L.C.A., current ed. p. 152).

34. L.C.A., op.172.

35. Delavenay, *loc. cit.*, Livre II, Ch. VII, pp. 506 *ff.*

36. W.L., Chapter XIX, 'Moony,' p. 258; Chapter XX, 'Excurse', p. 330.

37. L.C.A., p. 24.

38. L.C.A., pp. 172–3.

39. L.C.A., pp. 174–6.

40. L.C.A., p. 176.

41. L.C.A., pp. 176–7.

42. L.C.A., p. 178.

43. L.C.A., p. 179. The reader may compare this not only with 'Rose of the World', but with the flower and petals imagery and ideas on sex in '*Study of Thomas Hardy*'. *Phoenix*, pp. 400–4, 442–4, etc.

44. A.W., pp. 128–9.

45. L.C.A., p. 51.

46. 'Prologue' to *Women in Love*, *Phoenix II*, pp. 93, 95.

47. L.C.A., p. 55.

48. L.C.A., p. 53.

49. *Phoenix II*, pp. 92, 93.

50. *Ibid.*, p. 95.

51. *Cf.* Delavenay, *D.H.L., etc.*, Livre II, Ch. VII, p. 516.

52. L.C.A., p. 64.

53. L.C.A., p. 53.

54. *Cf.* L.C.A., pp. 53–4.

55. L.C.A., pp. 64, 67.

56. D.L.D., p. 239; Rw., p. 128. *Cf.* L.C.A., p. 162, D.L.D., p. 239, for a similar quotation from Ellen Key.

57. L.C.A., p. 76.

58. L.C.A., p. 83.

59. Rw., p. 315.

60. L.C.A., p. 94.

61. L.C.A., p. 99.

62. Wh.P., p. 460.

63. L.C.A., pp. 106, 108.

64. W.L., p. 372.

65. W.L., p. 373.

66. W.L., p. 376.

67. L.C.A., p. 112.

68. L.C.A., pp. 114–16.

69. L.C.A., p. 118.

70. L.C.A., p. 118.

71. See above, p. 93.

72. L.C.A., p. 122.
73. W.L., p. 373.
74. W.L., p. 507.
75. W.L., p. 46.
76. W.L., p. 267.
77. L.C.A., p. 28.
78. L.C.A., p. 30.
79. W.L., pp. 390–1.
80. C.L., p. 148.
81. *A Bibliography of E.C.*, pp. 74–6; *E.C.: In Appreciation*, p. 63: 'E.C. as I knew him', by Guido Ferrando.
82. Delavenay, *D.H.L., etc.*, Livre II, Ch. I, pp. 213 *ff.* and Livre II, Ch. II, pp. 250 *ff.*
83. S.&L., p. 288. For the dates, *cf.* C.L., pp. 154–84 *passim*; L., p. 95 *ff.*
84. S.&L., p. 355.
85. L., p. 104.
86. L.C.A., p. 178.
87. A. of C., p. 111.
88. L.C.A., p. 178.
89. L., p. 101.
90. L.C.A., p. 178.
91. L.C.A., p. 181.
92. L., p. 96.
93. L., p. 97.
94. L., pp. 99–100.

Chapter 4

1. C.L., p. 394; S.M., *passim.*
2. *The Christian Commonwealth*, 29 May to 10 July 1912. Among other contributions to this periodical, Carpenter's lecture 'The Inner Self' of 7 November 1912 was also published in 1912 as a supplement to *The Christian Commonwealth.* Carpenter wrote the following letter to the editor on 5 July 1912: "Sir, I just write to say, as the subject seems to have come up in your columns, that when writing '*The Art of Creation*', I had not then been fortunate enough to have come across Professor Bergson's work. In fact, I only read his "*Evolution Créatrice*" a year or so ago. Yours, etc., Edward Carpenter." (*Christian Commonwealth*, 10 July 1912.)
3. M.D.D., pp. 206–7. It should be noted that in Ps.U., Lawrence will react strongly *in words* against the second idea, while showing himself unable to replace it by any other. *Cf.* Ps.U., p. 32: "Ideal and material are identical. The ideal is but the God in the machine—the little, fixed machine principle which works the human psyche automatically."

4. M.D.D., pp. 207–08.
5. A. of C., pp. 2–4.
6. A. of C., pp. 4–5.
7. 'Foreword' to S. & L., pp. 95 *ff.*; '*The Crown*', R.D.P., pp. 1–18, etc.
8. A. of C., pp. 6–8
9. A. of C., p. 92.
10. A. of C., pp. 31, 34.
11. A. of C., p. 33.
12. *Cf.* C.L., p. 204: "Bergson bores me. He feels a bit thin."
13. A. of C., pp. 31–2.
14. A. of C., p. 33.
15. A. of C., p. 41.
16. A. of C., p. 44.
17. A. of C., p. 54.
18. A. of C., pp. 55–6.
19. S.M., pp. 135, 136–7.
20. *Ibid.*, p. 30.
21. A. of C., p. 56.
22. S. of T. H., *Phoenix*, p. 431. *Cf.* the whole passage which follows; *Cf.* also below, p. 144.
23. A. of C., pp. 56, 58.
24. C.L., p. 519.
25. A. of C., pp. 63–4.
26. A. of C., pp. 58–9.
27. A of C., p. 59.
28. A. of C., p. 59.
29. Rw., Ch. III, pp. 83–8.
30. A. of C., pp. 60–1.
31. A. of C., p. 62.
32. Rw., Ch. III, p. 88.
33. A. of C., p. 63.
34. A. of C., p. 69.
35. A. of C., p. 69.
36. W.L., p. 45.
37. Carpenter Collection, Sheffield, MSS 271–82.
38. Philadelphia, 1901, *Cf.* A. of C., p. 67, *n.* 1.
39. A. of C., pp. 113–14.
40. A. of C., pp. 116–17.
41. '"Thou art that," as his father says to Svetaketu, pointing to diverse objects, trying to make him feel that the subtle essence of all these things is his true Self'. A. of C., p. 65.
42. A. of C., p. 79.

43. A. of C., p. 79.

44. *Phoenix*, pp. 401, 403, 425, etc.; '*The Crown*', *Phoenix II*, p. 385. In other contexts (e.g. in the '*Hardy*', *Phoenix*, pp. 483, 487 on Tess), Hardy's "aristocrats" are shown as "detached", isolated—i.e. separate *in truth*, having achieved "being".

45. A. of C., pp. 88

46. A. of C., pp. 88–9.

47. A. of C., p. 90. An important difference between Carpenter and the Lawrence of *The Rainbow* is that the elder writer believes in some form of metempsychosis, while Lawrence does not suggest this in his novel.

48. C.L., p. 280.

49. *Phoenix*, pp. 515–16.

50. A. of C., pp. 109–10. We have stressed elsewhere (*D.H.L., etc.*, Livre II, Ch. VII, *Women in Love*) the influence of the Indian paintings of Ajanta on Lawrence's descriptions of Ursula.

51. C.L., pp. 281–3.

52. D.L.D., Ch. XV.

53. A. of C., p. 95.

54. A. of C., p. 96.

55. A. of C., pp. 96–7.

56. Ps. U., p. 47.

57. A. of C., p. 97.

58. A. of C., p. 99.

59. A. of C., p. 102.

60. John, 8, Chapter VIII VERSE 58.

61. A. of C., p. 102.

62. A. of C., p. 101.

63. True enough, he attenuates the exclusiveness of this belief by stressing that beyond the race-ego the individual is affiliated to the transcendent "world-self", "and that the individual . . . has still an access and an appeal to a region and powers beyond and prior to all heredity". A. of C., p. 134.

64. C.L., p. 478.

65. A. of C., p. 102.

66. A. of C., pp. 102–3.

67. A. of C., p. 103.

68. L., p. 96.

69. 'Rhythm', March 1913, in *Phoenix*, pp. 304–7.

70. L., p. 99.

71. L., p. 100.

72. See above, Ch III, *ad finem*.

73. L., p. 101.

74. L., p. 101.

75. D.L.D., p. 6. "generation is the superfluity, the ὕβρις of growth, and connects itself in the first instance with the satisfaction of hunger."

76. Delavenay, *D.H.L.*, etc., II, Ch. V.

77. *Cf. Phoenix*, pp. 433–4, and Delaveny *D.H.L.*, etc., Ch. V. *Cf.* '*The Crown*', R.D.P., p. 38.

78. W.L., pp. 94, 134, 208.

79. *Phoenix*, p. 432.

80. *Cf.* above, p. 137 and *n.* 67. On this train of thought, *cf.* below, Chapter VI.

81. W.L., p. 179.

82. W.L., p. 267.

83. A. of C., p. 105.

84. A. of C., p. 107.

85. A. of C., p. 98.

86. A. of C., p. 109.

87. D.L.D., p. 246.

88. *Phoenix*, p. 431.

89. A. of C., p. 110.

90. *Phoenix*, p. 431.

91. *Ibid.*, p. 431. *Cf.* A. of C., p. 85: "the mark of the individual Self is its differentiation, its distinctness, even in some degree its *separation* from the others. And so we find the first form in which the self fairly comes to consciousness is that of separation." [*My italics.*]

92. A. of C., p. 108.

93. A. of C., p. 109.

94. *Phoenix*, p. 404 *ff*, pp. 434, etc. '*The Crown*,' in R.D.P., pp. 40–1, etc.

95. A. of C., p. 25.

96. *Phoenix*, p. 433.

97. *Ibid.*, p. 433; *Cf.* W.L., Ch. XIX, p. 270: Will Brangwen "was not a coherent human being, he was a roomful of old echoes".

98. A. of C., p. 68.

99. A. of C., p. 64.

100. A. of C., pp. 68–9.

101. Ps. U., p. 122.

102. *Phoenix*, p. 419.

103. *Ibid.*, p. 434.

104. Ps. U., pp. 31, 47, etc.

105. *Ibid.*, p. 47. *Cf.* above, p. 143.

106. A. of C., p. 133. It is not clear whether or not Carpenter, who read German easily and was in touch with German psychologists, even knew of Jung's ideas by 1912, the year of publication of *Wandlungen und Symbole der Libido*. He could not know any of Jung's *books* by 1904. On the other hand his

own books were well-known in German medical circles and he was invited to speak in the summer of 1914 at a Berlin congress on sex-psychology. His lecture, which was not delivered because of the war, was entitled '*Die Homosexualität in der Kultur-Geschichte*'. Freud and Jung must have known his books.

107. A. of C., p. 134.
108. C.L., p. 290, 21/6/1914, and C.L., p. 300, 19/12/1914.
109. A. of C., p. 138.
110. A. of C., p. 153.
111. A. of C., p. 155.
112. A. of C., pp. 154, 156, etc.
113. A. of C., pp. 154–8.
114. A. of C., p. 161.
115. A. of C., pp. 163–4.
116. A. of C., p. 164.
117. A. of C., p. 165.
118. Delavenay, *D.H.L., etc.*, II, Ch. V.
119. On this *cf.* G.B.S's review of Chamberlain's *Foundations of the XIXth Century* in *Fabian News*, June 1911.
120. A. of C., p. 166.
121. A. of C., p. 140.
122. A. of C., p. 173.
123. A. of C., p. 173.
124. A. of C., pp. 174–5.
125. A. of C., p. 177.
126. A. of C., p. 178.
127. A. of C., pp. 178–9.
128. A. of C., pp. 180–1.
129. On this *cf. From Adam's Peak to Elephanta*, Chaps. VIII–XI, and below p. 192. On J. M. Pryse and the *chakras*, *cf.* Delavenay, *D.H.L., etc.*, II, Chap. VII.
130. R.D.P., pp. 47–8.
131. R.D.P., p. 47.
132. R.D.P., pp. 54–5.
133. R.D.P., pp. 38, 41.
134. *Phoenix*, p. 434.
135. R.D.P., p. 93.
136. R.D.P., pp. 96–7.
137. '*The Crown*,' R.D.P., p. 75. As for the swan, see also in *Phoenix II*, 'Art and the Individual,' p. 224 and below, Ch. V, p. 172.
138. '*The Crown*', R.D.P., p. 76.
139. *Phoenix*, pp. 463–4.
140. A. of C., pp. 209–12.
141. A. of C., pp. 212–13.

142. A. of C., pp. 216–17.
143. A. of C., p. 220.
144. A. of C., p. 225.
145. W.L., p. 335.
146. W.L., p. 331.
147. A. of C., p. 226.
148. *Cf.* above, Ch. II, p. 61.
149. A. of C., p. 227.
150. A. of C., pp. 228–9.
151. A. of C., p. 234.
152. Rw., pp. 294–8.
153. *The Virgin and the Gipsy*, p. 47.
154. D.L.D., p. 262.
155. C.L., p. 180.
156. C.L., p. 183.
157. D.L.D., pp. 263–4.
158. D.L.D., p. 264.
159. D.L.D., p. 267.
160. D.L.D., p. 269.
161. D.L.D., p. 271.
162. D.L.D., p. 237.
163. D.L.D., pp. 274–5.
164. C.L., p. 281.
165. *Phoenix*, p. 439.
166. C.L., p. 282.

Chapter 5

1. A. of C., p. 222.
2. A. of C., p. 234.
3. A.W., p.12.
4. A.W., p. 19.
5. A.W., p. 22.
6. A.W., pp. 22–3. *Cf.* below, p. 179, notes 43 and 44.
7. A.W., pp. 35–6.
8. A.W., p. 42.
9. A.W., p. 48.
10. A.W., p. 57.
11. A.W., p. 57.
12. A.W., p. 58.
13. A.W., p. 59.
14. A.W., p. 61.
15. A.W., pp. 65–6.

16. A.W., pp. 77–8.
17. A.W., pp. 79–80.
18. A.W., p. 80.
19. A.W., p. 81.
20. *Phoenix*, pp. 286, 419–20 (S. of T.H.), 439, 479–81, 513, 737–9; *Phoenix II*, pp. 224–5 (see below), 416, 420–1, 426, etc.
21. A.W., pp. 82–3.
22. Nehls, I, p. 74.
23. *Phoenix II*, p. 109.
24. E.T., p. 106.
25. C.L., p. 12
26. *Phoenix II*, pp. 225, 226.
27. *Phoenix II*, p. 223.
28. *Ibid.*
29. *Cf.* above, p. 165 and *n.* 6; p. 179, p. 8; A.W., p. 42; and below, p. 179.
30. *Phoenix II*, p. 225.
31. *Phoenix II*, pp. 565–70.
32. *Phoenix II*, p. 226.
33. *The New Age*, 17 March 1910.
34. *Loc. cit.*, p. 464, col. 2.
35. *Ibid.*
36. *Ibid.*, 20 July 1911, p. 286.
37. A.W. p. 122; '*The Crown*,' Ch. VI; R.D.P., p. 88.
38. A.W., p. 97.
39. A.W., p. 98.
40. Further on, Carpenter refers to "the new *phosphorescent shine of* Baudelaire or Verlaine"—a typical Laurentian phrase: *cf. Women in Love*, p. 179, "all our white phosphorescent flowers of sensuous perfection", itself suggestive of *Fleurs du Mal*. [*My italics.*] *Cf.* also 'Poetry of the Present' for a closely related sense of light in transient beauty, of "the still, white seething, the incandescence and the coldness of the incarnate moment". C.P., p. 183.
41. A.W., p. 122.
42. A.W., p. 130. Compare Lawrence's statement in 'Art and the Individual': "The same sentence in ten different mouths has ten different meanings." (*Phoenix II*, p. 225); here language is the artistic medium and the self (or selves) to be expressed, the "inexhaustible scene".
43. A.W., p. 132.
44. A.W., p. 134.
45. A.W., pp. 135–6.
46. *Phoenix II*, p. 226.
47. A.W., p. 210.

48. A.W., p. 215.

49. A.W., p. 216.

50. A.W., p. 226.

51. An allusion to Van Gogh's "yearning to procreate oneself with other horses, also free".

52. C.L., p. 327.

53. Delavenay, *D.H.L., etc.*, Livre II, Ch. V.

54. From a letter from Helen Corke (9 October 1968) we may quote the following: "I can't remember that we ever discussed or approached the subject of homosexuality—indeed, the word itself was probably unknown to me before 1914." The word may have been unknown to Lawrence until he wrote 'The Prussian Officer' and the '*Hardy*', or until he read Weininger and *The Intermediate Sex*.

55. *Phoenix*, pp. 512, 515–16.

56. C.L., p. 180.

57. C.L., pp. 96, 97, 98, etc.

58. *Fabian News*, June 1911.

59. *The New Age*, 4 April 1912. On T. E. Hulme and *The New Age*, *cf.* Wallace Martin, *The New Age under Orage*.

60. R.D.P., p. 24.

61. "I have always worshipped Siva," Lawrence said to Earl Brewster in 1927. See Brewster, *D. H. Lawrence, Reminiscences and Correspondence*, p. 112.

62. A.W., p. 224.

63. R.D.P., p. 94.

64. C.P., pp. 181–6; also in *Phoenix*, pp. 218 *ff.*

65. *Phoenix*, pp. 677–80.

66. *Phoenix*, p. 688.

Chapter VI

1. E. Lewis, *Edward Carpenter*, pp. 59–60.

2. C.L., p. 872. "I am never very fond of abstract poetry, not even Blake. And the theme of this I prefer in the old hymns and Vedas, in the original when it has a quivering which is gone here." What did Lawrence mean by "in the original"?

3. F.A.P.E., p. 185.

4. F.A.P.E., p. 187.

5. F.A.P.E., p. 194.

6. 'The Spirit of Place', S. M., p. 18.

7. *Civilization, Its Cause and Cure.*

8. *Angels' Wings.*

9. *Love's Coming of Age.*

10. *The Drama of Love and Death.*

11. L.C.A., pp. 28–9.
12. L.C.A., p. 28.
13. D.L.D., p. 27.
14. I.S., pp. 68–9.
15. D.L.D., pp. 29–30.
16. *Cf.* Letters, p. 97, last paragraph.
17. *Phoenix*, p. 399.
18. *Phoenix*, p. 403.
19. D.L.D., p. 5.
20. D.L.D., p. 29.
21. D.L.D., p. 7.
22. D.L.D., p. 8.
23. D.L.D., p. 17.
24. D.L.D., p. 21.
25. D.L.D., p. 23.
26. '*The Reality of Peace*,' *Phoenix*, p. 675.
27. '*The Reality of Peace*,' *Phoenix*, p. 681.
28. On this Whitman essay and an earlier 1918 version, see *The Symbolic Meaning*, p. 253.
29. *Cf.* below p. 224.
30. D.L.D., p. 31.
31. D.L.D., pp. 33–4.
32. D.L.D., p. 61.
33. We were unduly put off for a time from investigating Lawrence's considerable debt to Weininger by Havelock Ellis's disparaging general remarks on the Viennese in the course of a conversation on Lawrence in 1932.
34. Delavenay, *D.H.L., etc.*, II, Ch. V, pp. 383 *ff*.
35. W.L., p. 208.
36. C.L., p. 172
37. *Cf.* W.L., Ch. XIX, 'Moony', pp. 265–7.
38. D.L.D., pp. 237–8. *Cf.* '*The Crown*,' R.D.P., p. 99, with its promise of "a new heaven and a new earth" where "man is not man, as he seems to be, nor woman woman".
39. D.L.D., p. 229.
40. D.L.D., pp. 240–1.
41. *Cf.* above, Ch. IV, p. 149.
42. C.L., p. 136, 4 August 1912. If Lawrence did then have this idea in mind, it would suggest that he had read *The Drama of Love and Death* by August 1912, i.e. soon after publication. Similar thoughts seem to have been in his mind at the time of the final writing of scenes in *Sons and Lovers* dealing with the pre-natal life of Paul Morel.
43. The similarity of vocabulary with Carpenter is striking. For Carpenter

the Devil is "The Sunderer", and he presides over the period of civilization: *cf.* D.L.D., pp. 244–5.

44. S.M., p. 185, *Phoenix II*, 234–5.
45. *Ibid.*, p. 186, *Phoenix II*, p. 235.
46. Ps. U., p. 47.
47. Ps. U., p. 47.
48. Ps. U., p. 35.
49. Ps. U., pp. 108–9.
50. Ps. U., pp. 36–7.
51. *Fantasia*, pp. 137–8.
52. C.L., p. 454.
53. I.S., p. 42.
54. *Omoo*, quoted in I.S., p. 42.
55. W.L., Ch. XIX, pp. 265–7; Ch. XXXI, p. 507, etc.

55a. We are indebted to Professor Harry T. Moore for this information on the first U.S. edition.

56. *Phoenix*, p. 458.
57. I.S., pp. 45–9.
58. "I have begun the second half of *The Rainbow*. . . I feel I cannot touch humanity, even in thought, it is abhorrent to me. But a work of art is an act of faith, *as Michelangelo says*, and one goes on writing to the unseen witness." (To Barbara Low, C.L., p. 449.) [*My italics.*]
59. Heinemann, London, 1912.
60. C.L., p. 445; also p. 448.
61. *Phoenix II*, pp. 104–6.
62. *Cf.* Lawrence's description of Hermione as "prophetess", *Phoenix II*, p. 94, "maker of Gods"; *ibid.*, p. 97, etc.
63. In particular his lecture on Whitman delivered on 13 December 1922, before the British Society for the Study of Sex Psychology; see below, p. 222.
64. I.S., pp. 9–10, 11.
65. I.S., p. 11.
66. I.S., pp. 14, 15. It may be noted that Lawrence, in '*Education of the People*', a series of papers marked by a deep reaction against woman as mother and as "the goddess in the machine of the human psyche" (*Phoenix*, p. 630), as well as by a Whitmanesque apology of friendship between comrades, "sacred and inviolable as marriage" (*Ibid.*, p. 665), gives a special, mystical role to teachers as priests, expressions of "the living religious faculty" (*Ibid.*, p. 608).
67. I.S., pp. 27, 37, 54, 59–60, 62, etc.
68. I.S., pp. 64, 66.
69. I.S., pp. 55, 27.
70. I.S., p. 69.

71. I.S., p. 33.
72. I.S., pp. 33–4.
73. I.S., p. 35.
74. 'Prologue' to W.L., *Phoenix II*, pp. 103–6.
75. I.S., pp. 18–19.
76. I.S., pp. 34–5.
77. I.S., p. 18.
78. I.S., p. 121.
79. I.S., p. 122.
80. *Phoenix*, pp. 514–16.
81. *Cf.* Delavenay, *D.H.L.*, *etc.*, II, Ch. V, pp. 390 *ff.*
82. I.S., pp. 170–1. Carpenter quotes Charles G. Leland, *The Alternate Sex*, and Dr Jaeger, *Die Entdeckung der Seele*.
83. *Phoenix*, p. 468.
84. *Cf. Phoenix*, pp. 482–510 and Delavenay, *D.H.L.*, *etc.*, II, Ch. V, pp. 403 *ff.*
85. *The Occult Review*, XX–1. July, 1914, pp. 30–2.
86. *The Occult Review*, *loc. cit.*, p. 31.
87. I.T.A.P.F., p. 127.
88. C.L., p. 326. Lawrence's friendship with Bertrand Russell, Ottoline's lover, was then at its height: might there be a connexion between that feeling and the injunction to Ottoline to give up all 'physical' relationships?
89. 'Prologue' to WL, Ph. II, pp. 94, 97, etc.
90. S. of T.H., Ph., p. 496.
91. I.T.A.P.F., pp. 27–32.
92. *Cf.* Delavenay, *D.H.L.*, *etc.*, II Ch. V, pp. 384–5.
93. I.T.A.P.F., p. 71–82.
94. I.T.A.P.F., p. 47. Bastian, *Der Mensch in der Geschichte*.
95. I.T.A.P.F., Ch. V, 'The Dorian Military Comradeship'; Ch. VI, 'Its relation to the status of women.'
96. *Phoenix*, pp. 454–5.
97. *Phoenix*, pp. 405–6.
98. I.T.A.P.F., p. 111.
99. I.S., Ch. IV.
100. In 1915 Lawrence might have wished to show some reprobation of homosexuality, out of consideration for public feeling or for his publisher; in 1916 he may have felt he no longer had the same reasons for so doing, after *The Rainbow* had been destroyed by a magistrate's order.
101. *Phoenix II*, p. 105.
102. *Phoenix II*, p. 107.
103. Rw., p. 384.
104. W.L., p. 286.
105. I.S., pp. 50–1.

106. I.S., p. 56.
107. I.S., p. 65.
108. On this see Delavenay, 'Le Phénix et ses Cendres' in *Etudes Anglaises*, XXI–4, 1968.
108a. *Phoenix II*, p. 92.
108b. *Phoenix II*, p. 106–7.
109. S. Foster Damon, *Amy Lowell, A Chronicle*, 1935, p. 279.
110. *Phoenix II*, p. 107.
111. *Phoenix*, p. 479.
112. Book II, Ch. VII, pp. 516 *ff*.
113. *Cf. Phoenix II*, p. 98, etc., and W.L., Ch. V, p. 60, etc.
114. I.S., p. 57, quoting Krafft-Ebing, *Psychopathia Sexualis*.
115. I.S., pp. 47–8.
116. I.S., p. 70.
117. I.S., p. 73.
118. I.S., p. 74.
119. A. of C., p. 140.
120. D.W.W.W., p. 18. The reader who wishes to find Lawrentian comparisons will usefully turn to 'Poetry of the Present' (C.P., pp. 181–6) and to the 1924 Whitman essay in *The Symbolic Meaning*.
121. D.W.W.W., pp. 54–5.
122. D.W.W.W., pp. 151–2.
123. C.L., p. 556. *Cf.* above, Ch. I, pp. 34–35, *n.* 52.
124. S.F. of W.W., p. 14.
125. *Ibid.*, p. 14–15.
126. *Edward Carpenter, 1844–1929.*
127. *Cf. Phoenix*, p. 91. (*New Republic*, 15, XXI, 1920): "Whitman was almost conscious; only the political democracy issue confused him."
128. I.S., p. 75, quoting from *Democratic Vistas*.
129. Quoted from an interview with a daily newspaper, in M. Cowley, *Introduction* to *Complete Poetry and Prose of Walt Whitman*, p. 16.
130. I.S., p. 76, quoting *Democratic Vistas*.
131. I.S., pp. 77.
132. I.S., pp. 77–8.
133. I.S., pp. 107, 115–16.
134. I.S., p. 115.
135. I.S., p. 116.
136. I.S., p. 117. E. Bertz, *Whitman: Ein Charakterbild*, Max Spohr, Leipzig, undated.
137. *Cf.* 'Democracy' in *Phoenix*, pp. 699–718, probably written in 1922 or early 1923.
138. S.C.A.L., p. 169.

139. C.L., p. 25.
140. C.L., p. 258, December 1913.
141. See below, p. 254, *n.* 158.
142. Nehls I, 500–1. Letter to Godwin Baynes of "Summer 1919". "R." is G. Baynes's estranged wife.
143. S.M., pp. 262–3.
144. I.S., 75.
145. D.W.W.W. 'The Poetic Form of Leaves of Grass', pp. 107–15.
146. S.M. p. 264.
147. S.M., pp. 262.
148. S.M., p. 258.
149. S.M., 260.
150. S.M., p. 260.
151. S.M., p. 261. *Cf.* I.S. pp. 50, 55, 77, for similar allusions to Wilde.
152. '*Reality of Peace*', *Phoenix*, p. 673.
153. Ps. U., pp. 127–8.
154. S.M., pp. 262–3.
155. *Edward Carpenter: In Appreciation*, p. 77.
156. *Two Cheers for Democracy*, p. 217.
157. *Phoenix*, pp. 699–718.
158. *Phoenix*, p. 713.
159. '*Education of the People*', *Phoenix*, pp. 664–5.
160. S.C.A.L., p. 176.
161. T.D., p. 124. ('In the Drawing-Room'.)
162. *Letters*, pp. 704–5.
163. *Aaron's Rod*, pp. 126, 164, 312.
164. *Ibid.*, p. 312.
165. *Kangaroo*, p. 225.
166. *Ibid.*, p. 221.
167. *Ibid.*, p. 340
168. *Ibid.*, p. 390.
169. *Ibid.*, p. 389.

Chapter 7

1. C.L., p. 308, 27 January 1915.
2. *Fantasia of the Unconscious*, p. 11.
3. S.C.A.L., pp. 163, 167.
4. S.C.A.L., p. 167.
5. S.C.A.L., p. 168. On David and Jonathan, *cf.* Ch. V., p. 174.

BIBLIOGRAPHICAL NOTE

This note does not aim at providing a complete bibliography of Edward Carpenter: of the two that exist, one, Appendix II to *My Days and Dreams*, is quite adequate for most current purposes; the other, still in print, is available from Sheffield City Libraries, and is as complete as can be desired up to its publication date, 1949.

The basic bibliography of D. H. Lawrence is Warren Roberts's excellent work (1963), upon which it would be impertinent as well as useless to try to improve.

Selectivity is thus the guiding principle of the present note. The selection criteria followed are two: first, to assist the reader in finding bibliographical information; second, to record the titles of all books or articles quoted, mentioned, or to which the reader may have been referred, with as precise bibliographical information as is readily available at the time of writing. These principles lead to the deliberate omission of any titles by D. H. Lawrence which are not mentioned in the body of the study. Not all titles by Carpenter have been listed. Articles or essays by him are listed only in so far as they are mentioned in the study. Books about Edward Carpenter are listed, but not books about D. H. Lawrence unless directly relevant. Useful bibliographical information later than 1949 for Carpenter, and than 1963 for Lawrence, is also provided.

I. Bibliographies

(a) *Edward Carpenter*

A Bibliography of Edward Carpenter. A catalogue of books, manuscripts, letters, etc., by and about Edward Carpenter in the Carpenter Collection in the Department of Local History Books of the Central Library, Sheffield, with some entries from other sources; Sheffield City Libraries, 1949, pp. *ix* + 83.

N.B.—An annotated copy of this book, available to readers in the Central Library, contains much useful additional information on the Carpenter Collection.

Bibliography, Appendix II to *My Days and Dreams, q.v.* below, pp. 323–32.

(b) *D. H. Lawrence*

Roberts, F. Warren, *A Bibliography of D. H. Lawrence*, Rupert Hart-Davis, London, 1963, pp. 399.

Beebe, Maurice, and Tommasi, Anthony, "Checklist of D.H.L. Criticism", in *Modern Fiction Studies*, Vol. 5, No 1, Spring, 1959.

Delavenay, Emile, *D. H. Lawrence: l'homme et la genèse de son œuvre, les années de formation*, Note Bibliographique, pp. 711–28, Klincksieck, Paris, 1969.

II. Books and Articles by Edward Carpenter

The works listed are either analysed or cited in the text of this study, or are judged of special value in completing the reader's image of their author. They are arranged chronologically in order of publication; for each title the following information is added: important revised or enlarged editions, reprints, translations; an asterisk marks the edition to which reference is made in footnotes.

1883 *Towards Democracy*, John Heywood, Manchester and London, pp. *iv* + 119.

—1905, etc. Swan Sonnenschein, London; S. Clarke, Manchester; pp. *x* + 507.

—*1949 reprint of 1931 5th edition (17th impression), George Allen & Unwin, London, pp. 415.

—*Translations:* French, by Marcelle Senard, 1914; German, 1903–09; Italian, 1912; Russian, undated (partial), Japanese, 1915.

1887 **England's Ideal, and other papers on Social Subjects*, Swan Sonnenschein, Lowry & Co., London, pp. *iv* + 148.

—1933, 7th edition, George Allen & Unwin, London; Charles Scribner's Sons, New York; pp. *iv* + 177.

—*Translations*: German, 1912; Bulgarian, 1910; Spanish (partial), 1911.

1889 *Civilization, its Cause and Cure, and other essays*, Swan Sonnenschein London, pp. *iv* + 156.

—1906, "New and enlarged" 9th edition, Swan Sonnenschein, London; *Charles Scribner's Sons, New York; pp. 175.

—1921, "Newly enlarged and complete" 17th edition, George Allen & Unwin, London, 1921, pp. *vi*+299, Charles Scribner's Sons, New York, pp. *xi*+272.[1]

1892 *From Adam's Peak to Elephanta: Sketches in Ceylon and India*, Swan Sonnenschein, London; Macmillan, New York; pp. *xvi*+363.

—*1910, 2nd edition, Swan Sonnenschein, London; Dutton, New York; pp. *xx*+370.[2]

—1911, *A Visit to a Gñani or Wise Man of the East*, (four chapters from the above), George Allen & Unwin, London, pp. *viii*+67.

—*Translation:* Russian (partial), 1907.

1894 **Homogenic Love, and its place in a free society*, The Labour Press Society, Manchester (for private circulation), pp. 51. (Reissued in *The Intermediate Sex.*)

—*Translation:* German, by H. B. Fischer, Leipzig, 1895.

1894 **Sex Love, and its Place in a Free Society*, The Labour Press Society, Manchester, pp. 24. (Reissued in *Love's Coming of Age.*)

—*Translations:* French, by J. H. Menos, in *La Société Nouvelle*, 1895: German, by H. B. Fischer, Leipzig, 1895.

1896 *Love's Coming of Age: A Series of papers on the relations of the Sexes*, The Labour Press, Manchester, pp. *viii*+168.

—1906, Swan Sonnenschein, London; S. Clarke, Manchester; 6th edition, pp. *viii*+190.

—1915, Methuen & Co., London, 2nd [Methuen] edition.

—1916, Methuen & Co., London, 3rd [Methuen] edition. [Omitting the note on preventive checks to population], pp. *viii*+189.

—*1948, reprint, George Allen & Unwin, London, pp. 221 [Reprinted in 1897, 1902, 1903. Enlarged edition 1906. Reprinted in 1909, 1911, 1913, 1915, 1918, 1919. Further enlarged 1923. Reprinted 1930. Reprinted 1948.]

—*Translations:* French, by A. Marsen (Marcelle Senard), 1917; German, 1902; Italian, 1909; Swedish, Dutch, 1904.

1897 *Forecasts of the Coming Century, by a decade of writers*,[3] edited by Edward Carpenter, The Labour Press, Manchester; The Clarion Office, London; pp. *viii*+192.

---

1. Our copy is E.C's personal copy of the Scribner's edition, inscribed by him in pencil "Rec'd June 1921", paginated as indicated above for the Scribner's edition.

2. Copy kindly lent us by Sheffield City Libraries, Carpenter Collection.

3. Alfred Russell Wallace, Tom Mann, H. Russell Smart, William Morris, H. S. Salt, Enid Stacey, Margaret McMillan, Grant Allen, Bernard Shaw, Edward Carpenter.

1897 In Havelock Ellis, *Studies in the Psychology of Sex*, Vol. I. 'Sexual Inversion', London, The University Press, Watford.

(a) pp. 167–181. Carpenter is probably "Z", the author of Appendix B, 'Ulrichs's Views'.

(b) Carpenter's own case history, written by himself, appears as Case VI. (*N.B.*: Case VII in other editions, see M.D.D. 97, *n.* 1.) The case history begins with the words "My parentage is very sound".

1898 *Angels' Wings: a Series of essays on art and its relation to life*, Swan Sonnenschein, London, pp. *viii* + 248.

—*2nd edition, Swan Sonnenschein, London.[4]

1902 *Ioläus: an anthology of friendship*, edited by Edward Carpenter, Swan Sonnenschein, London, pp. *viii* + 191.

1904 *The Art of Creation: essays on the Self and its powers*, George Allen, London, pp. *xii* + 254.

—1907, "New and enlarged edition", George Allen, London; The Macmillan Co., New York; pp. *xii* + 266.

[Contains under the title 'Note on Matter' an essay published in *The Occult Review*, October 1906, 'The "X" behind phenomena'.]

—1927, George Allen & Unwin, London, 6th edition, pp. *xii* + 266.

—*Translations:* German, 1908; Italian, 1909; Japanese.

1905 *Prisons, police and punishment: an enquiry into the causes and treatment of crime and criminals*, Arthur C. Fifield, London, pp. 153.

—*Translations:* French, 1907; Russian, 1907.

*1906 *Days with Walt Whitman: with some notes on his life and his work*, George Allen, London, pp. *viii* + 187.

[Second edition 1906; reprinted 1921.]

1908 *The Intermediate Sex: a Study of some transitional types of men and women*, Swan Sonnenschein, London, pp. *vii* + 176.

—1912, 3rd edition, George Allen & Unwin, London; S. Clarke, Manchester; pp. *viii* + 176.

—*1952, 9th impression pp. *viii* + 176.

[Reprinted 1909, 1912, 1916, 1918, 1921, 1930, 1941, 1952.]

—*Translation*: German: *Das Mittelgeschlecht*, Munich, 1907.

1910 "On the connection between Homosexuality and Divination, and the Importance of the Intermediate Sexes generally in early Civilizations", in *Revue d'ethnographie et de sociologie*, 1910, pp. 301–16.

[Also published in *The American Journal of Religious Psychology and Education*, 1911, and, in German, in *Viertel-Jahrsberichte des* Wissenschaftlich-humanitären Komitees, 1911.]

---

4. See *n.* 2 on p. 270.

*1912 *The Drama of Love and Death: a Study of Human Evolution and Transfiguration*, George Allen & Co., London, 1912, pp. *viii* + 299.[5]
[New York Edition, M. Kennerley, 1912, pp. *viii* + 292.]
[4th reprint, 1926.]
—*Translations:* French, by George Bazile, 1918; German, 1924; Russian, by P. D. Ouspenski, Petrograd, 1915.

*1914 *Intermediate Types among Primitive Folk: a Study in Social evolution*, George Allen & Unwin, London; S. Clarke, Manchester; pp. 185.
[2nd edition, 1919.]

*1915 *The Healing of Nations, and the hidden sources of their strife*, George Allen & Unwin, London, pp. 266.
[Reprints: 1915, 1915, 1916, 1917, 1918.]
[American edition: Scribner's, 1915.]

1916 *My Days and Dreams: being autobiographical notes*, George Allen & Unwin, London, p. 340. (June.)
—†[2nd edition, October 1916.]
[New York, Scribner's, 1916.]
['*The Story of my Books*', reprinted from *The English Review*, February 1916, is an extract.]
[Reviewed in 'Notes of the Month', *The Occult Review*, XXIV–3, September 1916.]

*1916 *Never Again! A protest and a warning addressed to the peoples of Europe*, George Allen & Unwin, London, pp. 24.
—*Translations:* French, by A. Marsen (Marcelle Senard), Carmel, Genève, undated: *Plus Jamais!*; Danish, by Otto Jespersen, 1916; Norwegian, 1917; Japanese, 1917.
[Reviewed in *The Occult Review, XXIV*–5, November 1916.]

1917 *Towards Industrial Freedom*. George Allen & Unwin, London, 1917; Scribner's Sons, New York 1917; pp. *vi*, 224.
[2nd edition, 1918; reprinted, 1924.]

*1924 *Some Friends of Walt Whitman: A study in sex psychology*. The British Society for the Study of Sex-Psychology, Publication No 13. London, 1924, pp. 16.

*1925 *The Psychology of the Poet Shelley*, by Edward Carpenter and George Barnefield [G. C. Barnard], George Allen & Unwin, London, pp. 128; Dutton, New York, pp. 127.

III. Selected Books and Articles on Edward Carpenter

Beith, Gilbert, ed., *Edward Carpenter: in appreciation*, George Allen & Unwin, London, 1931, pp. 346.

---

5. File copy of second edition, August 1912, kindly lent us by Messrs George Allen & Unwin Ltd.

[Contributions by H. B. Glasier, Edward J. Dent, G. Lowes Dickinson, H. Havelock Ellis, Edith Ellis, Guido Ferrando, E. M. Forster, Laurence Housman, Charles Kingsmith, J. Ramsay MacDonald, W. S. Monroe, Henry H. Nevinson, Harold Picton, Henry S. Salt, Marcelle Senard, Raymond Unwin, etc.]

Crosby, Ernest, *Edward Carpenter, Poet and Prophet*, Fifield, London, 1905, pp. 52. [2nd edition.]

Ellis, E. M. O. (Mrs Havelock Ellis), *Three Modern Seers: James Hinton, Nietzsche, Edward Carpenter*, Stanley Paul, London, 1910, pp. 228.

Forster, E. M.—see Beith, above.

—'*The Life and Works of Edward Carpenter*': book talk broadcast by BBC, 25 September 1944.

—*Two Cheers for Democracy*, Edward Arnold, London, 1951, 371 pp. (Edward Carpenter, pp. 217–19): a reprint from "*Edward Carpenter:* A Centenary Note" in *Tribune*, 22 September 1914.

Glasier, G. B. 'Notes of the Month' in *The Occult Review*, Vol. XXI, No. 5, May 1915, pp. 245–56.

Lewis, Edward, *Edward Carpenter: an Exposition and an Appreciation*, Methuen, London, 1915, pp. *vi*+314.

O'Brien, M. D., *Socialism and Infamy; the homogenic or comrade love exposed: an open letter in plain words for a socialist prophet, to Edward Carpenter*, Sheffield, undated; 2nd edition, pp. 28.

[Correspondence concerning this scurrilous pamphlet is filed in the Carpenter Collection, Central Library, Sheffield.]

Reddie, Cecil, *Edward Carpenter, 1844–1929*. Publication No 16 of the British Society for the Study of Sex Psychology, London, 1932, pp. 12.

Senard, Marcelle, *Edward Carpenter et sa philosophie*, Librairie de l'Art Indépendant, Paris, 1914, pp. 106.

Sime, A. H. Moncur, *Edward Carpenter: His Ideas and Ideals*, Kegan Paul, London, 1916, pp. 146.

[Announced in *The Occult Review*, XXIV–4, October 1916; reviewed in *Id.* XXIV–6, December 1916, pp. 378.]

Swan, Tom, *Edward Carpenter: the Man and his Message*, reprinted from *Young Oxford*, Swan Sonnenschein, Manchester, 1901, pp. 28.

[New and revised edition, Jonathan Cape, London, 1922, pp. 89. (Reprinted 1919.)]

IV. Works by D. H. Lawrence Named in the Present Study

Order of publication of volumes, especially in view of the importance of the posthumous collections *Phoenix* (1936) and *Phoenix II* (1968), is often meaningless for the purposes of this study. Therefore essays named in our text are listed under their titles, in alphabetical order, as well as single-volume works or collections; the date of writing is indicated in square brackets, the edition used to which footnotes refer is shown by an asterisk; the current edition in the "Phoenix" collection, Heinemann, London, is given at the end of each entry for the reader's convenience.

—*A Propos of Lady Chatterley's Lover* [1929], Mandrake Press, London, 1930; *Phoenix II.*
—*Aaron's Rod* [1918–21], *Secker, thin-paper edition; The Phoenix Edition (*Novels*).
—'America, Listen to your own' [1920], *Phoenix.*
—*Amores* [1906–16], *Duckworth, 1916; *cf. The Complete Poems*, 1964.
—'Art and the Individual' [1908], **Phoenix II.*
—*Collected Letters*, *Heinemann, 1962.
—*Complete Poems*, *Heinemann, 1964.
—'The Crown' [1915], in **Reflections on the Death of a Porcupine, q.v.*; *Phoenix II.*
—'Democracy' [after 1919], **Phoenix.*
—'Education of the People' [1918, 1920], **Phoenix.*
—'England, my England' (Short Story) [1915, 1920]; 1st version, **The English Review*, October 1915; final version, **England, my England and other Stories*, Secker (1922), thin-paper edition; The Phoenix Edition, (*The Complete Short Stories of D. H. Lawrence*).
—*Fantasia of the Unconscious* [1921], *Secker, New Adelphi Library; The Phoenix Edition (*Essays*).
—'Foreword' to *Sons and Lovers* [1913], **The Letters of D. H. Lawrence*, 1932.
—*Kangaroo* [1922], *Secker, thin-paper edition; the Phoenix Edition (*Novels*).
—*Lady Chatterley's Lover* [1927], the Phoenix Edition (*Novels*).
—*The Letters of D. H. Lawrence*, edited by Aldous Huxley, *Heinemann, 1932.
—'New Eve and Old Adam' [1913–14], *The Phoenix Edition (*The Complete Short Stories*).
—*Phoenix: The Posthumous Papers of D. H. Lawrence*, *Heinemann, 1936.
—*Phoenix II, Uncollected, Unpublished and Other Prose Work* by D. H. Lawrence, *Heinemann, 1968.
—*The Plumed Serpent* [1925], *Secker, thin paper edition; The Phoenix Edition (*Novels*).
—'Prologue' to *Women in Love* [1916],[6] **Phoenix II.*
—*The Prussian Officer and Other Stories* [1910–14], *Secker, thin-paper edition; The Phoenix Edition (*The Complete Short Stories*).
—*Psychoanalysis and the Unconscious* [1920], *Secker, New Adelphi Library, 1931; The Phoenix Edition (*Essays*).
—*The Rainbow* [1914, 1915], *Secker, thin paper edition; The Phoenix Edition (*Novels*).

---

6. Our own dating on internal evidence.

—*Reflections on the Death of a Porcupine* (Collected Essays), *Centaur Press, Philadelphia; *Phoenix II.*
—'The Reality of Peace' [1917], **Phoenix.*
—Review of *Georgian Poetry* [1918], **Phoenix.*
—*Sons and Lovers* [1910–12], *Secker, thin-paper edition; The Phoenix Edition (*Novels*).
—*Studies in Classic American Literature* [1922–3], *Secker, 1924; The Phoenix Edition (*Essays*).
—*Study of Thomas Hardy* [1914] **Phoenix.*
—*The Symbolic Meaning,** Centaur Press, Arundel, 1962. (Early versions of *Studies in Classic American Literature.*)
—*Twilight in Italy* [1913, 1915], *Cape, The Travellers' Library; The Phoenix Edition (*Travel*).
—'The Two Principles' [1918], *cf* **The Symbolic Meaning*; *Phoenix II.*
—*The Virgin and the Gipsy* [1926], *Secker, thin-paper edition; The Phoenix Edition (*Short Novels*, Vol. II).
—*The White Peacock* [1906–10], *Secker, thin-paper edition; The Phoenix Edition (*Novels*).
—'Whitman': Version 1 [1918], lost.
Version 2, Revised [1920] edition of the 1918 essay, *The Nation and Athenaeum*, 23 July 1921; **The Symbolic Meaning, q.v.*
Version 3 [1922–3], **Studies in Classic American Literature*, Secker, 1924; The Phoenix Edition (*Essays*).
—*Women in Love* [1913, 1914, 1916], *Secker, thin-paper edition; The Phoenix Edition (*Novels*).

V. Works and Articles on D. H. Lawrence or Containing Biographical or Critical Material on Him to which Reference is Made

Brewster, Earl and Achsah, *D. H. Lawrence, Reminiscences and Correspondence*, Secker, London, 1939; pp. 319.
Carswell, Catherine, *The Savage Pilgrimage, A Narrative of D. H. Lawrence*, Chatto and Windus, London, 1932; pp. *xi*+296.
Chambers, Jessie, ("E. T."), *D. H. Lawrence, A Personal Record*, Cape, London, 1935.
Damon, S. Foster, *Amy Lowell, A Chronicle*, Houghton, New York, 1960.
Delavenay, Emile, *D. H. Lawrence: l'homme et la genèse de son œuvre. les années de formation*, 1885–1919, Klincksieck, Paris, 1969
'Le Phénix et ses Cendres', in *Etudes Anglaises*, Didier, Paris, XXIe année, No 4, October–December 1968.
Gray, Cecil, *Musical Chairs, or Between Two Stools*, Horn and Van Thal, London, 1948.

Peter Warlock: A Memoir of Philip Heseltine, Cape, London, 1934.

Lawrence-Ravagli, Frieda, *The Memoirs and Correspondence*, edited E. W. Tedlock Jr, Heinemann, London, 1961.

Luhan, Mabel Dodge, *Lorenzo in Taos*, Alfred E. Knopf, New York, 1932, pp. *viii* + 352.

Moore, Harry T., *The Intelligent Heart, The Story of D. H. Lawrence*, Farrar, Strauss and Young, New York, 1954.

Nehls, Edward, *D. H. Lawrence: a composite biography*, gathered, arranged and edited by Edward Nehls; 3 vols, University of Wisconsin Press, 1938–9: *xxv* + 614 (I), *xxi* + 537 (II), *xxxi* + 767 (III).

Pilley, W. Charles, "A Book the Police should ban", in *John Bull*, 17 September 1921.

Tedlock, E. W. Jr, "D. H. Lawrence's Annotations of Ouspensky's *Tertium Organum*, *Texas Studies in Literature and Language*, Vol. II, No 2, Summer 1960.

Tindall, William York, *D. H. Lawrence and Susan his Cow*, Columbia University Press, New York, 1939.

Vivas, Eliseo, "The Substance of *Women in Love*", *The Sewanee Review*, Vol. 66, No 4, Autumn 1968.

VI. General Sources and References

Asquith, Lady Cynthia, *Diaries*, 1915–1918, Hutchinson, London, 1968; pp. *xxvi* + 530.

Auger, Pierre, "Le régime des castes dans les populations d'idées", in *Diogène*, No 22, Gallimard, Paris, 1958.

Bastian, Adolf, *Der Mensch in der Geschichte, Zur Begründung einer psychologische Weltanschauung:* 3 vols; Leipzig, 1860.

Bertz, E., *Walt Whitman, Ein Characterbild*, Max Spohr, Leipzig.

Bucke, R. M., *Cosmic Consciousness, A Study of the Evolution of the Human Mind*, Philadelphia, 1901.

Calder-Marshall, Arthur, *Havelock Ellis, a biography*, Rupert Hart-Davis, London, 1959.

Clephane, Irene, *Towards Sex-Freedom*, John Lane, The Bodley Head, London, 1935; pp. *xii* + 243.

Cowley, Malcolm, *Introduction to the Complete Poetry and Prose of Walt Whitman*, Garden City Books.

Dalton, Hugh, *Memoirs: I. Call Back Yesterday*, 1887–1931, 1953; *II. The Fateful Years, 1931–1945*, Friedrich Muller, London, 1957.

Ellis, Henry Havelock, *My Life*, Heinemann, London, 1940; *Studies in the Psychology of Sex*, Vols. I–VI, Davis, Philadelphia, 1905.

Elton, Lord, *The Life of James Ramsay McDonald (1866–1919)*, Collins, London, 1939.

Ervine, St John Greer, *Bernard Shaw, his Life, Works and Friends*, Constable, London, 1956.

Ford, Ford Madox, *Return to Yesterday*, Gollancz, London, 1931.

Henderson, Archibald, *George Bernard Shaw, Man of the Century*, Appleton-Century-Crofts, New York, 1956.

Jaeger, Dr Gustav, *Entdeckung der Seele*, Leipzig, 1884–1885, a part of *Lehrbuch der Allgemeinen Zoologie*, 1871–1885.

Knight, William, *Thomas Davidson, 1840–1900: Memorials of Thomas Davidson, the Wandering Scholar*, Boston, 1907.

Krafft-Ebing, Richard von, *Psychopathia Sexualis*, authorized translation of the 7th enlarged and revised German edition, Davis, Philadelphia, 1894.

Leland, Ch. G., *The Alternate Sex, or the female intellect in man and the masculine in woman*, London, 1904.

Martin, Wallace, *The New Age under Orage, Chapters in English Cultural History*, Manchester University Press, 1967; pp. *xiii* + 303.

Morgan, Lewis Henry, *Ancient Society; or Researches in the lines of Human Progress from Savagery . . . to Civilization*, H. Holt and Company, New York, 1877.

Ouspensky, P. D., *Tertium Organum, a Key to the Enigmas of the World*, translated from the Russian by Nicholas Bessaraboff and Claude Bragdon, with an introduction by Claude Bragdon; Manas Press, Rochester, N.Y., 1920; pp. *xxii* + 344. (With a table of the four forms of the manifestation of consciousness.)

Raghavan, V., pp. 296, *The Indian Heritage, An Anthology of Sanskrit Literature*, Unesco Collection of Representative Works, The India Institute of World Culture, Basavangudi, Bangalore, India, 1956; pp. *lxxvii* + 494.

Rolland, Romain, *The Life of Michelangelo*, translated from the French by Frederic Lees, Heinemann, London, 1912; pp. *xiv* + 208.

Shaw, George Bernard, Review of Houston S. Chamberlain's *Foundations of the XIXth Century* in *Fabian News*, June 1911.

Snowden, Philip, *An Autobiography*, Ivor Nicholson and Watson, London, 1934.

Unwin, Sir Stanley, *The Truth About Publishing*, George Allen & Unwin, London, 1926.

Vatsayana, *The Kama Sutra*, Translated by Sir Richard Burton and F. F. Arbuthnot, George Allen & Unwin, London, 1963.

Weininger, Otto, *Sex and Character*, authorized translation from the 6th German edition, Heinemann, London, 1906; pp. *xiii* + 356.

INDEX

The signs below are used to designate works or characters as indicated:

* Works by D. H. Lawrence.
† Works by E. Carpenter.
‡ Characters from D. H. Lawrence's works.

*_Aaron's Rod_, 37, 43, 200, 205, 210, 237, 274
Abbotsholme School, 224
Abraham and Sarah, 136
Adam and Eve, 63
Adams, J., 172
Ajanta Frescoes, 257
Albany Review, The, 19, 82
Aldington, Richard, 207
Alexander (the Great), 212
Alexandra, Princess, 14
Allen & Unwin, 28, 29, 86
Allen, Grant, 270
Alma-Tadema, L., 167
*America, Listen To Your Own, 274
American Journal of Psychology, 129
*_Amores_, 274
†_Angels' Wings_, 99, 124, 154, 164–76, 179, 182, 238, 271
‡Annable, 57–8, 174
Aphrodite, 6, 147, 151
*_Apocalypse_, 116
Apollo, 149, 150, 212, 214
*_A Propos of Lady Chatterley's Lover_, 274
Aristogiton, 78, 221
*'_Art and the Individual_', 170–6, 180, 183–4, 231, 243, 259, 261, 274
†_Art of Creation, The_, 3, 36, 37, 60, 70, 88, 110, 111, 114, 115, 117, 118, 120–63, 164, 168, 173, 177, 180, 182, 193, 197, 222, 239, 241, 255, 271
†'Art of Life, The', 196
Ashbee, C. R., 224
Asquith, Lady Cynthia, 27, 29, 35, 248, 249, 276
Astarte, 65, 214
Athene, 149
Auger, Pierre, 2, 276

Baal, 214
Bachelard, Gaston, 124
Balonda Tribe, The, 207, 208
Bastian, Adolf, 214, 265, 276
Bastien-Lepage, J., 165
*_Bay_, 35
Baynes, Godwin, 267
Bayreuth, 30
Bazalgette, Leon, 223
‡Beardsall, Cyril, 52, 58
‡Beardsall, Lettie, 63
Baudelaire, Charles, 166, 183, 261
Beaumont, C. W., 35
Bedborough, George, 87
Beebe, Maurice, 269
Beethoven, Ludwig van, 165
Beith, Gilbert, 272

Belt, Thomas, 2
Bennett, Arnold, 22
Beresford, J. D., 207
Bergson, Henri, 46, 71, 113, 120, 123, 159, 239, 255, 256
Berkeley, George, 69, 119, 121, 122, 124
Bertz, E., 226, 266, 276
Besant, Annie, 11, 47, 54–5, 119, 193, 234
Bhagavad-Gita, 18, 47, 48, 54, 73, 191, 192
Binns, Henry R., 129
**Birds, Beasts and Flowers*, 42, 186
‡Birkin, Rupert, 59, 61, 64, 80–1, 90–7, 100, 101–2, 106, 107–10, 138, 142, 151, 156, 195, 198, 200, 201, 206–8, 210, 211, 215, 217–21, 252
Blake, William, 3, 165, 184, 187, 231, 262
Blavatsky, Helen, 2, 37, 39, 54–5, 94, 119, 130, 188, 193, 198, 219
Boehme, Jacob, 129
Bondfield, Margaret, 23
Boyle's Law, 68
Bradfield, 18
Bradlaugh, Charles, 11, 54
Bradway, 15, 17, 48
Brahma, 186–7
‡Brangwen, Anna, 103, 107, 128, 144
‡Brangwen, Gudrun, 61, 100, 103, 107
‡Brangwen, Lydia, 61, 104, 127–8, 156
‡Brangwen, Tom (the Elder), 61, 104, 127–8, 156
‡Brangwen, Tom (the Younger), 215
‡Brangwen, Ursula, 61, 71, 80–1, 90–7, 104, 105–10, 126, 132, 133, 156–7, 201, 215, 242, 252, 257
Brewster, Achsah, 275
Brewster, Earl, 193, 204, 275
Brighton, 12, 13
Brighton College, 13
British Museum, 6, 129
British Society for the Study of Sex Psychology, 35, 41, 223, 224
Brook Farm, 16
Browning, Robert, 169
Bucke, Dr. R. M., 42, 129, 149, 222, 276
Buddhism, 38, 122, 191
Burne-Jones, Sir Edward, 167
Burns, John, 16
Burroughs, John, 228
Burrows, Louie, 227
Butler, Samuel, 6
Byron, Lord, 212

Caesar, 212
Calder-Marshall, A., 246, 252, 276
Cambridge, 5, 13–14, 18, 34, 58, 190, 216
Campagni Bagnoli, Teresina, 111
Campbell, Gordon, 146
Carlyle, Thomas, 3, 53, 64, 66
Carpenter, Alfred, 13
Carpenter, Charles, 13
Carpenter, Edward, biography 12–21; links with Lawrence, 21–27; interest in *The Rainbow*, 27–33; tentative chronology of his influence on Lawrence, 36–8; as Victorian rebel, 44–47; *Towards Democracy* and *England's Ideal* 47–52; *Civilization, Its Cause and Cure*, 52–84; publishing troubles, 85–7; *Love's Coming of Age*, 88–110; translations of his works, 111–12; Carpenterian themes in Lawrence's works from 1912–13, 112–18; *The Art of Creation*, 120–63; *Angels' Wings*, 164–89;

Carpenter, Edward—(*contd.*)
religious outlook, 190–5; *The Intermediate Sex* and *Intermediate Types Among Primitive Folk*, 196–221; Carpenter, Whitman and Lawrence, 221–35; bibliography, 268–73
Carpenter, George, 13
Carswell, Catherine, 6, 275
Carter, John, 248
Casement, Sir Roger, 30
Cassandra, 213
Ceylon, 18, 54, 192, 240
Chamberlain, Houston S., 13, 30, 37, 137, 141, 142, 146, 149, 183, 185, 251, 259
Chambers, Alan, 174
Chambers, Edmond and Family, 19
Chambers, Jessie, 21, 22, 89, 170, 171, 213, 227, 240, 275
Charles II, 212
Charteris, Yvo, 35
Chesterfield, 15, 19, 20
Christian Commonwealth, The, 120, 255
Chubb, Percival, 16, 17
†*Civilization, Its Cause and Cure*, 19, 51, 52–84, 121, 164, 269
Clarence, Duke of, 14
Clarion, The, 19, 53
Clarke, Ada, 32, 159
Clephane, Irene, 8, 276
Coleridge, Samuel Taylor, 183
**Collected Letters of D. H. Lawrence*, 171, 274
**Collected Poems of D. H. Lawrence*, 50, 247, 274
Collings, Ernest, 112, 158, 184
**Complete Poems of D. H. Lawrence*, 274
Concord, 17
Coolidge, President, 232
Corke, Helen, 25, 32, 38, 55, 248, 253, 262
Cornwall, 33, 37, 40, 206, 207, 218, 240
Cowley, Malcolm, 266, 276
‡Crich, Gerald, 81, 100–2, 106–8, 144, 216–20
Crosby, Ernest, 273
*'*Crown, The*', 59, 71, 98, 99, 123, 124, 132, 141, 151, 177, 182, 183, 186–7, 274
Croydon, 23, 25, 36, 38, 174, 249, 253
†'Custom', 52, 77

Daily News, The, 19
Dalton, Hugh, 14, 276
Damon, S. Foster, 275
Dante, 98, 114, 116
Darwin, Charles, 7, 20, 42, 70, 75, 212
Daubeney, Lady, 13
David and Jonathan, 174, 243, 267
Davidson, Thomas, 16
Davey, J. G., 129
‡Dawes, Baxter, 211
‡Dawes, Clara, 21, 22, 64, 97, 113, 211
Dax, Alice, 11, 21–5, 26, 27, 36, 89, 171, 247, 248
†'*Days with Walt Whitman*', 222–30, 271
Debussy, Claude, 184
†'Defence of Criminals', 76, 78–82, 154, 196
Delavenay, Emile, 249, 253, 255, 259, 265, 266, 269, 275
*'Democracy', 274
Dent, Edward T., 273
Derby, 19
Despard, Charlotte, 23
De Villiers (*alias* Springmühl), 87
Diana, 65
Dostoievsky, Feodor, 184

†*Drama of Love and Death, The*, 36, 37, 41, 46, 88, 94, 110, 111, 117, 118, 139, 141, 154, 159, 162, 177, 182, 186, 193, 197, 198, 239, 241, 263, 272
Draper, Detective-Inspector, 248
†'Drawing-room Table in Literature, The', 175
*'Dreams, Old and Nascent', 25, 247
Duckworth, 248
Dying Gaul, The, 191

Eastwood, 9, 19, 21, 22, 23, 24, 26, 27, 32, 36, 170, 173, 174, 178, 215, 233, 238
Eder, Dr David, 219
Eder, David, Mrs, 70
*'*Education of the People*', 37, 70, 130, 141, 229, 239, 264, 274
Edward, Prince of Wales (Edward VII), 14
Ellis, Edith Lees (Mrs. Havelock Ellis), 11, 17, 45, 249, 273,
Ellis, Henry Havelock, 7, 9, 11, 16, 17, 37, 46, 86–7, 147, 171, 175, 198, 209, 212, 252, 271, 276
Elton, Lord, 246, 276
Engels, Friedrich, 9, 57
*'England, My England', 29, 274
†*England's Ideal*, 19, 51–2, 269
English Review, The, 27, 29, 176, 206, 238, 247
Ervine, St. John, 246, 277
Etudes Anglaises, 249, 266
†'Exfoliation: Lamarck versus Darwin', 70, 74

Fabian News, 185, 259
Fabian Society, The, 6, 11, 17, 19, 20, 34, 52, 54, 55, 57, 64, 67, 186, 232
**Fantasia of the Unconscious*, 70, 72, 130, 141, 163, 186, 204, 237, 251, 274
Farmington, 17
Fearnehough, Albert, 15, 18
Fellowship of the New Life, 11, 16–17, 26, 34, 232, 250
Féré, Charles S., 129
Ferrando, Guido, 111, 255, 273
Ferrier, James, 122
Florence, 14, 111, 239
Florida, 33
Ford, Ford Madox, 20, 247, 277
†*Forecasts of the Coming Century*, 53, 270
*'Foreword' to *Sons and Lovers*, 36, 112–17, 123, 138, 140, 158, 162, 184, 185, 197, 205, 241, 274
Forster, E. M., 8, 160, 231, 233, 248, 273
Fourier, Charles, 9, 187, 221
Fox, Charles, 15
Fra Angelico, 182
Fraser, Sir James, 2, 70, 72, 177, 214
†'Free Society, The', 196
Freud, Sigmund, and Freudian psychology, 2, 4, 39, 72, 113, 119, 125, 137, 188, 203, 239, 240, 259
Frobenius, 2, 39, 72
†*From Adam's Peak to Elephanta*, 18, 192, 193, 270

Garnett, David, 203
Garnett, Edward, 59, 60, 112, 135, 154, 158, 159, 161, 203
George V, 14
Georgian Poetry, 138, 275
Gertler, Mark, 137
Gandhi, 188, 234
Glasier, G. B., 273
Glenmore, 17
‡Goddard, 171

Goddard, H. H., 129–30
Goethe, 212
Gorki, Maxim, 174
Grant, Duncan, 161
Gray, Cecil, 248, 275
Gross, Otto, 113
Guildford, 15
Guild Socialism, 32–3
Gurdjeff, G. I., 41

Halifax, 14, 18
Hamlet, 64
Hardie, Keir, 23
Harding, President, 232
Hardy, Thomas, 162, 184, 212, 213
Harmodius, 78, 221
Harrison, Jane, 184
Harvard, 16
†*Healing of Nations, The*, 29, 272
Hegel, 119, 122, 169, 172, 174, 183
Henderson, Archibald, 247, 250, 277
Herakleitos, 2, 39, 72
Herbart, J. F., 172, 174
Hercules, 147
Hermes, 147
Heseltine, Philip, 37, 206, 219
Hilton, Enid Hopkin, 22–5, 38, 40, 247, 253
Hinduism, 121, 134, 192–4, 196, 214
Hocking, William Henry, 218
Home Office, 30
†'Homogenic Love and its Place in a Free Society', 86, 270
Hood, Thomas, 174
Hopkin, Olive, 23, 27, 247, 248
Hopkin, Sallie, 11, 22–5, 26, 34, 35, 36, 111, 223
Hopkin, William E., 11, 22–5, 26, 27, 31, 32, 34, 35, 58, 170–1, 174, 184, 206, 223, 238
Housman, Laurence, 273
Hull, 15
Hulme, T. E., 33, 186
Humanitarian League, The, 20
Huxley, Aldous, 22
Huxley, T. H., 124
Hyett, Lady, 13
Hyndman, H. M., 16, 19

Ibsen, Henrik, 167, 169
Icking, 111
†*Ioläus, An Anthology of Friendship*, 174, 271
Impressionists, The, 20
India, 18, 54, 73, 151, 192, 194, 240
‡Inger, Winifred, 215, 216
†*Intermediate Types Among Primitive Folk*, 12, 37, 110, 206, 212, 239, 272
†*Intermediate Sex, The*, 14, 28–30, 35, 37, 40, 88, 110, 158, 184, 196–220, 227, 228, 230, 239, 242, 262, 271

Jaeger, Dr Gustav, 265, 277
James, William, 129
Jennings, Blanche, 21, 27
Jesus, 122, 140, 149, 212, 224
Joyce, James, 2
Jung, Carl Gustav, 39, 41, 141, 145, 258–9

Kali, 177
**Kangaroo*, 37, 43, 200, 218, 235, 237, 274
Kant, 122
Kenny, Annie, 23
Key, Ellen, 254
Kingsmith, Charles, 246, 273
Knight, William, 246, 277
Koteliansky, S. S., 218
Krafft-Ebing, Richard von, 137, 191, 210, 266, 277

Labour Leader, The, 9
Labour Press, The (Manchester), 53, 85, 86, 87
Lady Chatterley's Lover, 97, 175, 240, 274
Lamarck, 70, 75
Lange, C., 129
Lao-Tze, 122, 166
Lawrence, David Herbert: links with Carpenter, 21–7; *The Rainbow* prosecution, 27–30; tentative chronology of Carpenter's influence, 36–8; reasons for silence re Carpenter, 38–43; *Towards Democracy* and *The White Peacock*, 42–52; *Civilization, Its Cause and Cure* and Lawrence's attack on civilization, 55–83; *Love's Coming of Age* and Lawrence's 1913–16 novels, 89–111; new themes in 1912–13, 112–17; *The Art of Creation, The Drama of Love and Death* and Lawrence's 'Philosophy' from the 'Foreword to *Sons and Lovers* to *Women in Love*, 120–63; *Angels' Wings* and Lawrence's aesthetic from *Art and the Individual* to *The Reality of Peace*, 164–89
Lawrence-Ravagli, Frieda, 23, 26, 29, 40, 111, 112, 113, 184, 201, 240, 243, 247, 276
League of Nations, The, 234
Le Bon, Gustave, 135
Leeds, 14, 18
Legitimation League, The, 87
Leighton, Lord, 172
‡Leivers, Miriam, 22
Leland, Charles G., 265, 277
Leonardo da Vinci, 153
Leopardi, 20
**Letters of D. H. Lawrence, The*, 22, 274
Lewis, Edward, 37, 46, 49, 192, 249, 262, 273
Liverpool, 18, 21, 27
Loercke, 129
†'Love as an Art', 196, 200
†*Love's Coming of Age*, 9, 22, 26, 36, 37, 63, 85, 86, 88–110, 111, 114, 116, 139, 158, 196, 198, 239, 241, 270
Low, Barbara, 70, 207, 217, 219, 264
Lowes Dickinson, G., 34, 214, 224, 273
Luhan, Mabel, 6, 41, 204, 276
Lycée Impérial (Hoche), Versailles, 13

MacArthur, Mary, 34
MacDonald, James Ramsay, 17, 23, 273
Mallarmé, Stéphane, 184
†'Man, the Ungrown', 88, 100
Manchester, 53, 86, 87
Manchester Guardian, 19
Mann, Thomas, 1
Mann, Tom, 270
*'Manifesto', 230, 253
Mansfield, Katherine, 41, 207
Marinetti, F. T., 161
†'Marriage', 85
†'Marriage: A Forecast—The Free Society', 88, 107
†'Marriage: A Retrospect', 88
Mars, 147
Martin, Wallace, 277
Marx, Karl, and Marxism, 19, 46, 52, 53, 54, 57, 63, 172, 181, 187, 235
Matthews, Sir Charles, 28
Maupassant, Guy de, 174
Maurice, F. D., 14, 54
McMillan, Margaret, 270
Melville, Herman, 205, 207–8, 217, 239

Merrill, George, 18, 24, 31
Methuen & Co., 27, 30, 248
Mexico, 43
Michelangelo, 153, 169, 191, 205, 208, 212, 224, 243, 264
Middleton-by-Wirksworth, 40
Millet, J.-F., 165
Millthorpe, 15, 18, 19, 24, 31, 40, 58, 235
Milton, John, 169
‡Minette, 103
†'Modern Science: A Criticism', 52, 67
Moore, George, 58, 174
Moore, Harry T., 247, 264, 276
Monroe, W. S., 273
Montaigne, 77
†'Morality Under Socialism', 82
‡Morel, Paul, 64, 97, 113, 210, 211, 263
Morgan, Lewis, 57, 277
Morrell, Lady Ottoline, 29, 182, 208, 213, 219, 265
Morrell, Philip, 29
Morris, William, 3, 9, 11, 16, 53, 66, 171, 196, 270
Moses, 63
*'Mr Noon', 171
Muirhead, R. F., 224
Müller, Max, 190
Mussolini, Benito, 231, 234
Murry, J. Middleton, 27, 207, 208, 210, 248
†*My Days and Dreams*, 12, 13, 15, 32, 53, 67, 268, 272

Nation and Athenaeum, The, 34
Nehls, Edward, 276
Nero, 216
†*Never Again*, 272
Nevinson, Henry H., 273
New Age, The, 11, 19, 22, 33, 82, 171, 175, 176, 186, 238, 248
*'New Eve and Old Adam', 253, 274
New Mexico, 43
†'New Morality, The', 52
Nicoll, Dr Maurice, 41
Nichols, Robert, 37, 206
Nietzsche, Friedrich Wilhelm, 20, 82–4, 113, 127, 185, 188, 238
Nottingham, 15, 18, 19, 20, 38
Nottingham University College, 240
Noyes, J. H., 88

O'Brien, M. D., 273
Occult Review, The, 37, 94, 171, 212, 238, 271
†'Ocean of Sex, The', 49
†'On the Connection Between Homosexuality and Divination', 271
Oneida Community, 16, 88
Orage, A. R., 11, 19, 22, 33, 41, 82, 171, 186
Ouspensky, P. H., 41, 204, 236, 249, 277
Ovid, 196
Owen, Miss Dale, 16
Owen, Robert, 16
Oxford, 18, 206

Pan, 151, 177
Paris and Helen, 172, 191
Parthenon, The, 191
Perugino, 166, 191
Picton, Harold, 273
Pilley, W. Charles, 276
**Phoenix: The Posthumous Papers of D. H. Lawrence*, 274
**Phoenix II: Uncollected, Unpublished and Other Prose Work by D. H. Lawrence*, 274
Plato, 15, 39, 64, 72, 74, 98, 119, 122, 124, 145, 146, 199, 212, 221

*_Plumed Serpent, The_, 37, 42, 43, 65, 146, 163, 200, 225, 234, 236–7, 274
Poe, Edgar Allan, 183
*'Poetry of the Present', 187, 261, 266
Potter, Joe, 24
Potter, Sallie (_see_ Hopkin, Sallie)
Priapus, 177
†'Prisons, Police and Punishment', 271
Progressive Association, The, 16
Progressive Review, The, 19
*'Prologue' to _Women in Love_, 26, 36, 40, 101, 175, 208, 213, 215, 239, 240, 242, 243, 247–248, 274
*'Prussian Officer, The', 262
*_Prussian Officer and Other Stories, The_, 29, 274
Pryse, James M., 3, 37, 39, 95, 130, 141, 151, 188, 193, 230, 259
*_Psychoanalysis and the Unconscious_, 136, 145, 203, 204, 230, 274
†_Psychology of the Poet Shelley, The_, 272

Raghavan, V., 277
*_Rainbow, The_, 5, 23, 24, 27–33, 36, 37, 40, 43, 60–1, 71, 80, 88, 90, 100, 101, 103, 105, 126, 127, 132–5, 139, 140, 151, 156–7, 159, 206, 211, 215, 219, 242, 248, 252, 257, 264, 265, 274
Raphael, 208
Rananim, 26, 66
†'Rational and Humane Science, A,' 52
Réal, Jean, 251
*'_Reality of Peace, The_', 182, 183, 187, 275
Reddie, Cecil, 41, 224, 249, 273
*_Reflections on the Death of a Porcupine_, 275
*'Restlessness', 250
*Review of _Georgian Poetry_, 275
Revista della Società Internazionale Degl' Intellettuali, 111
'Rhythm', 257
Ribot, Th. A., 129–30
Richardson, Dorothy, 2
Roberts, F. Warren, 268, 269
‡Roddice, Hermione, 61, 65, 142, 151, 156, 213, 219, 264
Rolland, Romain, 208, 277
*'Rose of All the World', 94, 98, 99, 197, 254
Rossetti, William, 14
Rousseau Jean-Jacques, 54, 58, 70
Ruskin, John, 3, 11, 52, 53, 66, 96, 171
Russell, Bertrand, 29, 33, 34, 70, 71, 265

St Edward's, Cambridge, 14, 58
St Francis of Assisi, 212
St John the Baptist, 181
St John the Evangelist, 2, 3, 39, 116
*_St Mawr_, 126
St Paul, 122
Salt, H. S., 270, 273
Sappho, 230
Satan, 151
Saturday Review, The, 85
‡Saxton, George, 52
*'Schoolmaster, The', 247
Schopenhauer, A., 113, 122
Schreiner, Olive, 11, 17
†'Science of the Future, The', 52
Scribner's, 29
Secker, Martin, 40
Senard, Marcelle, 273
†'Sex Love, and Its Place in a Free Society', 85, 270
†'Sex Passion, The', 88, 109
Shakespeare, 64, 212, 224
Shaw, George Bernard, 17, 33, 149, 185, 259, 270, 277

Sheffield, 9, 15, 17, 19, 20, 54
Sheffield Central Library, 10, 22, 268, 270
Sheffield Guardian, 19
Sheffield Independent, 19
Sheffield Telegraph, 19
Shelley, Percy Bysshe, 169, 212, 231, 272
Shirebrook, 21
Signature, The, 27, 29
Sime, A. H., 273
**Sisters, The*, 25, 36, 60, 80–1, 95, 99, 101, 103, 134, 139, 140, 158, 201
Siva, 149, 177, 186–7
‡Skrebensky, Anton, 126, 215
Smart, H. Russell, 270
Smillie, Robert, 34
Snowden, Philip, 19, 23, 34, 247, 277
Social Democratic Federation, 16
Socrates, 212
†'Some Friends of Walt Whitman', 76, 272
†'Some Remarks on the Early Star and Sex Worships', 88, 114
Sonnenschein, 54
**Sons and Lovers*, 21, 22, 36, 38, 59, 111, 112–14, 166, 211, 240, 241, 263, 275
Spectator, The, 176
Spencer, Herbert, 172
Spinoza, 122
*'Spirit of Place, The', 193, 262
*'Spiritual Woman, A', 249
Springmühl, 87
Stacey, Enid, 270
Stockham, Alice B., 88
†'Story of My Books, The', 32, 206
**Studies in Classic American Literature*, 38, 119, 208, 223, 227, 243, 275
*'*Study of Thomas Hardy*', 26, 36, 37, 50, 71, 73, 93, 94, 98, 101, 114, 116, 123, 124, 127, 132, 134, 138–40, 141–3, 144, 146, 149, 151, 154, 158, 161, 163, 179, 182–6, 195, 200, 205, 206, 211, 219, 239, 242, 256, 275
Sudermann, Hermann, 167
*'Sun', 65
Swan, Tom, 273
Swan Sonnenschein, 28, 86
Swedenborg, Emmanuel, 17, 104, 202, 250
Swinburne, Algernon, 50
**Symbolic Meaning, The*, 195, 263, 275
Symonds, John Addington, 17, 223

Taormina, 239
Taos, 239
Tedlock, E. W., Jr., 41, 249, 276
Tennyson, Alfred Lord, 169
Theosophy, 38, 54–5
*'These Clever Women', 249
Thoreau, Henry, 15, 64
Tiberius, 216
Times Literary Supplement, The, 248
Tindall, W. Y., 253, 276
To-day, 78
Tolstoy, Leo, 6, 162, 167, 169, 172, 173, 219
Tommasi, Anthony, 269
†*Towards Democracy*, 15, 17, 25, 36, 46, 47, 50–1, 86, 111, 192, 233, 241, 247, 269
†*Towards Industrial Freedom*, 272
**Trespasser, The*, 242
Tribunal for Civil Rights, 31, 32
Trinity Hall, Cambridge, 13
Tuke, Dr Hack, 87, 129
**Twilight in Italy*, 64, 151, 275
*'Two Principles, The' 121, 129–31, 194, 203, 251, 275

Tylor, Edward Burnett, 39

Ulrichs, K. H., 209
University Extension Lecture Scheme, 14
Unwin, Fisher, 86, 87
Unwin, Raymond, 273
Unwin, Sir Stanley, 27, 28, 30, 248, 277
Upanishads, The, 119, 122, 151, 155, 160, 191, 199

Van Gogh, Vincent, 262
Vatsayana, 196, 277
Verlaine, Paul, 178, 261
Versailles, 13
Virgin and the Gypsy, The, 260, 275
*'Virgin Youth', 247
Vishnu, 149
Vivas, Eliseo, 207, 276

Wagner, Richard, 20, 149, 165, 200, 238
Watford University Press, 87
Watts, G. F., 172
Webb, Beatrice and Sidney, 23
Weber, Alfred, 111
**Wedding Ring, The*, 161
Weininger, Otto, 37, 93, 137, 183, 198, 200, 206
Wells, H. G., 33, 176
Westermarck, Edward, 9, 212
Westmorland, 218
**White Peacock, The*, 36, 50–1, 57–8, 63, 65, 106, 123, 174, 175, 241, 275
Whitman, D. H. Lawrence's Essays on, 34–5, 37, 39, 200, 205, 221, 227, 229, 238, 239, 243, 266, 275
Whitman, Walt, 3, 8, 14, 15, 18, 34, 35, 37, 43, 46, 47, 48, 50, 55, 58, 76, 83, 113, 115, 122, 129, 149, 161, 165, 187, 189, 190, 195, 203, 208, 221–35, 241, 243, 250, 264, 266, 275
*'Wild Common, The', 248
Wilde, Oscar, 85, 86, 217, 230, 267
William of Orange, 212
Williams and Norgate, 87
†'Woman', 85
†'Woman, The Serf', 88
†'Women in Freedom', 88
**Women in Love*, 5, 25, 35, 36, 39, 40, 42, 43, 59, 60–1, 89–97, 100–5, 106–10, 122, 127, 129, 133, 134, 138, 151, 156–7, 160, 177, 179, 195, 198, 200, 207, 211, 215–21, 228, 239, 240, 241, 242, 275
Wordsworth, William, 169
Woolf, Leonard, 2
Woolf, Virginia, 2, 160

Yoga, 2, 3, 39, 72–4, 155, 156–7, 193, 240
York, 15

Zola, Emile, 167, 169, 174